LIVING BIOGRAPHIES OF
Great Painters

LIVING BIOGRAPHIES OF
Great Painters

By HENRY THOMAS AND
DANA LEE THOMAS

Garden City Books
GARDEN CITY, NEW YORK

Contents

CONTENTS

Introduction

IT HAS BEEN WELL OBSERVED that every good portrait is a
biography. It is not merely the representation of a living body; it
is the revelation of a living soul. What Santayana said of Shakespeare may be said with equal accuracy of Michelangelo: "God
doubled creation in creating thee."

The true artist is a biographer not only in his portraits but in
all his other paintings—whether he depicts a scene in action, a
quiet landscape, or an abstract idea. Any skilled artisan can faithfully reproduce an object. Like the photographer, he *imitates*
reality. But the superior artist *illumines* it. He defines, and in a
sense refines, the subject that he paints so that his brush brings
out the essential significance—that is, the life story—of his painting.

Every true picture, therefore, is a biographical poem. It illumines the mystery of life for our better understanding. It portrays not only an object, but its character. It transforms old
images into new beauty. It reproduces not only the manner but
the meaning of a sitter or a scene. The great artist interprets
whatever he represents. He adds to the painting the rhythm and

the color of his own personality. We may have observed, again and again, the original of his painting; but when we see it for the first time through *his* eyes, a fresh light comes into our *own* eyes. And then for the first time we see the object in its truer color and form.

In a sense, then, the true painter is more realistic than reality. He adds fresh dimensions to nature. This is perhaps what the Chinese biographers had in mind when they told the story of Wu Tao-tze, the greatest of their early painters. When the time came for him to die, they said, he painted an enormous landscape, stepped into the mouth of a cave he had pictured in the middle of the landscape, and disappeared forever from human sight.

This story, in the exaggerated humor of the old Chinese writers, expresses the idea that a great painting possesses not only outer but inner reality. It is the purpose of the artist to teach as well as to entertain, to illumine as well as to portray. Every good painting, in other words, is a biography with a body and a soul.

And every good biography is a painting in words. This, we trust, is true of the biographies in the present book. We have tried to portray the great painters as living teachers—to show that "the highest aim of the artist is to make new artists." Not necessarily painters, but people who understand paintings through a clearer understanding of the men who made them. This book is designed to play a part in everybody's training toward a degree of A. A.—Appreciator of Art.

H. T.
D. L. T.

GIOTTO

Great Paintings by Giotto

Assisi, Church of St Francis: *Frescoes.*

Florence, Bardi Chapel, Santa Croce: *Series of frescoes illustrating scenes from the life of St Francis.*

Florence, Peruzzi Chapel, Santa Croce: *Series of frescoes illustrating the lives of St John the Baptist and St John the Evangelist.*

Padua, Arena Chapel: *Series of Frescoes—Subjects taken from the parents of Mary, the Virgin and the Son of God—including Joachim and Anna, The Flight into Egypt, The Deposition, Pietà.*

Giotto di Bondone

1276–1337

Pope boniface viii, desiring to add some decorations to the sacristy of St Peter's Church, sent messengers throughout Italy to summon the greatest artists of the peninsula to Rome. One of these messengers entered the hut of a peasant painter in Tuscany. He had heard that this homely, jocular and uncouth artist, dividing his time between his brush and his plow, had painted some pretty pictures of his native countryside.

"His Holiness, the Pope, desires to examine your work, Master Giotto," announced the messenger. "He is summoning all good artists to Rome. Let's have a sample of your painting, so that we may decide whether we can employ you."

Giotto laughed and lustily dipped his brush into a pail of red paint. With a careless swish he drew a tremendous red circle on a piece of paper and handed it to the messenger. "This is my work. Look at it. Do you like it?"

"What kind of tomfoolery is this? I'm here on a serious mission."

The painter shrugged his shoulders, as if to say, "Take it or leave it. It's the best I can do."

"So this is Giotto's work," the pope remarked when the messenger returned with the sample. "A large red circle, and nothing more."

"He is a conceited ass, Father. The greatest opportunity ever offered him. And what does he do? He draws a big empty circle."

"Tell me," asked the pope, "did he have much difficulty in drawing it without the aid of a compass?"

"No, Father, just a dip into the pail and one careless swish."

"Well, well. It is not a very bad circle at all. As a matter of fact, it is a very round circle. He must have a good eye and a steady hand to do this. What manner of man did you find him?"

"He's an ordinary peasant, Father, and as ugly as Satan. People tell me he's full of homely anecdotes."

"And he claims he is an artist?"

"People say that he paints a sheep or a puppy on the wall, on a bit of broken fence. And, as if by a miracle, the spot immediately blossoms into life. But of course only the peasants say that."

"Peasants know. I've heard similar stories myself about this fellow. When he was a boy wasn't he apprenticed to the great Cimabue? They say that once, when Cimabue left the room, Giotto painted a fly on the nose of one of his master's portraits. Cimabue tried to brush the fly away when he returned. Did you inquire what sort of family he comes from?"

"He is the son of a blacksmith, Father. He was brought up tending flocks in the Mugello."

"Those hills in the Mugello are very green, I recall. And the folk who live there are simple folk. But from time to time there arises among them a man with a vision. You understand?"

"I do."

"This man will entertain us, if not with his genius, at least with his simple folk. When you hi ... Rome."

II

GIOTTO DI BONDONE came to Rome (in 1296) and painted frescoes for the pope. He painted scenes from the life of Christ. While he stood on the scaffold and painted, a crowd of good-natured homely fellows like himself peered up at him and watched his every stroke. Here was their countryman standing so unbelievably high above them. Wasn't he uneasy at this height? Didn't he wish he were down on the ground, by the side of these people among whom he belonged? Wouldn't he rather tell jokes than paint? He didn't know why it was that everything his peasant hand touched was transformed into a miracle of beauty. To be sure, he was rather fond of drawing. But for years he had never taken his talent seriously. When he was a lad of nine, watching his flocks in the pasturelands of Tuscany, he whiled away his time in sketching rude portraits of his sheep with a piece of slate on stone. And one day a great man who had been traveling through the countryside stood over the shoulder of the boy and quietly watched him at work. This man was Cimabue, the foremost painter in Italy. And as he stood silently at the birth of genius who knows what thoughts came to him? Perhaps his mind went back to the star-guided, wise old men who had stood at Bethlehem, at the scene of another simple birth twelve hundred years before.

Cimabue prevailed upon Giotto's father, the village blacksmith, to have his son apprenticed to the painter's trade. Cimabue took Giotto to his shop.

In the early days of the Italian Renaissance the painting of pictures was as much of an industry as the grinding of lenses or the cobbling of shoes. The master painter lived on the commissions he received from the popes, the bishops and the lay nobility for portraits, wall frescoes, enamelware and bronze. He had a flock of trained assistants who ground his colors and executed the details in the pictures after the master had drawn the general plan.

To Cimabue's shop went Giotto. He left the heritage which had been handed down to him from generations—labor in the hot Italian sun. Before his death every large city, every important church in Italy bore witness to his strange genius. He was the first giant to appear on the scroll of immortal painters in more than a thousand years.

III

THE TIMES in which Giotto lived were years of storm and stress. The Italian peninsula was dotted with small independent cities which recognized no other authority than their own sovereignty. They pitted their small armies and navies against one another in a million squabbles for the greater glory of the merchant leagues that controlled the civic life of the people. In addition to the constant trade wars, bands of professional robbers, or *condottieri*, swooped down from the mountains and plundered travelers of their wealth. It was an age of political and social anarchy. Feudalism had made comparatively little headway in the Italian peninsula. Italy was very largely a land of free men, *bondone*, like the stock Giotto himself had sprung from. Giotto was proud of his political independence. Once he had been summoned to Naples to paint some pictures for His Majesty, Prince Robert, one of the few tyrants in Italy. Giotto painted, among other subjects, a piece which he announced was a representation of the kingdom of Naples. He drew an ass with a saddle on its back, sniffing at another saddle that lay at its feet.

"What in the world does this picture represent?" Robert asked him.

"Your kingdom in miniature, Sire," Giotto replied. "The ass bearing the saddle stands for your people. There is no one bearing the saddle stands for your people. There is no one off his ruler. And see, he sniffs at the saddle on the ground, looking for someone else to ride him. Upon my word, Sire, every bit of this will happen if you do not unsaddle the ass and treat him as a man."

Giotto was bold, with his brush even more than with his tongue. His genius took wings and alighted with its message of color in every nook and cranny of Italy. It broke the silence of a thousand years and began once more to recognize the aspirations of the common man. Crushed by the trampling of the barbarian hosts who had surged into the Roman Empire during the days of its decline, the common man had been chained to the soil. He had become, under the institution of feudalism, a slave with a finite intelligence but with an infinite capacity to bear pain. He lived on his lord's domain and plowed his soil and grew his crops and paid his taxes. He had no personal or legal rights. He was a chattel, with as much dignity as a piece of household furniture. He imagined, in a vague sort of way, that the angels inhabited the sky and the devils lived in hell. That heaven was meant for him in the end, he was certain—if only he were patient and uncomplaining and good. So he gathered the grain for his master and drove his oxen until he himself, like a harnessed animal of the fields, dropped dead from exhaustion.

Yet these inarticulate masses formed the body of true Christianity. And one day a Messiah arose to give them a voice. This man was Francis of Assisi. He renounced the princes and the prelates and he placed himself at the head of the underprivileged. And in so doing he worked a great bloodless revolution. In some respects, to be sure, Francis was no greater than his age. He was characteristically medieval, for instance, in his profound belief in miracles, in his painful asceticism, in his childlike faith in the anthropomorphic qualities of pigeons, to whom he preached as a brother. But in his humanistic spirit, in his ability to recognize the true dignity of his fellow men, he was one of the princes of the human race. While the other religious leaders were content

[7]

to sing the glory of God, Francis raised a hymn to the dignity of man. While others concentrated on the kingdom of heaven, Francis set about to build a kingdom of heaven on earth. The saintly man of Assisi began the first chapter in the social history of Western Europe—a thoroughgoing reconstruction in the material plane of human existence.

It followed that there would be great changes from the old order on the artistic plane also. But who was there to carry on the work from where Francis had left off? Now that the masses were beginning to awaken from their sleep, who would open their eyes to the beauties of the new day that was dawning over the world?

IV

GIOTTO DI BONDONE came to the Church of Francis at Assisi on a commission to paint a series of frescoes illustrating the life of the saint. As he stood in the chapel above the ashes of this holy man he must have trembled at the thought of the deep responsibility before him. He was to paint a great sacred subject, and yet he had not been initiated into the rituals of ecclesiastical art. His native background was the soil, the sky, the pasturelands where the sheep grazed, not the rigid golds and silvers of the Byzantine panels. He was most alive when he told homely anecdotes to his rustic companions. Like our own Lincoln, Giotto had an uncommon genius for the homely story. Everything came to his mind in the form of the concrete, the pictorial, the dramatic. He was a simple soul grounded on a deep religious faith. No one was better qualified to interpret the legend of Francis of Assisi, if only he could be made to realize that. Why all that trembling as he stood on the spot ready to paint? Now for a time he was alone with Francis, and Francis was ready to listen to him, to make friends with him—if only he would tell the proper anecdote for the occasion. And suddenly the anecdote came to his mind. Now Francis would have laughed to hear it, this story of the clumsy pig. One day, as Giotto had been standing and talking to a number of friends, a pig ran into their midst and bowled the artist over into the gutter. Giotto got slowly to his feet and pardoned the presumptuous pig. All his life he had borrowed the hair of pigs for the bristles of his brush, and now at last the debt was repaid. An appropriate story, this, for the man who had talked to the birds and who understood the souls of all living things. Now, there, the tension was broken. Giotto took up his brush and painted the first broad stroke upon the wall. The Renaissance had begun in earnest.

V

Giotto painted twenty-eight frescoes on the life of St Francis. And in these frescoes he revolutionized art. Hitherto the artists had depicted not men but graven images. Giotto introduced on canvas men and women who felt and hated and loved. Hitherto it had been considered blasphemy for an artist to introduce into a religious painting a tree, a flower, a brook or any other object of natural scenery. But Giotto made an effective use of nature as a background for his series of frescoes. St Francis would have felt no more at home on a background of rich gold and silver than Giotto himself. For Francis, too, had been a shepherd. The painter would have done violence to the spirit of the saint had he not broken with the conventional art of the day and put his own simple genius to the interpretation of his fellow artist in human simplicity.

Step by step Giotto interpreted the major incidents in the life of St Francis. In the first fresco the young Francis is confronted by an elderly man who throws himself at his feet and prophesies that someday he will become a saint. In the second fresco Francis gives his clothes to a beggar and accepts the poor man's garments in return. Henceforth he realizes that he must enlist as a soldier in the great army of Peace. He hands his worldly

possessions over to his father and thereby signifies that he re-
nounces all the paternal protection of the home and the Church
and that he commends himself to the protection of God alone.
In one very beautiful fresco Francis is shown in an attitude of
prayer, beating his breast and whispering to the Lord, "I am the
most unworthy of thy sinners." Kneeling behind Francis is a
disciple, Fra Leone, who gazes up to heaven where he sees,
suspended in the blue, four golden thrones. The throne in the
center, larger than the rest, is empty in its rich splendor. An
angel looks down at Leone and points with one hand to the
empty throne and with the other to Francis. The throne had
belonged formerly to a rebellious archangel, and now it is await-
ing the arrival of the humble Francis. All the frescoes are touching in their simplicity and profound in their religious faith.
St Francis and Giotto—two of the gentlest brothers of the common man!

With the introduction of landscape into painting Giotto made
his first great contribution to modern art. With the landscape as
a background he worked out the first general scheme of three-
dimensional perspective. He replaced the grotesque Byzantine
representations of flat and lifeless anatomy with solid, lifelike
men and women. The colors lack the subtle gradations of the
later Renaissance, to be sure. Giotto has not as yet mastered the
problem of light and shadow. His pigments are rich and simple,
masses of tints that "stare right out from their depths." He had
an uncanny feeling for the dramatic, the animated gesture, the
impulsive act. He painted as he lived—zestfully, vigorously,
spontaneously, with every fiber of his being. The genius of
Giotto, like the genius of Abraham Lincoln, was grounded in a
sound, athletic body, toughened by perpetual contact with the
out-of-doors. In his veins flowed the rhythm of the swinging ax.
All his paintings, even those of his death scenes, are full of
motion. They tell vivid stories in a concrete manner. Every
figure in every picture plays its part in the telling of the story.

And always there is a dramatic unity to the picture. In his fresco on the death of St Francis, for example, the focal point is the head of Francis in his death sleep. There are three groups of monks gathered about the bed in grief. In the first of these groups stand five monks, rigid and upright as a row of poplars. They form a solid frame behind the beloved head, a bulwark to protect the body from the profane. The other two groups are arranged, in various attitudes, on either side of the bed. Some of the monks kneel reverently; one kisses the feet of the dead man; another kisses his lifeless hand; still another gazes steadfastly into the face as if to trace the soul as it begins its flight. One of the Franciscans holds the banner of their order, slightly inclined, as if in salute to the dead man. Around the head of Francis there is a halo which forms the center of the composition. The monks at the bedside are merely subordinate themes climaxed by the halo. And then there is an epilogue, painted in a line diagonally upward from the body of the picture. Once the eye of the observer has arrived at the head of St Francis, it follows the diagonal that traces the ascent of the soul to heaven. A very simple invention on the part of the artist leads the eye irresistibly to this vision of St Francis as he is borne aloft by four angels. For right by the corpse kneels a monk who turns his eyes heavenward in fascinated wonder at the transfiguration of the man of Assisi. The entire picture is a dramatic moment—the ascent of a human soul.

To Giotto no idea was too abstract for pictorial representation. In the series of frescoes on St Francis he painted an episode of the saint's marriage to My Lady Poverty. This picture is a study in which the moral idea is given material form. My Lady Poverty appears in the shape of a woman of sorrow whose feet are walking among thorns but whose head is crowned with the fragrance of a blossoming rose bush. At first Francis is painfully embarrassed at the meeting, but Jesus smiles upon him and gives him to the woman in holy matrimony. Two malevolent little boys in the foreground toss sticks and stones at her. But behind her, in the background, a man gives his coat to a beggar; and high above, in the heavens, an angel wings his way to the gates of St Peter, bearing the coat in his hands. This picture constitutes one of the most touching eulogies on poverty in the history of art. Yet just before his death, ironically enough, the artist composed a satirical poem on poverty, characterizing it not as the bride of holiness but as the mistress of despair. Giotto had lived long enough to recognize the reverse as well as the obverse side upon the mysterious coin of human destiny.

Fortunately for Giotto, his knowledge of poverty, especially in his last years, was objective rather than subjective. He observed it as an outsider. For he had become prosperous in his chosen art. He traveled the length and breadth of Italy and collected a tidy fortune for his work. He had acquired the double technique of making pictures and making money. He pitied his fellow artists who lacked his business acumen, and he pitied his fellow businessmen who lacked his artistic vision. How this vision had come to him, one of the Lord's most humble servants, he could not understand. But it was his. It was as easy for him to paint a great picture as to whistle a simple tune—a feat that amazed even the most understanding of his friends. Once, when he was a struggling young artist just out of Cimabue's shop, he had painted a scene from Dante's *Paradise* in the chapel of the Podesta at Florence. Dante, an official of Florence and the admiration of the entire literary world, had offered himself as a flaming torch at the altar of the beautiful Beatrice. Giotto met Dante in Florence and painted his portrait—the only picture that ever caught the ecstasy of Beatrice in Dante's eyes. Dante had interrupted the routine of his own successful political life to give the young and struggling artist advice about his art. They became fast friends. Giotto left Florence and traveled to fame and fortune. He married a homely peasant girl and helped her to raise six homely peasant children. He built a comfortable homestead and entertained his neighbors at a sumptuous board. Here, in 1306, came a lonely, sorrowful exile to beg for shelter. It was Dante, once prosperous and proud. Accused of political corruption by his enemies, he had been banished from his native city. How reversed were their positions when he sat down at Giotto's board! As he broke bread with his friend and looked at the faces around him he recalled his own house and hospitality in those better days, when the most beautiful faces in the land had paid homage to him. "How does it happen," he burst out involuntarily, "that a man with so homely a family can find the inspiration in his soul to paint such beautiful pictures!"

VI

Giotto's last Testament of Beauty, just before his death in 1336, sent him into the very heavens, so to speak. The Campanile at Florence, better known as Giotto's Tower, is a miracle of architecture, rising two hundred and ninety-two feet in the air—a monument of iridescent marble under the blue Italian sky. For Giotto, like many of the other artists of the Renaissance, was an architect as well as a painter. His was the genius to create solid as well as surface beauty. The Campanile consists of four stories. There are no windows in the first and second stories. Instead there is a façade of brilliant bas-relief. The two upper stories have Gothic windows set off by bands of mosaic. Giotto felt right at home as he stood on the greatest of his scaffolds, under the open sky, to paint upon this tower his final hymn to the glory of God. And this painting, like all his other work, is a mixture of rustic simplicity and realistic humor. On one of the bas-reliefs a little puppy watches a flock of sheep go by. John Ruskin once showed a photograph of the puppy to a class of young students he was instructing in England. Here was an unkempt and bedraggled little Socrates of the canine world, staring with a fooolish-wise look across the centuries out of the mists of the Middle Ages. The sight of this picture moved Ruskin's pupils to shouts of joyous admiration and Ruskin himself to tears.

This little puppy was worth the splendor of all the medieval art that had gone before Giotto. For it ushered in a new age. It opened the eyes of the world to a new kind of beauty—the beauty of the commonplace.

MICHELANGELO

Great Paintings by Michelangelo

Florence, Uffizi Gallery: *Holy Family*.

London, National Gallery: *Madonna and Child*, *The Entombment* (unfinished), *St John the Baptist* (unfinished).

Rome, Pauline Chapel: *The Conversion of St Paul*, *The Crucifixion of St Peter*.

Rome, Sistine Chapel, Back Wall: *The Last Judgment* (200 figures).

Rome, Sistine Chapel, Ceiling: *The Creation and the Fall of Man* (343 figures).

There is a copy of the *Holy Family* at the Boston Museum of Fine Arts.

Michelangelo Buonarroti

1475-1564

ONE DAY LEONARDO, elegant, smiling, trim, was walking down the Piazza della Trinita in Florence. A number of prominent citizens were sitting on a bench discussing a passage in Dante. One of the citizens looked up and saw Leonardo. "Gentlemen," he said, "here is the man who can settle our argument."

Just at this moment a young man appeared on the other side of the square. His face, with its flattened, broken nose, seemed to hold a perpetual grudge against the world. His short tumbled hair fell untidily over his forehead. His clothes were crumpled, his boots were covered with marble dust, and his hands were rough, with bits of clay clinging to the nails. Leonardo pointed to him. "There comes Michelangelo, gentlemen. You had better ask *him* to explain Dante."

Michelangelo, always on the watch for insults, took Leonardo's words as a direct challenge. "Explain it yourself!" he shouted in derision. "You can do everything, you know. Didn't you make a model of a horse and then quit the job because you couldn't cast it in bronze?"

Michelangelo passed on but turned back for a final fling:

"And those fat geese of Milan entrusted *you*, of all people, with that job!"

This explosion of ill will was the outlet for Michelangelo's resentment against his fate. For he was still young and comparatively unknown, whereas Leonardo, who was his senior by twenty-three years, was already acclaimed as one of the leading artists of the day. Later on Michelangelo was to outstrip his older rival both in fortune and in fame. But at this moment he was as yet unaware of his great destiny.

II

HIS FATHER, Ludovico di Lionardo Buonarroti, was the mayor of Caprese. The little boy grew up in a family of men. For he had four brothers and no sisters, and his mother died when he was six years old. The elder Buonarroti, of noble birth but poor and often out of a job, was ill-tempered and violent and hard on his children. He was especially irritated at Michelangelo's repeated declaration that he wanted to be an artist. No Buonarroti, he was determined, should be allowed to waste his time with the plebeian instruments of the chisel and the brush. His five sons must go into business. They must become bankers, like the famous families of the Pitti, the Sforzi, the Medici! And so he took his young dreamer of a son and tried to whip some sense into him.

But in vain. In spite of all his beatings and his scoldings, Michelangelo still insisted that he wanted to be an artist. And so, reluctantly, he apprenticed the thirteen-year-old boy to Messer Ghirlandajo and washed his hands of him.

Ghirlandajo was at that time painting the walls of Santa Maria Novella. He set his apprentices to the task of grinding the colors and copying bits of drapery from his carefully prepared sketches. But the copies of Michelangelo were better than the originals, and this made Ghirlandajo extremely jealous. He showed his jealousy in a hundred and one petty annoyances; and the sensitive young boy, having endured the misunderstanding of his father, now suffered from the envy of his teacher. He therefore conceived a mistrust of his fellow men, and this mistrust was to remain with him to the end of his days.

It was a fortunate thing, however, that Ghirlandajo disliked Michelangelo. For, in his determination to get rid of him, he palmed him off upon Bertoldo, the old man who was teaching youngsters the sculptor's art from the recently excavated antiques in the Garden of the Medici. This place was a veritable Garden of Eden to Michelangelo. For here he learned the work for which God had shaped his hands, and here he met the man who introduced him to the world of learning, of art, of music, of poetry, of beauty, of wit—everything for which his eager young soul was so passionately athirst. One day, as Michelangelo was chiseling out the face of an old man in the garden of Lorenzo de' Medici, Lorenzo the Magnificent himself happened to be strolling through the garden. He stopped when he came to Michelangelo's bit of statuary. He examined it and then turned to the young sculptor. "My boy," he said, "don't you know that an old man must have lost some of his teeth?"

Michelangelo was all excitement at the thought that Lorenzo had spoken to him. Seizing his tools, he knocked out one of the teeth and then turned to Lorenzo. "Is this better?"

"Yes," laughed Lorenzo. "Very much better!"

Lorenzo became interested in this quick-witted and talented youngster of fourteen. He took him into the Palazzo Medici, he allowed him to sit at his table, he encouraged him to play with his children, he presented him with a violet cloak, he offered him five ducats (equivalent in purchasing power to about fifty dollars) a month, and he opened his eyes to the glories of the pagan world. Here Michelangelo drank beauty and wisdom from the lips of the mystic Ficino, the philosopher Pico Mirandola, the poet Poliziano and the numerous scholars and writers and artists who came to the Medici palace from all the corners of the earth. At the Medici table, the center of the civilization of the day, Apollo was the Lord of Light and Plato his leading prophet and saint.

It was under this pagan influence that Michelangelo was encouraged to produce his first original work—the *Battle of the Centaurs*, modeled in relief—a living, fighting entanglement of half men, half horses, full of the symmetrical beauty of Greek nakedness, a myth of the dead past reborn into the world of the Renaissance.

It was a world in which Michelangelo felt perfectly at home. For at this period of his life he was supremely happy. But then there came a tragedy, and he was to bear the physical and mental scars of this tragedy throughout the rest of his days. One of his talented fellow apprentices was the quick-tempered and strong-fisted Torrigiano. This fellow could fight even better than he could paint, and it was an evil hour that prompted Michelangelo to criticize his painting. What happened after that is best told in Torrigiano's own words: "On that day I was more than usually annoyed by his criticism. I clenched my fist and gave him such a whack on his nose that the bones and cartilage felt as soft as a wafer. So he bore my mark as long as he lived."

Michelangelo was carried home for dead. When the wound was healed he saw his disfigured face in the mirror. From that time on he withdrew into himself and began to look with suspicion upon the entire human race. He never fully recovered from this tragic disfigurement of his body and the equally tragic distortion of his soul.

III

AT ABOUT THIS TIME Michelangelo heard the preaching of Savonarola, the apostle politician who inveighed against the pagan immorality and the unrepentant savagery of the secret rulers of the city. This preaching exerted a tremendous influence upon the sensitive young artist. One of his brothers, under this influence, entered a Dominican monastery. Michelangelo, too, was tempted for a time to renounce his art and to shut himself away from the world. There began in his soul a violent struggle between skepticism and religion, between beauty and duty, between the ideas of the old world and the ideals of the new. But after a time the struggle ceased and, fortunately for his art, Michelangelo was able to reconcile the two apparently irreconcilable elements. After all, he concluded, there is no good reason why an artist cannot subscribe to the best features of paganism *and* of Christianity. Perhaps the highest kind of art lay precisely in the *marriage* of the two, in the ultimate union of the holiness of beauty and the beauty of holiness. This reconciliation between paganism and Christianity brought peace to Michelangelo's spirit and proved to be the harmonizing principle of all his future masterpieces.

While this struggle was going on in Michelangelo's soul his patron died. The passing of Lorenzo the Magnificent precipitated an age of political turmoil. Savonarola had aroused the populace against the wanton frivolity of Piero de' Medici, the son of Lorenzo. King Charles of France was marching against the city. A mob of penitent fanatics was tearing down the pictures and the statues of Florence. The treasures of the centuries lay about the streets in heaps of ruins. Michelangelo, his young dream of art temporarily shattered, fled from the city.

He went to Bologna, where he received a commission to make a statue for the parish church. It was a light-bearing angel, a sort of baptized Apollo, a symbol of the reunion between the old world and the new.

But again Michelangelo was pursued by the resentment of his fellow artists, who were jealous of the fact that this young upstart was already surpassing their own best achievements.

—Literally hounded out of Bologna, he went back to Florence; and after a brief but not altogether welcome sojourn in his native town he went on to seek his fortune in Rome. When he arrived in the City of the Vatican he had just turned twenty-one.

IV

ROME, the eternal city of faith. But the guardians of the faith had betrayed their trust. What Michelangelo found on his arrival in 1496 was a city of music and murder, of culture and beauty and debauchery, of dancing and feasting and poetry and poison, of beautiful temples and ugly prison cells, of piety in the homes of the humble and lust in the palaces of the rich. And for two years he found himself a stranger there, out of tune with the world. "I have no friends," he said, "I need none, and I will have none."

At twenty-three, however, he found recognition even in this city of savage self-interest and merciless rivalry. He applied for a commission to model a statue of Christ and the Mother for the Church of St Peter. "The work," he wrote in his application, "will be such that no living master could do it better." He won the competition and made the statue. All the artistic people in Rome flocked to see the work. The dead Christ, his arms emaciated (they had actually been modeled from a corpse), was lying across the lap of a very beautiful woman much younger than himself. The spectators admired and were amazed. They asked the sculptor why he had made the Mother so much younger than the Son. "Don't you know," retorted Michelangelo, "that any woman who is pure preserves her youth for many years? How much more true is this of the Madonna, who has never yielded to human desire and whose features, moreover, have been transfigured by divine love!"

Throughout his life Michelangelo was to paint and to model figures, not in accordance with the conventions of the day but rather in accordance with the promptings of his own philosophy. He was one of the first of the moderns to apply psychology to art.

When this statue was finished Michelangelo yielded for the first and the last time in his life to the weakness of vanity. He had himself locked into the church at night; and there, under the light of a candle, he chiseled his name and his native town upon the statue. Thereafter he never signed any of his other completed works. Like the trees and the mountains of nature, the masterpieces of Michelangelo have no need to bear the signature of their creator.

V

MICHELANGELO returned to Florence at the age of twenty-six. Passing one day through the courtyard of the Cathedral, he stopped to examine a magnificent block of marble that had been lying there idly for forty-six years. He offered to do something with this marble if given the chance. The offer was accepted. Michelangelo began the work on August 2, 1502. On January 25, 1504, the colossal statue of David was completed.

This Giant, as it was called, became so epoch-making that for decades the people of Italy reckoned their time by it. "The year the Giant was set up" came to be known as the first year of the New Era. For the statue of David is indeed the introduction to a new era in sculpture. The statue now stands in the Florentine Academy of Arts—a naked athletic figure with a small head, huge body, slender waist, thin arms and strong hands whose veins stand out like whipcords. With his left hand he takes the sling from his shoulder, and in his right hand he holds the stone ready for its flight against the foe. But the most arresting part of the statue is the face. It is the face of a virile, determined, scornful and at the same time compassionate young man—the idealized face of Michelangelo himself. Like David, he too was ready to challenge the Goliaths of the day. The singer of Judea and the sculptor of Florence, two men with resolute, sensitive souls, two artists who knew how to fight!

The fame of the Giant brought Michelangelo back to Rome. The new pope, Julius II, was anxious to perpetuate his memory with a tomb such as the world had never seen. And the one man to do the job was Michelangelo. For Michelangelo, like himself, was a dreamer of stupendous dreams. Together they planned this magnificent tomb. It was to consist of forty over-lifesize figures who were to stand guard around the body of the pope. Two of the figures were to portray Moses and Paul; two others were to be allegorical symbols of heaven and earth; the rest were to represent the greatest saints and heroes of the past. "How much," asked the pope, "will this monument cost?"

Michelangelo thought it better to aim too high than too low. Accordingly he replied: "One hundred thousand scudi."

"Suppose we make it two hundred thousand." And before Michelangelo could recover from his astonishment the pope waved him away. "Don't stand there gaping, young man. Get to work!"

Elated with his commission, Michelangelo betook himself to Carrara, where he selected a thousand ducats' worth of marble. When these "mountains of stone" arrived at St Peter's Michelangelo began to hew them into life. But the progress was slow, and the payments from the pope were too irregular for steady work. Once more the genius of Michelangelo was being hampered by the jealousy of his rivals. One of these rivals was Bramante, an artist with a great talent and a puny soul. Anxious to win for himself the favor and the ducats of the pope, he told him that to dig a man's grave in his own lifetime would be an evil omen. Why not, he suggested, build a church instead of a tomb? He, Bramante, would be the architect. He would rebuild St Peter's and make it a landmark for the ages!

[*24*]

The pope listened to Bramante. Michelangelo, in conversation with one of the pope's jewelers, heard that he was to receive not another penny from the Vatican. "This news," he wrote to a friend, "alarmed me very much. I came to beg for the money that was due me, so that I might go on with the work. His Holiness told me to come again on Monday. I went on Monday and on Wednesday and on Thursday and on Friday. Finally a groom of the chambers said to me, 'I have orders not to admit you.' At these words my anger flared up, and I shouted: 'Then tell the pope that in the future, if he wants me, he will have to look for me himself!'"

And so, snubbed by the pope, he fled from Rome and went back to Florence. His distrust of humanity was now more intense than ever. The whole world, he felt, was against him. In all his business deals he was convinced that the other fellow was trying to rob him. If his tailor made his vest a little too tight, he believed that it was done deliberately, in order to vex him. He refused to receive presents from anybody. "Beware," he said, "of the Greeks—or of the Italians—bearing gifts." He always locked his workshop, for fear that his fellow artists might steal his ideas. As for ideas of their own, he believed they had none. All of them, he remarked caustically, were imitators. Once he was called upon to criticize a portrait painted by another artist. "Very nice," he said, "but everything in this picture is borrowed." And then, with a sarcastic smile, he continued: "I'm just wondering what will happen to this picture on the Day of Judgment, when all the bodies will want their limbs back again."

Whenever he was hurt he withdrew into the shell of his pride and wouldn't let anyone come near him. The pope ordered him again and again to come back, but Michelangelo refused. He would brook no commands from anyone. "He who begins by being a prince's pack mule," he said, "will have the load on his back till he dies." Finally the pope *entreated* him to return, for an artist of Michelangelo's genius was an asset to the Vatican. Michelangelo yielded to the entreaty and went to meet the pope. Not, however, at Rome, but halfway, at Bologna.

"You are a strange man," said the pope. "Instead of coming to us, you have waited until we came to you."

"Your Holiness has done me a great hurt."

"But I shall heal it, I promise you." Laying his hand on the kneeling artist's head, he blessed him.

And thus their quarrel was patched up. "Michelangelo," wrote Soderini, the ruler of Florence, "is one of those men from whom you can get anything by kind words. . . . You must show him affection, assure him of your esteem—and then he will produce such works as will amaze the world."

VI

As a result of the pope's kindness Michelangelo now produced one of those works that amazed the world. The project of the tomb had been abandoned, at least for the present. For the pope was still superstitious about the matter of planning for his death during his lifetime. Instead he asked Michelangelo to paint the ceiling of the Sistine Chapel—the twelve figures of the apostles, conceived in such dimensions as no painter before him had even dared to imagine.

Here, then, was another undertaking worthy of Michelangelo's genius. For four years he literally locked himself into the chapel, admitting no one except the color grinder and, occasionally, the pope. He painted most of the work with his head thrown back and his eyes looking upward. Long after the painting was finished he was obliged to hold every letter and every book that he wanted to read high above his head. For the muscles of his eyes had become accustomed to this peculiarly abnormal point of view.

When the pope beheld the completed work he was enchanted

with it—except for one detail. Most of the saints and apostles in the earlier pictures had been painted with gilded embroidery lavishly displayed over their garments. "Why," asked the pope of Michelangelo, "have you omitted the gold trimmings?"

"Holy Father," replied Michelangelo, "in those days the men and the women were poor and honest. They had faith, but they had no gold."

VII

IN ONE OF HIS SONNETS George Santayana writes that God doubled creation when he created Shakespeare. The same may be said of Michelangelo. For the painting of the Sistine Chapel is creation created anew. The pope's original plan of the twelve apostles had now grown into a complete vision of heaven and earth. At first there is darkness and divine loneliness—the expectant moment before the birth of the world. And then—the Eternal, borne aloft by clouds of angels. He divides the light from the darkness; He fashions the sun and the moon; He separates the water from the land; He stirs Adam into life with the touch of His finger (to Michelangelo God is the Divine Sculptor); He shapes Eve out of the flesh of Adam; He displays before her the trees of the garden and the tempting fruit; He dispatches the angel to drive Adam and Eve out of Paradise with his flaming sword; and He sends down the waters of His wrath upon the sinful race of men. And round about this central picture of creation and destruction sit the sibyls and the prophets, looking on, reflecting, hoping, exhorting, praying—the eternal intermediaries between God and Man.

VIII

POPE JULIUS DIED, and his heirs requested Michelangelo to complete the tomb which he had begun during the pope's lifetime.

The times were tragic. War and pestilence ravaged the land. Buildings were torn down, paintings were demolished, and bronze statues, including some of Michelangelo's best works, were melted into cannon. But Michelangelo, in spite of all these discouragements, went on. New popes were elected, ruled and died; new wars came and devastated the country; new promises were made and broken; and throughout it all Michelangelo continued with his work on the monument. Illness came and still further ravaged his none-too-prepossessing features. Disappointments seared more and more deeply into his ravaged soul. But his fingers, fashioned by God for the creation of beauty, went on with their inspired labor. He was accused of laziness, self-interest, dishonesty. His rivals insinuated that he was being bribed by the owners of the Carrara quarries to purchase their marble for his commissions. The accusation was, of course, baseless. But Michelangelo's patrons listened to the evil tongues and compelled him to get the inferior marble of Saravezza. Michelangelo, "a lowly, impoverished, crazy human being," as he described himself at this time, went on with his monument and confided his bitterness and his vision to the silent marble figures that he was bringing into life. He has given us a vivid portrait of himself at the age of forty-seven—short curly hair, a forehead wrinkled with the furrows of suffering, thoughtful, penetrating, yet haunted eyes, narrow lips compressed into a defiant firmness, a short straggly black beard, and the entire face dominated by the broad, flat, broken nose—the features of a man who has known cynicism and sorrow, rebellion and beauty, stubbornness and resignation, the face of a satyr and a saint.

For twenty-three years he went on with his work on the monument, this lonely god lost in the world of men. The plague carried off his favorite brother and came near to costing him his own life. It was almost impossible, as he tells us in one of his sonnets, to struggle on:

In thraldom such as this, in such disgust,
With plans miscarried, spirit tossed and torn—
And then strike fire from marble, if you can!

But even under these circumstances he succeeded in striking
fire from the marble. At last, at the age of seventy, he finished
the monument of Pope Julius II. The central figure of the monument is the statue of Moses—"the supreme achievement," as it
has been called, "of modern sculpture." This statue is half god,
half man, a perfect blending of Christianity and paganism. Two
horns protrude from the narrow skull. He is seated, and his
beard descends like a tangled vine from his face to his knees.
His huge knotted arms are bare, and one of his hands, strong,
vibrant, sensitive, rests upon the tablet of the law. His right foot
is planted firmly upon the pedestal, and his left foot is thrown
back as if he is ready to rise and to thunder forth his commandments to a disobedient people. And there is thunder, too, in the
fierceness of his eye and the angry projection of his lower lip.
It is passion held back but ready, upon the least provocation, to
burst into fury. The terrible prophet of an angry God, the judgment of the superman upon the folly and the savagery of mankind.

And at this time Michelangelo himself, like Moses, pro-
nounced judgment upon the folly and the savagery of mankind.
He painted the *Last Judgment* upon the walls of the Sistine
Chapel. This painting is a companion piece to the *Creation*
which, a quarter of a century earlier, he had painted upon the
ceiling of that chapel. Again, as of old, he painted most of his
figures naked. "This work," said one of the cardinals, "is fit for
a tavern, not for a chapel." And when the pope suggested that
Michelangelo cover those figures with draperies the artist replied
bluntly: "Let His Holiness attend to the souls of the people and
let *me* attend to the bodies."

The *Last Judgment* is the painting of an innumerable swarm of human beings—the world—whirled along in a dizzy maelstrom around the figure of Christ. And Christ in this painting is not the God of Love but the God of Vengeance. He had come once to redeem the world, and the world had rejected Him. He now comes again, but this time to *judge* the world. There is now no pity in His judgment. There is only implacable justice, tempestuous grandeur, majestic force. The Virgin stands sorrowfully and helplessly by, with her eyes averted, as her Son waves the trembling multitude to their last place of retribution—a handful of them upward to their heavenly reward, the vast majority of them downward, to their eternal damnation. The everlasting struggle between Heaven and Hell. The history of the Human Race. The symbolical representation of the inexorable destiny of Man.

One day, as he was working on the *Last Judgment*, he fell from the scaffolding and severely hurt his leg. Discouraged over the accident, he crawled home and shut himself up to die. But a doctor climbed in through the window and nursed him back to health. He returned to his enormous task and completed it on Christmas Eve, 1541.

Michelangelo finished the *Last Judgment* at the ripe old age of sixty-six. He was rich now and famous and the envy of all the artists of the world. Yet he was more unhappy than ever. For he had to pay the penalty of a long life—the loss of his dearest friends, one by one. Within a very short time three of them died. The first was a boy of fifteen, a young artist whom the childless Michelangelo had loved with the tenderness of a father. The second was the boy's uncle, Riccio, Michelangelo's financial adviser and most ardent admirer. "This man," he said, "was to me more than a brother." But the greatest of all was the third blow—the death of Vittoria Colonna. This brilliant and beautiful mystic was the only woman who had shown more than mere admiration for Michelangelo. For years they had interwoven their sentiments toward each other into a garland of letters and sonnets which are among the treasures of Italian literature. And then, suddenly, his belated dream of love came to an abrupt end. As he stood by the body of the woman he had idolized but had never embraced he took her cold hand and kissed it. "Nothing," he later confided to one of his intimate apprentices, "grieves me more than the fact that, even on her deathbed, I dared to kiss only her hand and not her lips."

And thus was the lonely old artist deprived of his last chance at mortal happiness. The death of Vittoria Colonna brought about a breakdown in his health. For weeks he lay critically ill. His great life was apparently nearing its end.

But he recovered. For his labor was not yet completed. He was to give the world one more masterpiece—considered by many the greatest of all his masterpieces—before the final summons came. He was seventy-three years old when the pope asked him to design the new dome for St Peter's. He refused. For he felt too old to undertake so tremendous a task. But the pope insisted, and finally Michelangelo consented—on one condition. He would receive no pay for this work. At most he would be able to give only a few months to this task, perhaps a year or two if the fates would be unusually kind to him. How much longer could a man of seventy-three be expected to summon the physical and the mental vigor necessary for so tremendous an undertaking?

And so, with this reservation, he undertook the job. The pope died and four other popes after him—and Michelangelo was still busy at the task. For sixteen years he kept at it, the power of his body and his mind undiminished to the end. Finally, at the age of eighty-nine, he rested from his labor.

But not altogether. He spent the last months of his life designing and hewing out the statues for his own monument. There were to be four statues in all—Christ taken down from the cross, supported by the Madonna, who in turn is sustained by the helping hands of Mary Magdalen and Nicodemus. The face of

Nicodemus is covered by a heavy cowl. But the features showing through the cowl are the grief-stricken features of Michelangelo. Years ago, at the beginning of his career, he had represented himself as a fellow conqueror of David. Now, at the end, he depicted himself as a fellow sufferer of Jesus.

On February 12, 1564, he stood all day working on the figure of Christ. On the fourteenth he went out on horseback in a pelting rain. Four days later, still in his full consciousness, he died.

On his deathbed he regretted, not the cessation of his life, but the end of his labors. "I am dying," he said to Cardinal Salviati, who was ministering to him, "when I have scarcely got through learning the A B C of art. I was just getting ready for my real work!"

RAPHAEL

Baltimore, Epstein Collection: *Emilia Pia de Montefeltro.*

Bologna, Gallery: *St Cecilia.*

Boston, Gardner Museum: *Pietà, Portrait of Inghirami.*

Boston, Museum of Fine Arts: *Madonna and St Francis.*

Detroit, Institute of Arts: *Portrait of Taddeo Taddei.*

Dresden: *Sistine Madonna.*

Florence, Pitti Gallery: *Madonna della Sedia, La Donna Velata, Portrait of Pope Leo X.*

Florence, Uffizi Gallery: *Madonna of the Goldfinch, Portrait of Himself, Portrait of Pope Julius II.*

London, National Gallery: *The Ansidei Madonna, St Catherine, The Vision of a Knight.*

Milan, Brera Gallery: *The Marriage of the Virgin.*

New York, Metropolitan Museum of Art: *The Agony in the Garden, Madonna and Child Enthroned with Saints.*

Paris, Louvre: *Holy Family, La Belle Jardinière, St George.*

Philadelphia, Widener Collection: *Madonna and Child.*

Rome, Vatican: Seventy *Frescoes.*

Rome, Villa Farnesina: Fresco, *Galatea.*

St Louis, Schoenberg Collection: *Portrait of a Young Man.*

Washington, National Gallery: *Madonna and Child.*

Raffaello Sanzio

1483–1520

Raphael's father, Giovanni Santi, was a painter, poet and greengrocer all rolled into one. His paintings were mediocre; his poetry was labored and stilted; but his vegetables were rich and luscious and fresh. For the little duchy of Urbino, the mountain city in which the elder Santi lived and in which Raphael was born, enjoyed the triple blessing of a rich earth, warm sunlight and sweet rain. Young Raphael, named by his father after one of the archangels, absorbed into his soul the earth and the sunlight and the rain of his native province. And, above all, its rugged scenery and its artistic treasures. Few cities in the world were better calculated to feed the eyes of a growing young artist with the wonder of beauty. Urbino was a natural canvas of fertile valleys and smiling hills that suddenly started up into abrupt mountains. On the one side a jagged outline of fantastic peaks that towered into the sunset; on the other the blue shimmer of the Adriatic just barely visible in the distance. As for the city itself, it was one of the most precious jewels in the golden crown of the Renaissance. The pictures and the statues and the buildings of Urbino suffered but little in comparison with those of Florence, or even of Rome itself. Urbino was already famous as the mother of artists when Raphael was born (March 28, 1483).

Raphael's childhood was happy but all too brief. At the age of eleven he had lost his mother, a brother and a sister, and his father. The deep lines of suffering had been thus early engraved upon the etching of his character. The "archangel child" was from the very beginning destined for immortal glory and mortal sorrow.

When his father died Raphael was put into the custody of his uncle, Bartolommeo Santi. Fortunately his father had left him a sufficient inheritance to enable him to study art without the constant fear of hunger. He left his native city at sixteen, took up his residence at the Umbrian city of Perugia and apprenticed himself to the most famous of its artists, Perugino.

The talents of the pupil were infinitely superior to those of the master. Raphael, however, did manage to absorb from his teacher an instinct for coloring and an eye for perspective—two technical phases in which Perugino stood supreme among the Italian artists of that period.

The artists of Umbria, following the lead of Perugino, were experts in the technique of painting. But in the choice of their subjects they were behind the times. Looking down upon the pagan art of the Renaissance, they confined their efforts to the painting of religious themes. This exclusiveness, while it narrowed the scope of their work, was nevertheless good for their pockets. The peasants of Umbria were so deeply attached to their faith that they were eager to spend the savings of a lifetime on a religious picture for their village church. Food for their souls was to them more important than nourishment for their bodies. The Umbrian artists couldn't work fast enough to supply the constant demand for pictures of saints and Madonnas and Christs on the cross. It was an encouraging atmosphere in which

Raphael served the years of his apprenticeship. When, at the age of nineteen, he left Perugino he had acquired an expert technique and had laid the solid foundations of a fortune which, within a few years, was to be worth close to half a million dollars. But, above all, he had won a reputation for painting some of the most beautiful pictures that mortal eye had ever beheld.

II

LIKE MOST of the other great artists, Raphael prepared preliminary sketches, or cartoons, of his paintings. (These cartoons are not to be confused with the caricatures of our modern newspapers.) It is interesting to note the technique which he employed in making his cartoons. One of his earliest paintings was the *Coronation of the Virgin*. In preparing the sketches for this painting he used a young man as a model for the Virgin. The young fellow, dressed in tight-fitting hose that displays every line of his well-shaped body, sits with bowed head and with clasped hands while the crown is being held above him. In the finished picture the face and the figure assume the outlines of a woman and the body is covered with a flowing robe. But the position of the arms and the legs is exactly the same as in the preliminary sketch. Only the hands and the feet can be seen, but the rest of the body is there, in unmistakable outline. The position of every part of the body is so perfectly defined through the drapery because the artist has used an undraped figure for his original study. The preliminary sketches for many of the clothed figures in his later paintings were drawn in the nude. For Raphael was anxious that the parts of the body which were covered should be as accurately conceived as those parts which were exposed. At all times Raphael was as painstaking as a professional scientist in his exact observation and accurate representation of nature. No two faces, no two figures, no two poses, no two leaves upon a tree are exactly alike in the numerous paintings of Raphael. Like Leonardo and Michelangelo, Raphael was the perfect master of detail.

III

THE YEAR 1504 marked the beginning of the most eventful period of his life—travels, commissions, friendships with wealthy bankers and powerful noblemen, excursions into the beauties of ancient history and literature and art, lavish entertainments, incessant toil and fame. He was now a full-fledged citizen of the Renaissance, a lover of pagan beauty as well as of Christian purity, a painter of Venuses and Madonnas, of satyrs and saints, of Apollo, the Lord of Laughter, and of Jesus, the Prince of Sorrow. Seeking for the proper atmosphere in which this twofold aspect of his genius might find its full fruition, he came, at the age of twenty-one, to Florence.

Fiorenze, the City of Flowers. The art capital of Italy. The maelstrom of political rivalry, of military intrigue, of social pageantry, of religious controversy, of poetry and poison, of philosophy and debauchery, of fanatical asceticism and unbridled lust. Shortly after his arrival at this city with its dual personality Raphael became acquainted with both features through the influence of two of its leading citizens. These two men were the painter, Fra Bartolommeo, and the architect, Baccio d'Agnolo.

Fra Bartolommeo, a disciple of Savonarola, was prominent among those who, in 1497, had built a gigantic funeral pyre for all the ancient Greek and Roman books and paintings and statues that were to be found in Florence. Then, having "burnt and buried" the spirit of paganism, he had entered a Dominican convent to spend the rest of his days in praying and in painting sacred pictures. In spite of Bartolommeo's asceticism Raphael found in him a kindred spirit. For both of them possessed a stupendous imagination and a capacity for dreaming superb dreams in composition and in color. Their friendship, begun in Florence in 1504, lasted until the untimely death of Bartolommeo in 1517.

Bartolommeo had directed the eyes of Raphael toward heavenly things. Quite different was the influence exerted upon Raphael by his other friend, Baccio d'Agnolo. Baccio was a man of the world. His studio was the gathering place of the Florentine intelligentsia. Here the young Raphael rubbed elbows with the leading artists, poets, philosophers and wits of the day. And his own wit sparkled like a jewel in the general conversation. For Raphael was not only one of Italy's supreme artists but one of her most brilliant men. And he was as personable as he was brilliant. His face was like that of one of his Madonnas. There was as yet not the slightest suggestion of a beard upon his chin. His eyes held beautiful dreams in their liquid dark depths. His throat was long, slender and exquisitely shaped. And his mouth, when it opened in a smile, could turn even a carping critic into an admiring friend. The most ruthless noblemen and business-men of Italy, adventurers to whom killing was as natural as breathing, took Raphael under their protection and encouraged him and coddled him with an almost fatherly affection. They showered him with their commissions, they filled his purse with their ducats, and finally they brought his work to the attention of Pope Julius himself.

IV

IT WAS in the summer of 1508 that Raphael came into the patronage of Julius II. This soldier pope was more interested in the politics of the earth than he was in the glories of heaven. He had no taste for literature. "Why do you want to represent me with a book?" he said to Michelangelo. "I am no scholar. Give me a sword." He was a man of action and of boundless ambition. His interest in the arts was largely personal. He wanted to perpetuate himself as a lavish patron and to have his portrait immortalized by the greatest of the contemporary artists. He was a hard taskmaster. He treated his painters and his sculptors like talented worms. He got all the work that he could out of them, and then he crushed them under his feet. But to Raphael he was a kindly, smiling and indulgent protector. For Raphael had about him that gentle courtesy which transforms everything in its presence into a kindred gentleness.

When Raphael came to Rome he found the leading artists feverishly engaged in beautifying the city under the orders of Julius II. But immediately upon Raphael's arrival the pope dismissed all these artists, with the exception of Michelangelo and Bramante, in favor of his new protégé. The three titans now set out to produce the three wonders of the modern world—Michelangelo's monument of Pope Julius II, Bramante's restoration of the Church of St Peter and Raphael's decoration of the Vatican.

Raphael began his decoration in the Chamber of the Signature, so called because it was the room in which the pope signed the documents submitted to him by his ministers. For the theme of his painting Raphael took his cue from Petrarch, who in two of his poems describes the triumph of love and the triumph of fame. Raphael's pictures on the walls and the ceiling of the Chamber of the Signature represent the beauty of Hellenism and the glory of Christianity. On the one side we have a number of scenes taken from the history, the literature and the philosophy of the ancient world, and on the other a number of contrasting scenes taken from the Scriptures. The School of Athens and the Church of Rome; Plato and Dante; Venus and the Madonna; Apollo and Christ. The underlying motive of the theme is the superiority of Christianity at its best over Hellenism at its best. The composition has rhythm and cadence and perfect balance. The figures are set off, one against the other, like the phrases of a carefully constructed stanza. The picture is an immortal discussion between wisdom and holiness, between pleasure and sorrow, between laughter and love. It is, in short, an epic poem in paint.

The painting in the Chamber of the Signature is tolerant, thoughtful, serene. In the other rooms of the Vatican, however, it takes on a more turbulent tone. Pope Julius was a man of violent temper, of hasty decision, of stormy action. He wanted the winds of his own restlessness to blow through the atmosphere of the other paintings. And Raphael acceded to his wishes. He painted the conquests of the Church, the punishments of the heretics, the huzzahs of the multitude at the victories of the pope. The groups in these pictures are like swarms of bees buzzing and pressing one against the other—a whirlpool of passions let loose, of enthusiasm that knows no restraint. These paintings were meant to be a tribute to the greatness and the popularity of Pope Julius II, whose picture dominates the most important of them—*The Expulsion of Heliodorus from the Temple*. At the extreme right of this painting Heliodorus is being lashed out of the Temple by the whips of the infuriated angels, while on the extreme left Pope Julius II sits upon a throne, amidst the approving multitude, and looks with grim satisfaction upon this well-deserved punishment of the sinner. The pope had commissioned this painting in order to symbolize not only the expulsion of sin from the Temple but the expulsion of the French from Italy. In his desire to feed the vanity of the pope Raphael obliged himself to violate not only the purity of his conception but the chronology of his composition. He intermingled a sacred with a profane theme, and he inserted a modern pope into an ancient picture. It is easy to condemn Raphael for his easy acquiescence to the pope's wishes, to call him a man without backbone, or—as some of his extreme detractors have done— to accuse him of sycophancy, of insincerity and even of downright dishonesty. Let us remember, however, that the art of the sixteenth century depended upon patronage. Had Raphael antagonized his patrons, he could never have had the opportunity to enrich the world with his masterpieces. If, in so doing he also enriched his own pockets, it was merely an incident—and, as we shall see, a rather unlucky incident for Raphael.

V

RAPHAEL was still engaged in the decoration of the Vatican when Pope Julius died (1513). The new pope, Leo X, turned out to be an even greater patron of art than his predecessor. Unlike Julius II, Leo X loved art for art's sake. He had inherited his hunger for beauty from his father, Lorenzo the Magnificent, who had been the first and the most understanding of Michelangelo's admirers. The papacy of Leo X, like the reign of Lorenzo the Magnificent, was one continuous festival of intellectual and aesthetic epicureanism. Under his encouragement the genius of Raphael came to its full flower. And Raphael was but one of a numerous race of demigods at that period. The list of the names that graced the pontifical court of Leo X comprises one of the most brilliant pages in the roster of history's hall of fame. There were the sages and the poets—Ariosto, Bembo, Bibbiena, Castiglione, Beroaldus, Andrea Fulveo, Aretino; the architects, headed by Bramante and Fra Giocondo; the sculptors, under the leadership of Michelangelo; and the painters, Peruzzi, the two Sansovinos, San Gallo, Melzi, Signorelli, Beltraffio and Fanfaia. And over them all, lordly, proud, serene, presided that philosophical Prince of the Renaissance, Leonardo da Vinci. It was an age of magnificence, of great achievement and even greater dreams, of much genuine beauty and not a little artificial pomposity. It was an age of hard work and hard play, of feasting and flattery, of sparkling wine and brilliant epigrams. And it was an age of unlimited ambition. Everybody was desperately trying to outpaint, outmodel and outsmart everybody else. Good-natured deception was the order of the day. On one occasion the financial magnate, Agostino Chigi, gave a banquet to the pope. The feast was spread in a gorgeous pavilion that had been raised on the banks of the Tiber. Each massive silver plate, as soon as it was emptied, was ordered by the host to be hurled into the river. The guests looked on with open-mouthed amazement at the reckless extravagance of their host. But there was a cunning method in this apparent madness of Chigi. He had spread a number of nets under the surface of the water, and immediately after the departure of the guests he ordered the silver dishes to be fished up again.

Such was the material and cultural atmosphere of Rome under the papacy of Leo X. And it was in this atmosphere that Raphael was able to climb to the heights. His genius, his indefatigable energy and his unfailing courtesy combined to make him the most popular painter of his day. He received a host of commissions from the pope, from Chigi, from Cardinal Bibbiena, from all the influential and wealthy citizens of Rome. He had acquired a whole academy of pupils, who adored him like a young god. Whenever he walked in the streets an escort of fifty disciples followed worshipfully behind him. One day Michelangelo twitted him about this entourage. "You go about the streets," he said, "with a suite like a general." Whereupon Raphael promptly replied, "And you go about alone, like the hangman."

On occasion Raphael had the sharpest of tongues. When two cardinals, criticizing one of his paintings, remarked jestingly that the faces of the apostles, St Peter and St Paul, were too red Raphael retorted: "I have painted them so deliberately, Your Eminences. They are blushing in heaven to see their Church governed by such men as you."

He used the keen darts of his wit, however, only upon those who were in no position to do him any harm. To those upon whom he depended for his commissions he was always the courteous knight of the silent tongue and the willing hand. And the harder he worked, the more plentifully the commissions kept pouring in upon him—a constant stream of orders for frescoes, church and palace and bath decorations, theatrical scenery, plans for pageants, designs for cameos and wood carvings, portraits, tapestries—and Madonnas.

His Madonnas were something new in the history of art, gems of beauty in a setting of peace. Among the most touching of them—in a wealth of such equal splendor it is almost impossible to select the best—is the *Madonna of the Goldfinch*. In this picture the Virgin is seated on a moss-covered rock with her Child standing in front of her, supported between her knees. In her left hand, which rests upon her left knee, she is holding an open book. Her gaze, however, is directed not upon the book but upon the infant St John who, trembling with excitement, has rushed forward with a beautiful goldfinch which he has just caught. The eyes of the Virgin melt with tenderness as with her right hand she gently presses St John toward her Child. To complete the harmony of the picture the Child turns slowly around to face St John and, without lifting his foot, which rests upon that of his mother, he puts out his hand to stroke the bird. The framework for this scene of maternal tenderness is a meadow, with rivers and bridges and spires and mountains in the background. Every tree, every flower, every tuft of grass is brought out with a precision that shows Raphael's sensitiveness toward natural as well as human personality. Raphael was the painter of the individual soul.

VI

AT THE AGE OF THIRTY-ONE Raphael was at the peak of his power. In addition to all his other work the pope had appointed him as the chief architect for the rebuilding of St Peter's. Never had any artist accepted so many commissions, and of so stupendous a character, within so short a time. His patrons vied with one another in their eagerness to heap labors and honors and riches upon his all-too-willing shoulders. And this proved to be his tragedy. The greatest satirist in the world is Fate. Some of her victims she kills with too much neglect, others with too much glory. Raphael possessed a superhuman genius but only human strength. He broke down under the burden of his too-great popularity. In the spring of 1520 he was engaged upon a picture of the *Transfiguration*—the ascension of Jesus from his mortal crown of thorns to his immortal crown of gold. Raphael never finished the picture.

So sudden was his going that to this day the circumstances attending it are uncertain. On April 1 he was still hard at work; on April 6 he was dead. He died on Good Friday, which happened to be his birthday as well as his deathday. He was exactly thirty-seven years old when he died.

As he lay in his casket his last painting was placed beside him. It was a striking symbol of his destiny, of all human destiny—life, ambition, labor, death, transfiguration.

DA VINCI

Great Paintings by Leonardo da Vinci

Florence, Palazzo Vecchio: *The Battle of Anghiari* (unfinished).

Florence, Uffizi Gallery: *Adoration of the Magi* (unfinished).

London, National Gallery: *The Virgin with St Anne* (drawing).

Milan, Brera Gallery: *Head of Christ.*

Milan, Monastery of Santa Maria delle Grazie: *The Last Supper.*

Paris, Louvre: *Madonna of the Rocks, Mona Lisa, St John the Baptist, Virgin with St Anne.*

Rome, Vatican: *St Jerome* (unfinished).

Turin: *Portrait of Himself.*

Leonardo da Vinci
1452–1519

LEONARDO DA VINCI represented the most perfect type of manhood in the modern world. That was his great glory—and his great tragedy. He had the unlimited dreams of a god but the limited powers of a man. His ambition was to do all things and to do them flawlessly. He conceived a thousand and one projects, and he completed only a handful. For he left his works undone the moment he discovered that the execution fell short of his vision. His life was an unfinished roadway, littered with the débris of sublime fragments. "I have never," he wrote bitterly toward the end of his life, "achieved a single work."

II

THIS MAN, who "never achieved a single work," dreamed a greater number of dreams, in a vaster variety of fields, than any other man of the Renaissance. And the men of the Renaissance were noted for the universality of their intellect.

The universality of Leonardo was the astonishment of his

generation. "And still they gazed, and still their wonder grew, that one small head could carry all he knew." The scope of his artistic, mental and moral activities embraced the entire world. He tried to re-create its beauty, to measure its immensity and to interpret its mystery. He was a painter, a sculptor, an architect, an engineer, a musician, an anatomist, a mathematician, a naturalist, an inventor, an astronomer, a stage designer and a philosopher all rolled into one. At his death he left about five thousand pages of unpublished manuscript. A brief glance at only fifty of those five thousand pages will perhaps serve as the best introduction to the versatility of his mind.

Here, then, is a partial list of the subjects which Leonardo includes in those fifty pages: ancient fables and medieval philosophy; the causes of the tides in the sea and the movement of the air in the lungs; the measurements of the earth and the distance between the earth and the sun; the nocturnal habits of the owl and the physical laws of human vision; the nature of flame and the formula for squaring a circle; the law of gravitation and the rhythmical swaying of trees in the wind; the sketch of a flying machine and a medical prescription for a stone in the bladder; a device for swimming with an inflated leather jacket and an essay on light and shade; a design for a pleasure garden and a new set of war engines; a recipe for making perfume and a list of original geometrical theorems; a series of hydraulic studies on the pressure of water in a fountain, a host of observations on the habits of birds and beasts, an article on vacuum, a device for using steam as a motive power, a chapter of original maxims and a disquisition on the nature of the moon.

This comprises about one fifth of the subjects treated in only fifty out of the five thousand pages of Leonardo's notes. Add to this the fact that Leonardo painted probably the most perfect portrait of the ages (*Mona Lisa*), created perhaps the most beautiful fresco known to man (*The Last Supper*) and modeled an equestrian statue (of Sforza) which was i it d y ard l as the eighth wonder of the world, and then try, if you can, to measure the boundaries of Leonardo da Vinci's genius.

Every once in a while the Great Sculptor designs a model of the superman He is to create in the future. Leonardo was one of the most perfect of these divine experiments in human clay.

III

HE WAS the illegitimate son of Ser Piero Antonio, a Florentine lawyer who lived among the Tuscan foothills in the Castle of Vinci. The rocky paths of the countryside exercised the boy's body, and the lights and shadows that played over the hilltops gave nourishment to his soul. Even as a child he dazzled everyone with his beauty. With his rose-colored cloak and golden hair he looked like an angel of Botticelli descended from the clouds. And he could sing divinely. At an early age he learned to accompany himself on the lute, and he improvised both the words and the music as he sang to the astonishment of his father's guests.

But not satisfied with his musical genius, Leonardo tried to master every phase of human thought. He had an observant eye, a firm hand and an artistic soul. Once as a young boy he lost his way in the mountains. He came upon the entrance of a dark and yawning cave. Writing of this experience in his later years, he said, "Suddenly two emotions arose in me, fear and desire: fear of the dark cavern, desire to see whether there were any marvelous things within." Throughout his days he was to be mastered by these two emotions—fear of the dark mystery of life, or rather of his own inability to penetrate it, and desire to bring the wonder of this mystery into the light, to study it, to explain its meaning and to paint its glory. He decided early in life to be an investigator, a teacher and, above all, an artist.

He begged his father to apprentice him to a painter. But his father objected. Painters in those days were looked down upon as inferior creatures. Ser Piero wanted his son to be a lawyer.

like himself. One day Leonardo, without his father's knowledge, painted upon a wooden panel the blackness of the cave in which he had been lost and, leaping out of it, a frightful dragon with fiery eyes, wide-open jaws and distended nostrils that spurted flames and poisonous vapors.

When the work was finished Leonardo asked his father to come into his room. With true dramatic instinct he had half covered the window and had placed the easel in such a position that the light fell upon the fiery dragon. Ser Piero stepped into the room, and the first thing he saw was this horrible monster ready to spring upon him. With a cry he leaped back toward the door. "Don't be afraid, Father," smiled Leonardo. "It's only a painted dragon." And then, with a wisdom beyond his years, he added, "I see I've done an adequate job."

Ser Piero, too, admitted that his son could do an adequate job in painting. Accordingly he apprenticed him (in 1470) to the famous Florentine painter, sculptor and architect, Andrea del Verrocchio.

When he entered upon his apprenticeship Leonardo was eighteen years old. Verrocchio, his master, was his senior by seventeen years. Like Leonardo, he was interested in the sciences as well as in the arts. Painting, to him, was a mathematical demonstration of three-dimensional beauty. All art must be based upon a geometric design. It must be concrete and solid; it must have not only length and width but depth. Verrocchio was one of the first Italian artists to realize the importance of perspective in painting. His scientific attitude toward art exerted a powerful influence, as we shall see, upon the developing genius of Leonardo.

A hard worker himself, Verrocchio kept all his apprentices constantly at work. Yet Leonardo managed somehow to find time for his scientific and his philosophic studies. As a young boy he had fallen under the influence of Toscanelli, the naturalist, philosopher and mathematician whose daring pronouncements were the amazement of Florence and whose theory about the roundness of the earth was destined a few years later to launch Columbus upon his dream of discovery. Leonardo, too, as a result of his conversations with Toscanelli, began to dream great dreams of discovery. But he confined his adventures to the mental instead of the physical world. He began to busy himself with the problems of geography, astronomy, physics, natural history and engineering. He invented labor-saving tools, he drew maps, he observed the flights of birds, he designed machines for turning and grinding and transportation, and he began to fill his notebooks with scientific and artistic sketches. Dozens of them. And again and again, at the bottom of a sketch, he would write: "This is simple and good. But try to do better."

This was to be his motto throughout his life—*good, but try to do better.*

IV

His work at Verrocchio's studio brought him into contact with the fashionable world of Florence. His eyes were dazzled by the gold and the silver, the pearls and the diamonds and the rubies, the silks and the brocades and the satins and the velvets, the waving plumes and the prancing horses—all the extravagant splendor which the Medicis, headed by Lorenzo the Magnificent, displayed with such proud abandon. Accumulated wealth meant power, and wealth displayed meant the respect and the admiration of your fellows. Young Leonardo's heart was filled with a hunger for luxury. His fine figure must be set off by equally fine garments. Let the Florentines recognize him for what he was—a young god living for a while among mortals.

Yet this young Florentine god had the most abstemious of appetites. He spent nearly all his earnings on his clothes, leaving very little for his food. His own tastes were simple, but he must cater to the tastes of the mighty. To make an impression. To curry their favor. To win their patronage. To bring his artistic and his intellectual visions into the concrete world of reality.

And so, in spite of his private modesty and his innate simplicity, he presented himself in public as a dashing cavalier and incomparable master of all knowledge. His business was to dazzle. At thirty-one he applied to Ludovico Sforza, the Duke of Milan, for a position as general director of Milan in the arts of peace and the arms of war. The letter which he addressed to Sforza, and in which he enumerated his talents, could have been written, as Jean Paul Richter points out, "only by a genius or by a fool." In a tone that seemed cold and businesslike and matter-of-fact this amazing young artist informed Ludovico that he could build portable bridges for the pursuit of the enemy and that he knew how to destroy the enemy's bridges; that he was able to drain ditches and rivers; that he possessed a secret whereby he could ruin any fortress that was not built on a stone foundation; that he could build a new and destructive type of cannon; that he had discovered a noiseless method for constructing tunnels under rivers; that he knew how to build covered tanks for attacking the enemy; that he possessed plans for the making of strange submarine weapons of defense and attack; that, furthermore, in times of peace he could equal anyone in architecture, and in painting he could "do as much as any other, be he who he may"; and that, finally, he would engage to execute an equestrian statue of Sforza's illustrious father, a colossal sculpture the like of which the world had never seen!

Instead of committing the young Leonardo to the nearest insane asylum the count invited him to come to the palace. Leonardo impressed the gentlemen and charmed the ladies of the court of Milan. He remained in the service of Ludovico Sforza for twenty years.

At Milan he became the official engineer and the unofficial master of gaiety. He planned the entertainments, he wrote the music, he painted the scenery, he designed the costumes, and he took the leading role in the pageants of the court. He was, in short, the most active participant in the frenzied life of his day.

Active, yet aloof. Like the cynical court jesters of old, he despised the men and the women whom he flattered. And he despised himself for the part he was obliged to play in this stupid and artificial life of the court. He was compelled to stoop in order to conquer, to turn himself into a buffoon in order to secure his commissions as an artist. But he had his revenge. In a series of bitterly brilliant fables which he wrote at this time he lashed out savagely against that most shameful and most pitiable of living creatures—Man. "Men," he confided to the pages of his notebook at this time, "are nothing else than passages for food, augmenters of filth, and fillers of privies. . . . Nothing else in the world is effected through them, and they are without any virtue. . . . There can surely be no question that Nature must desire to extinguish the human race as a useless thing."

He despised the miserable human race and yet he was anxious to help it out of its misery. While he was at Milan he tried to build and to beautify and to ennoble the City of the Renaissance. He planned roads with two levels for safer travel. He advocated wider streets for safer sanitation. He dreamed of transforming the landscapes of Italy with a network of temples and cataracts and canals and lakes and gardens. He designed a system of small cities, each of them to consist of five thousand houses with no more than six inhabitants to a house. For he believed that humanity was too congested to be happy. "We must separate this great congregation of people who live crowded together like herds of goats, filling the air with stench and spreading the seeds of pestilence and death."

The cities that he planned were to be built along riverbanks. For in this way he could introduce into each city a sanitary sewage system—something undreamt of in his day—nothing less than a series of underground canals that would carry all the refuse of the city into the river.

His model cities were to have no ugly sights or evil smells. They were to be full of space and air and beauty and cleanliness and freedom and culture and joy. The great dream cities of a healthier, happier race of men.

But they remained dreams. For Sforza was not interested in advancing money for so utopian a project. Instead he gave Leonardo an assignment of another sort. He commissioned him to model an equestrian statue of his illustrious father, Francesco Sforza. This equestrian statue, or, as it was popularly called, "the horse," was as colossal in size as it was magnificent in conception. In 1493 the clay model was unveiled for exhibition. Displayed under an improvised triumphal arch, it became a thing of wonder to all Milan. Here, on the verge of realization, stood one of the most stupendous and one of the most beautiful dreams in the entire history of sculpture. All that was necessary to fulfill the dream was to cast the statue in bronze. But the casting was never done. It required too much bronze for so tremendous a job. Milan was at war with France, and all the spare metal within the city had to be melted into arms and ammunition. Destruction won a victory over creation. Leonardo's statue remained unfinished. In 1499 the French troops occupied Milan, and Leonardo's noble and masterly work became a target for the Gascon bowmen. Today, thanks to the war, not a trace is left of this "Eighth Wonder of the World."

V

LEONARDO was now a man of great fame and meager purse. Ludovico Sforza was the sort of patron who paid his artists with golden phrases rather than with gold coin. And of late even his admiration for Leonardo's genius had cooled off. Too close proximity had bred contempt. He began to neglect Leonardo and to give out his best commissions to other and inferior artists. And so Leonardo, with a heavy heart, sat down to write a letter to Sforza. "Your Excellency," he began, "it vexes me deeply that you are giving me no further commissions . . . I know that your thoughts are turned in other directions . . . I should like to recall to Your Magnificence my poor services . . ." And then he went on, hesitantly, to remind Sforza that there were payments still due him for three years' work and that he was at present in "great financial difficulties . . . And may I conclude, Your Lordship, that my life is at your service. I hold myself in readiness to obey you . . ."

This letter shamed Sforza into giving Leonardo a new commission. And this commission was to make the name of Leonardo immortal. He finished this "most sublime of all human paintings" in 1498. It was *The Last Supper*, depicted upon the front wall of the dining room in the Church of Santa Maria delle Grazie. This fresco has become blurred and cracked with the passage of time. Leonardo mixed his colors with oil, a fatal innovation for a fresco painting. The paint has peeled off in many places, and the faces of Jesus and his disciples have been retouched by less skillful hands. Yet the soul of beauty still shines through the crumbling paint of *The Last Supper*. Like most of the other paintings of Leonardo, it is geometric in design. For Leonardo's art, like Plato's philosophy, is based upon the symmetry of mathematics. A long narrow table, with its white cover embroidered in blue like a Jewish prayer shawl, stands in front of three windows. Through the center window the light streams in upon Jesus, who sits with his back to the window, with six disciples on either side of him. Jesus has just spoken the bitter words, "One of you shall betray me." The twelve disciples, each group of six further subdivided into groups of three, show their reaction to the words of Jesus by the expression of their faces and the motions of their bodies. James the elder, his mouth open in amazement, seems to be repeating the words of Jesus. Thomas, the everlasting doubter, is raising his index finger, as if about to ask a question. Philip, his arms crossed over his breast and his eyes dimmed with tears, is protesting his innocence. John, his hands clasped together, looks on with a helpless despair. Peter, the man of action, has sprung from his seat, with a knife clasped in his hand. Judas, immersed in shadow, shows his guilt in his almost imperceptible recoil and in his shifty eyes. Matthew, his arms outstretched, seems to be appealing to the others: "No, we must not let this happen!" And so on, down to the last psychological and geometrical detail of the painting—one of the supreme achievements of the human mind. In this painting, as one of Leonardo's biographers has remarked, "science is wedded to art, and philosophy imprints a kiss upon the perfect union."

It took Leonardo a long time to paint *The Last Supper*. Aiming at perfection, he did his work slowly and meticulously, always revising what he had done the day before and never quite satisfied with the results. "When setting to work to paint," writes his biographer, Lomazzo, "it was as if he were mastered by fear. . . . His soul being full of the sublimity of Art, he was enabled to see in his own pictures faults which others hailed as miraculous creations." Another of his biographers, Signor Bandello, tells us that "he would often come to the church at early dawn . . . Hastily mounting the scaffolding, he worked diligently until the shades of evening compelled him to cease, never thinking to take food at all, so absorbed was he in his work. At other times, however, he would remain there three or four days without touching his picture . . . standing with folded arms, gazing at his figures as if to criticize them himself."

It was this perpetual self-criticism that prevented him from completing another masterpiece, *The Battle of Anghiari*. In spite of his scientific interest in military engines he was one of the few men of the Renaissance who saw war in all its realistic ugliness. Writing about it in his notebook, he called it "that insanity most bestial." When, therefore, he received a commission from his native city to celebrate the Florentine victory at the Battle of Anghiari he proceeded to paint not the glory but the fury of war.

[58]

He drew sketches of the battle such as Tolstoy might have painted had he been an artist. And as an accompaniment to the sketches he wrote a word picture of the battle which is worthy of the great Russian novelist at his best. The dust and the smoke of the conflict, the reddish glare of the sun upon the agonized faces of the combatants, the tangled heaps of wounded men and horses, the thick rain of arrows falling in every direction, the backward-flying hair of the pursuers, the furrows made by the horses as they drag their riders through the slippery and blood-stained mud, the broken shields and spears and swords and helmets scattered on the ground between the legs of the dead and the dying, the winding trickle of blood from the gaping wounds, the staring eyes, the clenched fists and the grotesque poses of the slain soldiers, the dirt and the sweat and the blood upon the faces of the exhausted soldiers—all these are but a handful of the thousand and one details which Leonardo introduces into his description of the battle. It is a pity that he did not match his verbal pictures and his sketchy outlines with a completed painting. This painting, like so many other of his grandiose conceptions, remained an unfulfilled dream. He felt that it was a job beyond the power of a genius even like himself. The *art* of man, he believed, was not quite equal to the task of painting the *cruelty* of man.

VI

BEHOLD HIM NOW at fifty: tall, noble, erect, dressed in a scarlet velvet cloak, his mustache carefully waxed, his long hair and beard gleaming like threads of finespun copper embroidered here and there with a touch of gray, his hands white, slender, aristocratic, yet strong enough to bend a horseshoe or break a sword, his eye bright and his step elastic and firm—a poet in quest of beauty, a philosopher in search of truth. From now on to the end of his life he will be a restless wanderer, going from

Milan to Florence, from Florence to Venice, from Venice to
Rome, from Rome to Amboise, seeking everywhere for new
patrons, new ideas, new dreams, new ways to make men less
stupid, less cruel, less sad. And wherever he goes there plays
about his mouth a strange smile. There is wisdom in that smile,
and sorrow and cynicism and contempt. But, over and above
all, there is pity in it. And frequently he transfers this smile of his
to the faces of the portraits that he paints—St Anne, Leda, the
Virgin Mary, John the Baptist, Bacchus and Mona Lisa. They
call him "Leonardo, the painter of the smiling faces."

And so he wandered about the world, this painter of the
smiling faces, dreaming, inventing, sketching, modeling, building, philosophizing and amusing the lords and ladies of the
court with his caustic wit, his worldly wisdom—and his magical
tricks. For this Dr Faustus of the Renaissance had acquired a
reputation as a great magician. He would put a saucer of boiling
oil on the table, pour red wine on top and "set the wine on fire,"
to the amazement of his audience. On festive occasions he made
mechanical lions that walked and glared and roared like living
creatures. Once, having procured the entrails of a sheep, he
showed them to his guests on the palm of his hand. Then, after
the manner of a professional juggler, he asked them to come into
his workshop. Here he began to inflate the entrails with a pair of
bellows. Gradually the handful of intestines blew up into transparent balloons, pushing through the door, filling the entire
room and compelling the astonished guests to flatten themselves
against the walls. When the trick was over he smilingly explained to his visitors that he had merely shown them a symbol
of human virtue, which at first may seem insignificant but which
by careful tending may be capable of infinite growth.

Always, even in his playful moments, he was the philosopher.
His notebooks are full of profound observations about life and
death. Much of his writing is hard to decipher. For he was left-
handed and wrote his Italian, as if it were Hebrew or Arabic,

from right to left. No attempt has been made as yet to systematize his philosophical aphorisms. Even in their fragmentary state, however, we can see in them the courage of a stoic tempered with the gentleness of a Christian. Leonardo was not a member of the Church. But he was a follower of Jesus. He showed this not only in his exquisitely sympathetic drawing of Christ's face but in his equally sympathetic understanding of Christ's thought. Like Christ himself, or like the stoics of Rome, he took his own sorrows lightly and sympathized with the sorrows of others. He suffered much from the malice of his enemies and the envy of his friends. But he bore his sufferings and his insults with a patient dignity. "Patience," he wrote in one of his manuscripts, "serves as a protection against wrongs as clothes do against cold. For if you put on more clothes as the cold increases, it will have no power to hurt you. So in like manner you must grow in patience when you meet with great wrongs and they will then be powerless to vex your mind."

He was willing to endure the foolishness of the individual. But he had a great contempt for the follies of mankind. "What do you think, Man, of your own species?" he asks. "Are you not ashamed of your stupidity?"

He was frequently amused by the struggles of the princes for empty honors. While his patrons tried to perfect themselves in the art of royalty, Leonardo devoted himself to the royalty of art. In beauty alone he found the solid satisfaction of life. All else he regarded, with the wisdom of a Koheleth, as the baseless hungering for nonexistent fruits. Ambition is vain, and hope leads only to disappointment. "Desire," he wrote, "is sweeter than fulfillment." It is ridiculous to break your neck, and other people's necks, in your scramble for fame. "The fruit that seems sweet on the tree often turns bitter in the mouth." We must learn the limitations of our strength. To aim too high is not only foolish but dangerous. Let us measure our ambition by our talents, and let not our desires outstrip our ability to fulfill these desires. "Since we cannot attain what we wish, let us wish only what we can attain."

Desire is sweet, but fulfillment is bitter. "There is no perfect gift without great suffering." Especially is this true in the case of an artist like Leonardo. The greater the capacity for beauty, the greater the sensitivity to pain. The artist achieves more because he suffers more. The Greek poets had a theory, based upon their profound understanding of life, that knowledge comes through sorrow. *Pathei Mathos.* We are able to learn because we are ready to suffer.

Leonardo's learning and Leonardo's art and Leonardo's gentleness were the result of his suffering. He showed pity toward all because very few showed pity toward him. Having suffered humiliation all his life at the hands of his patrons, he refrained from hurting or humiliating anyone else. The very thought of inflicting pain upon any living creature was abhorrent to him. His biographer Vasari tells us that "when he passed the market place where birds were sold, he would frequently take them from the cages with his own hands; and having paid the sellers the price that was asked, he would let them fly away in the air, thus giving them back their liberty."

His pity for all living things led him to be a vegetarian. Life to him was sacred. As we have no power to create life, we have no right to destroy it. "It is an infinitely atrocious act," he wrote, "to take away the life of any creature. . . . The soul wills not that rage or malice should destroy life. . . . He who values not life does not deserve to have it."

Leonardo knew whereof he spoke. For he had observed the pity and the irony and the cruelty of life at first hand. At the court of Ludovico Sforza, at the castle of Cesare Borgia, at the palace of King Francis I, in the cities, the towns, the villages, the military camps—everywhere he had seen men imprison and slaughter their fellow men for the pettiest of ambitions and the flimsiest of prizes. His contemplation of the beauty of man had

[*62*]

made him an artist. His observation of man's barbarity turned him into a philosopher.

VII

AND A PHILOSOPHER he remained to the end of his days. He had good need of his philosophy, for he possessed very little else. He offered to the world his superb statues and paintings, and he was repaid with empty praise. He tried to build great buildings, to design beautiful cities and to conquer the sea and the earth and the air with his inventions of the submarine, the steam carriage and the airship, and he received no encouragement from his patrons. At last, toward the end of his life, he did receive some encouragement and a chance to make a good living. Doing what? Making mirrors and building stables! Pearls to the swine, luxurious stables for the horses. Such are the tasks to which humanity reduces the most precious of its souls.

VIII

HIS LIFE, as he saw it, ended in failure. "He was passed over not only for great commissions but for high offices." His dreams, his ambitions, his plans, his inventions, his hopes, all lay about him in ruins. "We always hope for the future," he wrote in his last years, "but the future has only one certainty in store for us— the death of all hope." His whole existence, he observed, had been nothing but a preparation for death. "When I thought I was learning to live, I was but learning to die."

Yet he accepted the necessity of death, as he had accepted the uncertainties of life, with the resignation of the stoic. When the final summons came he was ready, like a tired child, to go to his rest. "As a well-spent day brings happy sleep," he wrote just before the end, "so does a well-used life bring happy death."

He died in France on May 2, 1519, at the age of sixty-seven.

The only mourners who followed his coffin were a handful of faithful servants who had lost a gentle master, and the paid poor of the village who raised their professional lament for a stranger they knew nothing about. There was only one man at that time who was able to measure Leonardo's greatness. This man was Leonardo's pupil and friend, Francesco Melzi. "The death of Leonardo," wrote Melzi, "is a loss to everyone. . . . It is not in the power of nature to reproduce such another man."

TITIAN

Baltimore, Epstein Collection: *Portrait of a Man.*

Berlin, Museum: *Titian's Daughter.*

Boston, Gardner Museum: *The Rape of Europa.*

Cincinnati, Museum Association: *Portrait of Philip II of Spain.*

Detroit, Ford Collection: *Andrea Navagero.*

Detroit, Institute of Arts: *Man with a Flute.*

Florence, Pitti Gallery: *La Donna Bella, Head of Christ.*

Florence, Uffizi Gallery: *Flora, Portrait of Catherine Cornaro, Portraits of Duke and Duchess of Urbino, Venus.*

Kansas City, Nelson Gallery: *Cardinal Granvelle.*

London, National Gallery: *Bacchus and Ariadne.*

Madrid, Gallery: *Portrait of Philip of Charles.*

Munich, Old Pinakothek: *Christ Crowned with Thorns.*

New York, Frick Collection: *Portrait of a Man in a Red Cap.*

New York, Metropolitan Museum of Art: *Portrait of Andrea Gritti, Venus and the Lute Player.*

Paris, Louvre: *Entombment, Madonna with St Agnes, Man with a Glove, Woman at Toilet.*

Philadelphia, Widener Collection: *Venus and Adonis.*

Rome, Borghese Gallery: *Sacred and Profane Love, Education of Cupid.*

St Louis, City Art Museum: *Christ at the Temple.*

Venice, Academy: *Assumption of the Virgin, Presentation of the Virgin.*

Washington, National Gallery: *Toilet of Venus.*

Tiziano Vecellio

1477–1576

IT IS NOT ALWAYS TRUE that those whom the gods love die young. For the gods certainly loved Titian, and yet they gave him more than his mortal share of years. He lived to the ripe old age of ninety-nine, outspanned the reigns of three kings, fourteen popes and fourteen mayors of Venice and finally succumbed (in 1576) to a plague that took off half of the city's population along with him. Only a few weeks before the end he had held drinking parties in memory of his friends and had cast longing eyes on the lovely young Venetian girls whose mothers and grandmothers he had known and desired. For an entire century there seemed to be no Achilles' heel whereby death could touch the constitution of this tough, pleasure-loving old graybeard artist. At ninety-nine he bargained for every penny of his income with the sharpness of a man of forty-five and painted love in its various manifestations with the gusto of a youth of twenty-one. Safely ensconced in a magnificent villa fronting the Venetian lagoons, he hid himself away from mortality itself and laughed till his sides ached to see its futile gestures to entrap him. He was a history of memories and a contemporary of Henry VIII, Martin Luther, Calvin, Francis I and Charles V, all of whom he outlived. He was a sturdy old oak who had outlasted the forest of his time, a lone, straggling, sole surviving member of the old flock walking among the herds of new generations. Yet the gleam of the epicure remained in his eye.

Old age, a season of tragedy for many, was nothing of the sort for Titian. Immensely wealthy, he was the darling of his fellow artists and of the aristocratic patrons of the fine arts the world over. The King of Spain and the Holy Roman Emperor sought to be his companions. To the end he was tended by a daughter and worshiped by a son. And as long as he lived the energy and the desires of life never left him. Old age for him was a picturesque landscape of snow with the sunlight beaming down warmly upon it. No blasts of the north wind ever came to disturb the serenity of his last years.

II

HE WAS BORN (1477) in Piave di Cadore, a little mountain town lying in northern Italy between southern Bavaria and the Adriatic Sea. At the age of twelve his father took him on a trip to Venice. The great city of the west had by this time passed the zenith of her queenliness. In 1453 the Turks had overrun Constantinople and had cut off most of Venice's eastern trade through the Black Sea. None the less, Venice was still the chief city of Europe. It was sometimes called the most "westerly" city of the Orient. The barbaric outposts of London and Paris could not hold a candle to this city of water boulevards and sparkling temples. Venice was the city of an Oriental dream, a fantasy of exotic shapes and colors such as might be found at the end of an opium pipe. Indian jugglers, sailors and traders from China, snake charmers, Frenchmen clad in silks and satins, Spaniards with pointed beards, Muscovite princes, Greek courtesans, the spirit of the carnival with its marked revelry—all this cosmopolitan pageantry had become embodied into the very personality of the city that lay mirrored in her silver lagoons.

Venice was a cathedral that had been erected for the worship of worldliness. Obviously a St Francis or a Giotto, men who were humanists of the spirit rather than of the flesh, would be out of place in this city that sat like a priceless jewel on the edge of the Italian boot. But the great epicureans of art, the conjurers who possessed the genius of turning naked canvas into warm, delicate, human flesh, came to Venice to practice their magic just as the snake charmers and sorcerers had come to practice theirs. In this new city of Babylon beauty rather than duty reigned supreme. In this terrestrial Eden a thousand apples had been plucked and eaten by a thousand pleasure-loving inhabitants, and a thousand more were bending the boughs of the trees.

What an impression the visit must have made upon the boy of twelve! As an artist Titian was to become a perfect product of this cosmopolitan spirit. The art of the Venetian school had been derived basically from the Oriental tradition. But, like Cimabue and Giotto in Rome a century earlier, the Bellini brothers, Gentile and Giovanni, were leading a movement in Venice to throw off the old Byzantine artificiality and to paint the true outlines of the human form. And Titian, a short while after his visit, was apprenticed to one of the Bellini brothers, Giovanni. The lad overbubbled with energy; he had an impulse to cover the canvas with everything he saw, everything he felt. The master restrained him and put a leash on his mighty creative powers. The boy had a marvelous genius for color; the master forced him to concentrate on form. The boy had visions of Venus and Bacchus and laughter-speckled landscapes; the master made him paint Madonnas and saints. The boy was forced to sheathe his vision and to bide his time. Day after day he worked in the drab, businesslike shop, perspiring over devotional subjects, while at his side labored a fellow dreamer. This fellow apprentice was Giorgione, the handsomest young blade in Venice, an Apollo who looked like a god and talked like a devil, who played the lute and made the hearts of all the young girls dance to his intoxicating tunes. As he was a little older than Titian and already somewhat of a master in his craft, Titian worshiped him. Giorgione had the magic of color in his fingers—and such color! The like of it had never been seen on canvas. But Giorgione at this time was no more recognized as an artist than Titian. One day, after a night of escapades, they were thrown out of Bellini's shop by the irate old master himself. They were left without a cent in their pockets, having spent everything on their previous night's adventures. What were they to do now?

"Well," said Giorgione, "we ought to thank God we've been given a chance to quit this miserable shop."

"*Quit?*" countered Titian. "We've been thrown out. We haven't got the price of a meal between us."

"Wait," said Giorgione. "Someday we shall be painting for kings and queens."

"That's fine! But how are we going to eat today?"

"We'll get along. Today I think I shall begin my professional career as a painter by painting my—ah—mistress—the young lady I picked up on our unfortunate excursion into the realms of Venus."

"I think I'll do my mistress too," agreed Titian.

Somehow they managed to scrape together a little money. They took a tiny room overlooking the Grand Canal which was filled night and day with gondoliers. Giorgione was a poet of color and a connoisseur in the various vintages of love. All he had to do was to lead, and Titian was sure to follow. He piped his way with his lute into brothels and brawls and ordered the spiciest tidbits at the table of life with the instinct of an epicure.

Titian tried desperately to copy the technique of Giorgione in his love-making and his art. And he succeeded.

Giorgione was the youngest and best hope in the Venetian school. Few people had appreciated the true splendor of a Venetian sunset until Giorgione filtered it through his eyes and caught its essence in paint. Few people had ever studied the fine shading of the Venetian landscape, with its dark slopes and jagged, stormy rocks, until Giorgione put the mark of his genius upon it. The man had the technical touch and the grand imagination of the ancient Greek masters. His nude women reclining with shepherds in the fields had been summoned to life again from the workshop of the sculptors of Athens after a lapse of sixteen centuries. This young pleasure-loving Venetian was a natural child of Venus born into a Christian world, and Titian knelt in adoration at his feet.

III

THE PAGAN GOD and his disciple managed to find enough work to get along. They received their first big commission when a Venetian warehouse, which had been destroyed by fire, was rebuilt. Secular as well as sacred buildings were at that period decorated with frescoes and murals. Titian and Giorgione were assigned to the embellishment of the warehouse. Titian did most of the work, but Giorgione appropriated most of the credit. He basked in the congratulations of his friends and acknowledged the assistance of Titian with a mere wave of his graceful hand.

As the work progressed a coldness sprang up between the two. This coldness gradually grew into an icy barrier that put a complete end to their friendship. And, strangely enough, it was not the resentment of Titian but the jealousy of Giorgione that brought about this break in their friendly relationship. Giorgione could not bear to be second in anything. He began to realize that Titian was on the point of surpassing him in the art of color, and it was a mortal blow to his pride. He shut himself up in his rooms for days at a time and refused to see Titian. Bewildered at the change in Giorgione's manner toward him, and scarcely comprehending the reason, Titian finally left Venice to continue his career alone. Giorgione returned to his riotous night life in order to forget his disappointment; and at last, worn out with dissipation and discouragement, he died at the early age of thirty-two.

IV

THE YEARS PASSED. Titian, in the course of his wanderings, came to Padua and was entertained at the home of Luigi Cornaro. Luigi had led the wildest of lives up to the age of forty-five and had then drawn in the reins and put a curb upon his passions. At the age of eighty-one, sitting in a splendid villa, this model of abstinence told the story of his reform to Titian.

"To keep healthy and mentally fit, my son, I eat twelve ounces of food each day. And I drink fourteen ounces of wine," he added, with the devil lurking in his eye.

Luigi lived more than a century and wrote comedies when he was eighty-five. The Renaissance was full of such patriarchs who knew how to love lustily and live long.

Titian had now reached the maturity of his powers. Following in the Giorgione tradition of realistic color and the human touch (his angels looked like chubby babies with superadded wings, and his Madonnas were the lifelike portraits of his female friends), Titian was beginning to be hailed everywhere as one of the masters of the Renaissance. He was hardly the ideal youth of the sixteenth century. If the truth must be told, Titian the man fell far below the stature of Titian the artist. He longed for money and adulation. He had the uncanny knack of insinuating himself into the good graces of the high and mighty. Like Voltaire, he bent his knee to authority and basked in the sunlight of the royal smile. Like Voltaire, too, he had a very shrewd head for business. If he hadn't been blessed with the genius for the brush, he would have made an excellent trades-man. And finally, like Voltaire, he was a religious skeptic and a very devil with the ladies.

At the age of thirty-seven he was summoned to the most brilliant court in Italy, that of Alphonse I of Ferrara, a remote ancestor of Queen Victoria. But there was nothing Victorian about this dashing young duke. He was the fifth husband of that "innocent of innocents," Lucrezia Borgia, the virtuoso in poison. In spite of the pleasant distractions during his stay at Ferrara, Titian managed to turn out two masterpieces—the *Bacchus and Ariadne* and the *Tribute Money*. The god Bacchus, resplendent in a chariot drawn by two panthers, is descending upon the Island of Naxos. Captivated by the grief of the beauti-ful Ariadne, who has been abandoned on the island by her lover Theseus, he promises the girl that every one of her tears shall be transformed into a shining star in heaven. The scene is full of a realistic voluptuousness possible only to an artist who has sampled the bittersweets of life at first hand. Quite different is the *Tribute Money*. There is tenderness in this splendid study of Christ, and thoughtfulness, and adoration that comes very close to worship. Here, too, there is realism. The texture of Christ's beard is true down to the very last hair. But the face has a Rembrandtesque softness. The hands of the Saviour are beautiful, and the gesture of the fingers as he gives the coin is gracefully divine. Titian spent his days not only in good living but in high thinking. He absorbed beauty, filtered it through his philosophy and transmuted it into living art.

But he was, above all else, a practical man of the world. He was now married and the father of a family—an additional inducement to his ever-growing ambition. And just at this time a man came along to further his ambition. The name of this man was Pietro Aretino, and he met Titian over a bottle of wine. Pietro, who typified the less pleasant side of the Renaissance, was the Alcibiades of Venice. He possessed an abundant gift of humor, a talent for poetry, social charm, imagination—in short, everything but character. He had sought refuge in Venice after he had been hounded out of every other city in Italy. Wherever he had taken up his residence he had composed vulgar lampoons against the citizenry. He was gallant, however, whenever he chose to be so, and he had managed to worm his way into the confidence of the petty princes. In this way he frequently burrowed to the bottom of state secrets and demanded money for blackmail. He was privy to every scandal; his finger was in every political pie. Sadistic by nature, he loved to torture his closest friends by revealing their private lives in ribald verse. In spite of all this he possessed a few good qualities. At times he was generous to a fault. He contributed a good deal of his ill-gotten wealth to the upkeep of women of the slums. He took ragged street urchins into his house and fed and clothed them as if they were his sons. In addition, this amazing man was a connoisseur in art. Kings sought his advice as to what they should buy for their palaces. He kept a lavish house full of Renaissance painting and sculpture, and he supported a great number of needy artists at his own expense. He was a master of flattery and the coaxing word. He wrote wheedling letters asking favors of prostitutes and prelates. On one occasion, when Titian was summoned to the court of Charles V, he sent along with the artist a written petition presenting himself as a candidate for the office of cardinal of the Holy Church. His hair was luxuriant, his eyes were wide apart and frank, his forehead was round. If it were not for the numerous scars that revealed the constant sword fights he engaged in, his face might have been mistaken for that of a saint. Indeed, he called himself the "Divine Aretino." And he became a sort of press agent for Titian. "With your genius and my connections," he had told Titian when they first met, "we'll make a fine partnership."

[74]

This became one of the strangest "partnerships" in all history. And it lasted over thirty-five years, until the death of Aretino brought it to an end. Aretino trumpeted Titian's name abroad. He sold Titian's paintings to his ruffian friends in all parts of Italy—adventurers like himself with ill-gotten wealth and a hobby for art. He even intrigued to get Titian an invitation to the court of the Holy Roman Emperor, Charles V. This emperor had conceived the ambition to crush the whole European continent under his heel and to become a second Charlemagne. He was an enemy of Italian liberty. Titian, however, was far from being an Italian patriot. He gladly accepted an invitation to Charles's court.

At this court Titian met an official who happened to have an Italian mistress. Charles had invaded Italy, and this woman was one of the fruits he had plucked on that occasion. Titian painted a very convincing portrait of her. At least it convinced Charles V to such an extent that he ordered Titian to paint a royal portrait. He had no hesitation in doing this, although he was at that very moment preparing for another invasion of the artist's homeland. Once more Titian obeyed the crack of the whip. God had built him with superhuman genius and with the weaknesses of a man. And so, with his customary complaisance, he bent the knee to the conqueror of Italy. And when he finally returned to Venice it was with a noble title and with a purse full of money. Always the businessman, he invested his money in real estate and settled down to enjoy a life of careless plenty and fruitful toil.

There was another artist in Venice at the time—a visiting artist, a man with an iron soul and a tender passion for art. He had both the strength and the tears of the devotee to a noble cause. He was a mighty, elemental man, as stanch and as pure and as majestic as the poetry he wrote in marble. And he was a tremendously lonely man, with the intellectual integrity of a great soul who rebels against all the little souls of his day. This man was Michelangelo, and he was everything that Titian, was not—except, of course, that both were artists of the very highest order. If Michelangelo was the first great titan of the human trinity, the older brother of Shakespeare and of Beethoven, Titian was the last of the pagan priests, a man who loved the parade and not the prayer.

The two artists met in Venice, but only casually and without good will. Michelangelo soon left Venice on his restless pilgrimage, and Titian moved into a spacious villa where, except for a few minor trips, he spent the remaining forty years of his life. Seated in his garden that fronted the sea, with the music of the waves as they swept into the lagoon singing in his ears, he painted over a thousand pictures before the plague of 1576 called him to his rest. Here his daughter grew to womanhood and his second son Orazio learned to sketch and to mix paints under his eye. His wife brought him his daily meals as he sat with his brushes and watched the blue hills of Cadore climb heavenward and the glassworks of Murano belch out their smoke. His older son, Pompinio, was full of the devil and gave his father no end of trouble. He had taken the robes of priesthood but had bolted the Church and had become a worthless profligate. From time to time he drifted home to the villa and demanded money from his indulgent father. At such time the "Divine Aretino," who now was a regular guest at the family table and who had served as godfather to the boy, would proceed to give Pompinio a lecture on character and morals. Age had forced Aretino into paths of decency. Behind an old white beard the devil himself would look respectable and could play the role of a father-confessor.

V

TITIAN was in his late sixties. From a self-portrait in the Berlin Museum we know how he looked at this time. His small keen eyes are clear, and in them we can still see reflected the desires of youth. The sensitive hands, with the long spiderlike fingers, seem restless to build a web in which to keep the fame of their owner forever secure. The mouth droops in angry jealousy that the sun can throw brighter colors over the landscape than he. And there is sadness in the face. It is a lean, vibrant face with a heavy beard and a look of restless, hungry, unsatisfied ambition.

In his old age Titian was a hypochondriac. He complained to his physician that his years were slowing him up. Nevertheless his fingers tightened at the glimpse of a ducat. With an incredible rapidity and an endless rapacity he continued to paint portraits, devotional subjects and landscapes for the paying clientele. He had the artistic soul of a chameleon, with a veritable kaleidoscope of colors in his repertoire. He would put the countenance of Venus on the torso of ugliness for the right sum. He flattered his wealthy patrons by painting them not as they actually were but as they would like to be. By a few master strokes he smoothed the wrinkles of age and put love in the eyes of wealthy matrons who sat for their portraits and paid to be fooled. And, above all, he put magic into the color of their hair—a golden, red-yellow tint (known to this day as Titian) that turned ordinary auburn or red hair into a crown of glory. Aretino, who seemed to be capable only of recognizing the most superficial qualities in Titian's art, wrote to a friend a letter in which he boasted of the ease with which Titian was able to throw off one mood in favor of another and to paint anything at all to order. "And never below the market price!" Due to Aretino's maneuvering, Titian received stupendous prices for his works. He did several portraits of Charles V, the most famous of which is the emperor at Mühlberg, done in 1548. Here we see featured a characteristic background of sky with a swish of somber clouds. Charles, in a suit of armor gleaming with life and holding a long, dangerous-looking lance in his hand, sits on an ebony charger and frowns at the world in his most warlike fashion.

This done, Titian painted a portrait of Charles's fellow monarch, Philip of Spain, who had come to Germany for the purpose of ingratiating himself with the German people. Philip was a narrow-chested, bowlegged, thick-lipped mongrel of a king. But Titian's portrait was concealing rather than revealing. It is said that Bloody Mary of England, to whom Philip was betrothed, fell in love with the picture though she could scarcely stand the original. Titian had indeed done a masterly underemphasis of painting. He had been especially careful to tone down the famous Hapsburg protruding jaw. For all his seventy years, Titian hadn't lost his skill at pole-vaulting his way into the favor of a king.

VI

IN ADDITION to the huge income he received from his artistic labors Titian earned quite a sum from a position he held at the Customs House in Venice. This position had been given him by the political leaders of the city in 1516, on condition that he cover the walls of the city hall with murals describing an epic land fight. But for twenty-one years Titian was too busy carrying out private commissions to perform his part of the bargain. Finally, in 1537, the politicians threatened to revoke his salary if he did not begin the project immediately. Titian responded with unusual alacrity. He painted the picture known as *The Battle of Cadore*. This huge picture is strikingly similar to the sketches in Leonardo's notebook on *The Battle of Anghiari*. The canvas is a confusion of horses and men writhing, twisting, plunging on the points of spears and dying in an agony of distorted faces and convulsive muscles. The politicians were apparently displeased with Titian's neglect of this job for twenty-one years, for when the Ducal Palace needed repairs they gave him a slap in the face by awarding the job to a much inferior artist.

Titian could afford to take the insult with gallant nonchalance. He was famous the world over. Aretino had brought Vasari, the most notable journalist of the century, to Venice to write Titian's biography. And Vasari paid the great artist the usual salaams. He remarked that no one else in Italy, neither Raphael nor Leonardo, could equal Titian's genius for painting. He might have paid homage to the old man's genius for living, as well. Titian was a patriarch in a magnificent white beard. He was overwhelmed with invitations from every great monarch in Europe. Charles offered him a palace to live in, if only he would come to Germany. Philip begged him to spend his remaining years in Spain. Francis I, whose mighty nose in profile has been preserved for all time in one of Titian's portraits, asked him to live in France. The pope offered him a state position if he came to Rome. To Rome he went, but only for a temporary visit. He was given a princely convoy by the Duke of Urbino. Unbowed by his seventy years, he rode like a conqueror into the papal city and was wined and dined at the tables of the great. Then from Rome he traveled to the court of Charles V at Augsburg. He went over the mountains in the thick of winter and arrived none the worse for the trip. Melancthon, a scholar of Latin and Greek who happened to be staying in Augsburg at the time, wrote in genuine, jealous admiration of this artist Methuselah, this ancient playboy whom the pleasures of youth, the summer dissipations and the winter journeys, the banquets, the adulation, the wine, the women, the long succession of pleasures and the years of uninterrupted toil could not kill. A trip of hundreds of miles over a donkey path in the dead of winter was nothing at all to this tough old rascal with the brush, as long as glory awaited him at the journey's end. After a season with the wine cups at Augsburg he returned to his villa and settled down to twenty more years of hard work and hard play.

At eighty he continued to paint his nude Venuses with an incredible gusto. Indeed, the female nude reached its highest expression with Titian in his old age. It lay with breath-taking sincerity in the foreground of a hundred landscapes. The Venus of Venice was plump to an extent that would have shocked the modest intentions of the ancient Greeks. Love was not a weasel tune for the bagpipes; it was a robust song on the lips of the Renaissance poet and artist and man about town. And Titian sang it in his wine cups long after the bedtime of the ordinary man's life. These last twenty summers were no different from the first seventy-nine. He gathered in his ducats with a shrewd eye. He collected every penny that was due him through the generations. The hoary head still stooped to wheedle and cringe. The fingers clung with the tenacity of a hungry little boy to the petticoats of Glory. Days he worked assiduously at his easel. Nights he gave suppers that lasted far into the morning. At these villa entertainments were the architect Sansovino, the historian Samito and the "Divine Aretino"—all old men. But they drank strong wine and ogled the maidens who passed the lantern-lit shores in the gondolas. They quoted sonnets and discussed art and raised their bowls in toasts to the future. They were three aged children who refused to leave the party of life and to be put to bed while others celebrated.

At one of these celebrations Aretino was in remarkably good humor. He spoke eloquently under the influence of his cups. He presided over the table like Dionysus, and a cascade of jests fell from his thick lips. It was well toward three in the morning. The air was cold and still. He told one last obscene joke and died suddenly where he sat, with the laughter clinging to his throat. What a final chapter for the ribald novel of this man's career!

Titian had only one close friend left. This was Sansovino, the architect. Both men were over ninety; both refused to give in to old age. In each other's presence they vied for youth. They took long exhausting walks and pretended not to puff. They kept late hours and concealed their weariness. They talked of life and of love, and they hid the catch in their throats. Then one day Sansovino talked no more. And Titian took his walks alone. Not quite alone, for very often he was accompanied by his daughter Lavinia. Titian was a familiar legend in his walks. The people in the streets always made way for the man with the snowy beard, dressed in a fur tunic and a black velvet cap. He might have been a monarch or a god. Indeed, very often a monarch would be entertained at his villa—and it was surprising the gods didn't come.

Titian was immensely wealthy, yet he never ceased to cringe for an extra ducat. In the tones of a young artist struggling against starvation he sent a bill to Philip of Spain for a commission he had just fulfilled. Here is what he said: "Please send the money at once, so that I may terminate in peace what few days I have left to live in the pay of Your Majesty . . . I am forced to throw myself at the feet of my most Catholic Majesty, to beg in the name of his clemency that he may put an end to my misfortune."

However, it remained not for Philip but for the plague to put an end to Titian's "misfortune." In 1575 the plague swept down on Venice. The dead were numbered in the thousands; the streets were lined with hearses. Thoughts on mortality rushed through the head of Titian, and he began to lay plans for his place of burial, just in case . . . He went to a church of the Franciscan order and told the priests that he was willing to paint them a devotional scene on any subject provided they promised to defray the expenses of his burial in one of their plots. This business proposition was accepted, and Titian painted a study of Mary holding the dead Christ in her lap. But even then he could not resist the temptation to do a little more bargaining over the disposal of his body. He thought he could squeeze a few more feet of burial ground out of the

Franciscans if he withheld his painting for a higher price. It is a great tribute to his business ability that he was successful in the deal. They allowed him to rot in more spaciousness.

The plague did not get him the first year. But in 1576 it came again, and this time it sought him out in his villa on the north shore. The long game of hide-and-seek was over. He succumbed at the age of ninety-nine.

RUBENS

Antwerp, Cathedral: *Elevation of the Cross, Descent from the Cross.*

Antwerp, Museum: *Adoration of the Magi, Crucifixion.*

Berlin, Museum: *Raising of Lazarus, The Stag Hunt.*

Boston, Museum of Fine Arts: *Peace and Plenty, Portrait of Isabella Brant, Rubens' Master and His Wife.*

Brooklyn, Museum: *The Risen Christ.*

Chicago, Art Institute: *Samson and Delilah.*

Cleveland, Museum of Art: *Triumph of the Holy Sacrament.*

Detroit, Institute of Arts: *Philip Rubens—the Artist's Brother, St Michael.*

Harvard University, Fogg Art Museum: *Portrait of a Lady.*

Kansas City, Nelson Gallery: *Portrait of Thomas Parr.*

London, National Gallery: *The Judgment of Paris, The Rape of the Sabines, The Straw Hat.*

London, Wallace Collection: *The Rainbow Landscape.*

Los Angeles, Keeler Collection: *The Duke of Mantua.*

Madrid, Museum: *Garden of Love.*

Munich, Old Pinakothek: *Battle of the Amazons, Fall of the Angels, The Lion Hunt, Portrait of Rubens and His First Wife, Portrait of His Second Wife.*

New York, Frick Collection: *Portrait of Ambrose Spinola.*

New York, Metropolitan Museum of Art: *Adoration of the Magi, The Holy Family, Pyramus and Thisbe, St Cecilia,* several *Portraits.*

Paris, Louvre: *The Flemish Kermis, Portrait of Elizabeth of France.*

Sarasota, Ringling Museum: *The Departure of Lot from Sodom, Danaë and the Golden Shower.*

Toledo, Museum of Art: *The Holy Family.*

Vienna, Belvidere Gallery: *Assumption of the Virgin, Ignatius Loyola Casting Out Devils.*

Peter Paul Rubens

1577–1640

RUBENS WAS BORN IN 1577, one year after Titian's death. His father at the time was living at Siegen, Germany, an exile from Cologne whither, in turn, he had been exiled from his native city of Antwerp in the Netherlands. John Rubens was a doctor of laws and a professor of love. While at Cologne he had become an intimate counselor of Prince William of Orange and an even more intimate counselor of the prince's pretty young wife. Prince William's subjects began to talk of a court scandal. The unsuspecting prince went away on a military campaign with the army, leaving Dr Rubens to continue the romantic campaign at home. Dr Rubens was a handsome devil with a quicksilver tongue that pushed the mercury of a woman's passion up many degrees when he spoke. Anne, the prince's wife, was a lissome bundle of royal charms, all ears for the silver words of love minted from her admirer's heart. When Prince William returned from his battles he found his wife in the arms of Rubens. Anne's condition was indeed interesting. It was whispered far and wide that she was to have a child by the famous doctor of laws. Now that William had returned home, Rubens' condition became interesting also. He was thrown into jail under sentence of death. The lips that had dared to kiss a princess of the blood were to be forever silenced for their audacity.

From his prison John Rubens wrote the prince a letter in which he apologized for his conduct. He reminded William of all the illustrious rulers in history whose wives had strayed into other men's arms. He concluded with this consoling thought: "Your indignity, Sire, could have been much greater. After all, your wife carried on her flirtation with John Rubens, a doctor of laws, a person who ranks next to a baron. Just think, it might have been a butcher!"

Won over by the charm of this facile-tongued roué, Prince William pardoned him and sent him into exile. The doughty doctor packed his belongings, settled down at Siegen and for the rest of his mortal days shut his eyes to the blandishments of forbidden love.

II

IT WAS AT SIEGEN that Peter Paul Rubens first saw the light. Shortly after the baby's birth his father died. His mother brought her four children back to Antwerp and sent them to an excellent public school. Peter Paul was ignorant of his father's past, but the germ of the Lothario was in his blood. Tall, easy-tongued, handsome, alert, he became a page, at the age of thirteen, at the palace of the Princess Margaret de Ligne-Aremberg. Here he learned to sniff at the perfumes of the great ladies and to sneeze with the manners of a gentleman. Even at thirteen he was a polished little courtier of the sixteenth century. But Peter had another and more important asset—a talent with the brush. He remained at court until the age of twenty, and then he could stand it no longer. He slashed his laces, rolled up his sleeves and offered himself as an apprentice to three Flemish artists whom he was soon to outshine in fame and fortune. First he studied under Tobias Verhaegt, to whom art was not a personal expression so much as a decorative handicraft for commercial consumption. The influence of this man, though the apprenticeship lasted only six months, remained with Rubens to the end of his life. Painting, to Verhaegt and to all of his contemporaries, with the exception of Rembrandt, was not a medium for delineating the autobiography of the artist's soul. It was a means for executing clever little essays in color descriptive of the life and manners of the elite society in which the court painters moved. Titian had begun the tradition of turning an epoch into a series of individual portraits of wealthy patrons who paid high prices. The artist rarely, if ever, dared to express his own views. He was merely a mirror reflecting the tastes of his clientele. Titian, as it happened, was a mirror that reflected with unequaled genius the color of his surroundings. If sometimes the artist sought refuge away from his own epoch, it was practically always an escape into classical antiquity. But here also the artist was incapable of doing personal pictures. To be sure, his hands were eager to catch the roots of the vitality that was classical art. But this vitality, which sprang from the immortal gods of Olympus, afforded no outlet for the personal story of a mortal artist. There was no room for a man's tears where the sun of Apollo blazed. This was the atmosphere in which Rubens served his apprenticeship under Verhaegt.

He passed from the tutelage of Verhaegt to Adam van Noort, who had a great reputation as a boor and a drunkard but a very small reputation as a painter. He was coarse and cantankerous down to the very marrow of his bones. While his hands mixed the paints his lips were wet with alcohol and his eyes were bleary with lascivious thoughts. He was no fit master for the elegant young courtier, who left him after a while and offered himself to a third instructor, Otto van Veen. This gentleman was a connoisseur of classical culture. He carried, Atlaslike on his shoulders, the traditions of Italian art from Rome and Naples to Northern Europe. He laboriously copied the paintings of Titian and Tintoretto and breathed the spirit of the Renaissance through petrified nostrils. He passed a whiff of this spirit on to Rubens in the form of classical precepts and textbook rules. From this influence Rubens was to emerge only after two decades of hard labor.

Shortly after his sojourn at the house of Otto van Veen Rubens applied for membership in the artists' guild of St Lukes at Antwerp. He was accepted without hesitation. He was scarcely above twenty at the time, but he received, through this connection, a commission to do some civic decorations. Three years later he took his first trip to Italy and made a careful study of the great Renaissance masterpieces.

III

HE WAS NOW TWENTY-THREE, with a dashing eye, a sprightly step and the polished affectations of the courtier. He loved gaiety in the parlor and walks in the garden. He adored the minuet tempo of social intercourse and the flute calls of polite conversation. He inherited the Nordic complexion, along with the intelligent eyes and the aristocratic mouth of his father. He was quiet and dignified and at all times reserved. Every word that dropped from his lips was passed by the censor of his own restraint. He had not the artistic passion of a wild mountain cataract but the gentle enthusiasm of a rock garden stream. He spoke and wrote Greek, Latin, French and Italian in addition to his native Flemish. And when he spoke there was the barest suggestion of a swagger to his mouth and a sense of supreme self-control. Not one of his letters shows a single trace of spontaneity or warm feeling or self-revelation. When he expressed himself in painting, as we shall see, he did so in opaque, fantastically brilliant colors, which served as a hallowe'en mask over the spirit of the man.

IV

WHILE HE WAS IN ITALY he stopped at Venice. The bright warm decorations of the Venetians greatly impressed him. And he set about to become a virtuoso in the handling of pigment. Vincenzo Gonzaga, the Duke of Mantua, met him, took an instant liking to him and offered him a job. The duke was a genuine lover of art who incurred heavy debts in the pursuit of his treasures. He emptied his pockets and covered his walls. He served exotic meats and pastries prepared in elaborate shapes that took away the breath of his guests. By the time they had recovered and were ready to eat he would order a second banquet, an exact duplicate of the first, which had grown cold. The duke entrusted Rubens with a series of portraits of his household members. "P. P. R. succeeds perfectly in this form," he wrote to a friend. Peter Paul also succeeded perfectly in winning the entire confidence of the duke. He was prudent, very prudent, with tight lips that compressed secrets between them, that smiled fetchingly to solicit further secrets, that asked for information but rarely spoke advice and that always were ready to kiss a lady's hand—especially if that hand was bedecked with jewels.

In 1603, three years after he met the duke, Rubens was sent along with a party of messengers to the King of Spain, Philip III. He had charge of a series of pictures to be given as presents to the monarch. The trip was made entirely in the rain. The pictures got damp and were spoiled. Rubens refused to retouch them. "I am not willing to confound myself with another man, however great," he remarked. But he painted two pictures of his own to replace those that were most seriously damaged.

When he reached Spain he turned up his nose at the paintings of the local artists, but he sought the gallery of imported Italian works. The native artists painted the familiar scenes of the countryside—landscapes, animals, portraits of humble folk. But Rubens' eye looked for the altarpieces of the Italian Renaissance. His mind was like a house haunted by the ghosts of Tintoretto, Titian, Raphael—spirits that were only too capable of casting their spells of color over the imagination of impressionable young men. He felt that he must dip his brush in wine and cover his canvas with flaming strokes. He had the obsession to re-create the Venus of a Titian or a Giorgione, to learn anew the secret they possessed for reproducing the warm tints of the flesh. To recapture the art that was born in the Italian sun, wasn't that too bold an undertaking for the painter from the North? Yet this was exactly what he undertook to do— and he almost, but not quite, succeeded.

He returned to Rome from Spain. He took a trip to Milan, where he made a copy of Leonardo's *Last Supper* and painted several religious pieces for the Jesuits. What were his assets at this period of his life? For one thing, he had heroic ambitions. He would rather attempt a *Last Judgment* after the manner of Michelangelo than anything else. He must paint whole worlds on canvas. His powers of execution fell somewhat short of his ambition, however. His composition was faulty and unoriginal. He was not able to manage a crowd of figures in scenes. His drawing was by no means flawless. And his taste was open to question. Attracted by the exaggerated naturalism of Michelangelo's art, he imitated his mannerisms rather than his manner. He accentuated the disproportion and the lascivious postures without reflecting the vitality and the dynamic power of Michelangelo. He was like a novice poet copying the sensuous imagery of Byron without the poetry that turns such sensuousness into art. We are confronted with the strange paradox of the young Rubens, the very model of courtliness and restraint as a man, painting, in this early period, with extreme abandon and carelessness. He painted an *Assumption of the Just* that looks like "a rain of little nude figures." He was fascinated by the human flesh on canvas. He neglected a meticulous technique that would please the mind for a lavish display of color that pleased the eye. He depended upon the lighting effect of the picture gallery to conceal the defects in his pictures. He used shadows to cover up the mistakes in his colors. He painted a Madonna on slabs of slate so that the tints might lie smoothly and not be affected by adverse light reflections. "I need not trouble myself to make it very good or highly finished, because no one can ever judge it in this bad light," he remarked. It is to be suspected that the bad light concealed a recklessness and unsavoriness that Rubens had inherited from his father. In the shadowy recesses of his own portrait lurked the obsession to go completely pagan, while in the well-lighted places he danced the minuet.

V

IN 1618, while he was living at Rome, his mother died. Rubens had been deeply attached to her and he took the blow keenly. He remained in seclusion for several months. Then he resigned from the service of the Duke of Mantua and set out for himself. He returned to Antwerp and lived with his brother Philippe, the secretary of the town council. Philippe was married to Maria de Moy, daughter of a fellow politician. And Maria had a niece whose eyes reflected heaven. She was eighteen years old, and her name was Isabella Brandt. Rubens met her and fell in love with her. They were married the following year. She was the first woman of any real significance in his life. He commenced to use her as a model for his art. Her ample figure and her smiling dimples enliven several of Rubens' finest pictures.

He was only thirty-two at the time, but, like Titian, he had already achieved financial success. The Duke of Mantua had given him a comfortable salary. His brother Philippe managed to get him a score of commissions from the good burghers of Antwerp. He built himself a house designed after the manner of an Italian mansion. He acquired a large collection of art treasures from Italy and settled down to live in great style. He was a thoroughgoing classicist in everything—including his fondness for Venus. All day long he painted. And then, as twilight settled on the town, he mounted his horse and rode along the river Scheldt, lost in reverie. He would fix his eyes on the Dutch barges that sailed lazily down the stream against a sad and quiet countryside—green fields and gray buildings, and in the background the gloomy tower of the weather-beaten old cathedral. Slowly the solid rustic beauty of the scene etched its way into him, and he began to forget about the colored spires of Venice and the spicy Italian sky. Here was rough, honest nature that begged to be painted. The smoky clouds of Antwerp, as well as the Italian sunsets, were worthy of representation on canvas. And who could paint them better than a son of Flanders? There is little doubt that Rubens was slowly weaned away from his love of all things Italian by the horseback rides along the river Scheldt. Instead of copying the gold and the glitter of what others—the Italians themselves—had done so well, Rubens decided to reproduce the simple beauty of his own country. He was determined to place himself at the head of the Flemish school of painting. Henceforth he would cease to attempt to transplant his Northern genius into the exotic soil of Italy.

The members of the Flemish school of painting, such masters as Brueghel, Van Bolen and Jordaens, were experts in brushwork. They painted the homely scenes of life in town and country. They cared less about the tassels and the ornaments of the great than they did about the flat toe of a peasant's shoe. They were artists not of the court and of the grand nobility but of the bourgeoisie, the rising, ambitious and industrious middle classes. They were quite liberal, almost photographic in their representations. The texture of a brick in a wall, the minutest description of a cobblestone in a street—these they painted with amazing craftsmanship. And they were masters of the medium of light and shadow. Unlike the Italians, who depended on broad masses of color, working from black to tints of the deepest luminosity, the Flemish school started with high color values and by subtle gradations scraped down to delicate suggestions and nuances. They cared little about decorative effects. They dealt mostly in low tones.

Rubens at no time during his life, even when he joined the Flemish school, was able to break completely with the Venetian tradition. To the very end Rubens was, like Titian, a supreme colorist. In a sense he became the *enfante terrible* of the Flemish school. Nevertheless his masterpieces date from this second period of his art, when he learned how to apply the principles of chiaroscuro—that is, the balanced distribution of light and shadow to produce a perfect harmony of color.

He was swamped with commissions. He did a very unusual thing. He opened a painting factory, so called, and recruited a school of pupils to fill in the minor details of his paintings once he had drawn the general design. He had become so popular that he was obliged to refuse more than a hundred aspirants to his factory. To this day there is a controversy as to the genuineness of many of the paintings that bear the name of Rubens. We don't know how much was done by the master hand and how much by the pupils. His pupils were by no means novices at their art. As a matter of fact, one of them was the famous Van Dyck, who ranks next to Titian and Velasquez in portraiture. Rubens was a businessman. Of that there is no doubt. Many people were scandalized at the factory. However, Rubens' genius, unlike that of Rembrandt, did not consist in the vitality of his personal expression and his individualistic insight. He was chiefly a decorator. He was one of the most objectively minded painters on record. He was frankly interested in the commercial aspect of his art. Let the pupils do the bulk of the work. A few master strokes from his brush, and the painting could command the very highest price. Art was a business, not a divine impulse.

Those who search for the romantic artist, and for everything that we associate with the romantic movement, had better turn away from Rubens before they become disillusioned. Much of the sensitive value of life, much of the value of truth, was wiped out in an orgy of color when the painters of that period sat down to their work. Intellectually and artistically, the seventeenth, perhaps, was the most hypocritical of all the centuries.

At first Rubens' customers did not take too kindly to paying large sums of money for paintings that had only a touch here and there of the master hand. But soon they became reconciled to the idea. A sweep from the brush of Rubens, a few hasty corrections, and nobody could tell the pupils from the master. In this way Rubens was able to undertake large-scale church decorations, genre pictures and family portraits, all jumbled together in a fever of mass production. Since the majority of the paintings were hung in ill-lit palaces and churches, the blemishes were not revealed to the eye of the layman. In addition to swelling the entrepreneur's bank roll the factory served a social purpose. It employed half a hundred artists who had technical excellence, if no creative initiative, and it kept them constantly at work when otherwise they might have been starving. Yet the system stifled all originality on the part of the pupils and encouraged the mannerisms of their master. The bulk of the output is colorful and pleasing to the eye but lacking in conviction. Perhaps a score of the paintings are masterpieces. This is especially true of the work of Van Dyck. So successfully did this pupil imitate the master that today the art critics are uncertain as to which of the two men is to be credited for many of the pictures that go under the name of Rubens.

As for the layman, he is completely lost when he tries to search for a genuine Rubens. The reason for it appears from the following letter which he sent to a patron: "A Prometheus Enchained on Mount Caucasus, with an eagle that devours his liver: an original work of my own hand, the eagle done by Snyders (an assistant), 500 florins. Daniel in the midst of many lions, done from nature: original work entirely from my hand, 600 florins. Leopards painted from nature, with satyrs and nymphs: original picture by my hand, except a fine landscape done by an artist clever at this kind of work, 600 florins. A Last Judgment begun by one of my pupils . . . As the present piece is not quite finished, I will retouch it altogether by myself, so it can pass for an original, 1200 florins . . . A piece representing Achilles disguised as a woman: painted by my best pupil and entirely retouched by me, a very agreeable picture, and full of graceful young girls, 600 florins." And so on and on . . .

Rubens was a classicist in his art. And he had a classic sense of business. He once wrote: "To reach the highest degree of perfection as a painter, it is necessary not only to be acquainted with the ancient statues, but to be inwardly imbued with a thorough comprehension of them." Undoubtedly he thoroughly comprehended the image of the golden calf as well.

VI

RUBENS WAS NOW FORTY-ONE. Strongly pro-Spanish in his politics, he was a diplomat as well as a painter. Kings and queens could use him. The political situation of Europe at this time was a potpourri of mismanagement. The queens gambled with their jewels, and the kings gambled with their people. The impertinent poker game which the royalist egocentrics played around the table of Europe was euphemistically called *diplomacy*. And Rubens was shrewd enough and perhaps egocentric enough to fit snugly into the council chambers of the state. He was a sworn subject of the Stadtholder's wife, the Archduchess Isabella. His knee was ready to bend obsequiously at the very sound of her name. The archduchess had two political objectives: first, to crush the people's desire for independence in the United Provinces; and second, to gain the alliance of England in her constant quarrels against the other European countries.

But England at that time was flirting with France. Buckingham, that potent, swashbuckling nobleman with the flowing mustachios whom Alexandre Dumas has incorporated into his romance, *The Three Musketeers*, had gone to France on a diplomatic mission for his sovereign. However, he found time to kiss the French queen, and thus created a major scandal. It was at Paris that Rubens met the gallant duke. He had been summoned by Marie de' Medici to decorate the Luxembourg Palace. He took the necessary measurements, gave Marie his official opinion about the beauties of the French court and managed to enjoy himself hugely at the palace. Here he met Buckingham, the playboy of Western Europe. Buckingham saw Rubens' work, liked it and insisted on posing for a portrait. Rubens accepted the offer. For many afternoons Buckingham posed. Rubens, quiet and reserved though he was, did much more than paint. He had come to France not only as an artist but as an envoy. He painted Buckingham and sounded him out. Would England be favorably disposed to a Spanish alliance (now that Buckingham's love-making in France had exploded all hopes of an Anglo-French rapprochement)? "Hold your head a little to the left, please ... King Philip of Spain could do a great deal for the Stuart cause against the English Parliament ... Hold the smile now ... The archduchess is greatly desirous of King Charles' good will ..." That sort of business. The seventeenth century was an age of intrigue. A traveling painter was not merely a painter. Likely as not he was also a secret spy. People spoke in quiet tones to conceal their turbulent thoughts. Rubens was a master of silent observation. He could be entrusted by Isabella to paint pictures with his hands and to gather news with his ears. It is interesting to note that just before his French journey he had been knighted by the Spanish king. He had smiled and slipped his tongue into a title.

His diplomatic duties were a godsend to Rubens. In 1626 his wife died, and it was only his constant travel and turmoil and labor that restored his peace of mind. The archduchess, now that England seemed ready to listen to terms, sent Rubens on a trip to Spain to sound out her overlord, Philip, on the English alliance. It was a subtle business. But the shrewd artist diplomat was more than a match for the job. Armed with his easel and his brushes, he set out for Spain. Here he met the young Spanish court painter, Velasquez. In only one respect were Rubens and Velasquez alike. Both of them believed that the fates had shown great wisdom in selecting them as their favorites. On almost every other point the two disagreed. Rubens spent many hours instructing the young Spaniard. He told him to study the Italian Renaissance as a model for his art. He advised him to copy the antique. But Velasquez had an eye for nature—a faculty that was entirely beyond Rubens' powers of comprehension. Rubens went so far as to urge Philip IV to send his young court painter to Italy. But, after all, what could Velasquez learn there? Why copy others when he had the makings of a giant in his own right? He was something Rubens could never be. He was dark and Spanish, and he had poetry in his fingers. He was a creator. At this period Rubens was still more or less of a master copy boy. But Velasquez had visions and dreams of his own. Rubens saw beauty only in the masterpieces of the past, which he tried to emulate. Velasquez, however, had the rare and greater gift of seeing beauty in ugliness and divinity in things humble and small. After all, Rubens was merely the servant of greatness, while Velasquez was its master.

Rubens, however, was by this time in the full swing of the second period of his art. He was slowly mastering the medium of his greatest asset, his color. In this field Velasquez could never surpass him. Furthermore, he was learning to overcome his greatest failing, his carelessness in the handling of his composition. In his early work much of the dramatic action and Michelangelesque mannerism lacks conviction. His *Last Judgment* looks like a sack of potatoes. But now he was slowly accustoming himself to the intricacies of form and design.

And at the same time he was also perfecting himself in the form and design of European diplomacy. He went to England as a representative of the Spanish crown. He managed to collect an honorary degree from Cambridge, and he received a commission from King Charles to decorate the ceiling of the banquet room at Whitehall. Charles had just deprived England of its Parliament, and England was soon to deprive Charles of his head. He was up to his neck in mischief with that master of intrigue, Richelieu, and he was ready to plunge the whole country into war in order to take the minds of his subjects away from the constitutional fight at home. Rubens did not like to see England go to war, especially if it was to be a war against Spain. And so, with the shrewdness of a diplomat and the genius of an artist, he painted for Charles a great allegorical picture that represented the terrors of war and the blessings of peace.

Rubens' pleasant stay in England was not graced by the friendship of Buckingham. For at that time it was a moot question as to whether Buckingham was friendly with anyone other than Beelzebub, inasmuch as he had been assassinated the previous year by a disgruntled underofficer. Some moralists were pleased to see in his untimely end the principle of good vanquishing evil. There was, however, as much good as there was evil in Buckingham. He was a connoisseur of art as well as of kisses. Rubens had succeeded in selling him his entire collection of Italian art, charging him "ten thousand pounds for what had not cost above a thousand," as one contemporary put it. That same collection today would be worth many, many times ten thousand pounds, since it contained nineteen pictures by Titian, thirteen by Veronese, seventeen by Tintoretto, three by Raphael and thirteen by Rubens himself.

When Rubens returned from England he undertook the obligations of matrimony for the second time. His first wife had been dead three years. The new bride was a robust young lady of sixteen. Rubens was fifty-three. He had known Helen since childhood. In fact, she was a distant relative of his first wife. They were married in 1630, and Rubens proceeded to paint her in every state of dress and undress imaginable. Helen has come down to us as a baggy woman made notorious by her husband's art. At fifty-three Rubens was a gentleman with the cravings of a satyr. And Helen was his buxom dryad. Rubens has been condemned by some of his critics for the manner in which he exhibited his wife. But these critics have made the mistake of confounding art with morals. Helen herself made this mistake. At his death she was about to destroy several of the pictures, but she changed her mind when the Duke of Richelieu offered her a large sum for them. Helen overcame her moral scruples, to the enrichment of herself—and of the rest of the world.

VII

AFTER HIS SECOND MARRIAGE Rubens plunged once more into the maelstrom of diplomacy. Neither the attacks of the gout nor a pretty wife could stop him. He became so busy in his political affairs that, when he wrote letters to his friends, he "stood on one leg," as he expressed it. But in 1633 he burned his fingers with a political firecracker and retired from the scene. The Archduchess Isabella had ordered him to stay at Antwerp and on no account to allow certain important state papers to get out of his hands. But one of the leaders of the people's party, the Duke of Arschot, demanded to see the papers. Rubens sent him a letter refusing to show them. Whereupon the duke exploded. He wrote him a curt note which ended with the comment, "I hope in the future you will learn how persons of your caste should write to persons of mine." Rubens immediately sent him a letter of apology, and the duke went around showing the letter to his friends. With the death of his patron, Isabella, Rubens renounced the role of diplomat. From then on he was only a painter. A very sick one at that. He suffered from severe attacks of the gout—a strange penalty for a man who had been a moderate eater all his life. When the brother of the Spanish king arrived at Antwerp to succeed Isabella as viceroy Rubens was unable to move from his bed to receive him. However, in between his attacks he managed to design eleven arches with decorations for the festive occasion.

From now on his road led not to the palace but to the grave. He had reached the third and finest manner of his painting. For thirty years he had labored painfully to achieve the secret of color. And now he had finally mastered the art. He had learned, too, the art of composition, as those who have seen his series of paintings on the life of Marie de' Medici will testify. Perhaps the most famous painting of this series is the one in which Henry IV of France receives the portrait of the Italian queen from the hands of angels. The stately and romantic figure of Henry, as he stands in his armor and gazes at the portrait, is Rubens at his noblest. For once there is feeling as well as color in his work. Another masterpiece of this period is the portrait of his second wife, Helen Fourment, holding a fan. The picture consists of a series of horizontally sloping lines—the clouds in the background, the slanting hat, the feathered fan—a well-nigh perfect blending of composition, color and technique. There is restraint, warmth and a marvel of chiaroscuro in this painting, as well as in *The Descent from the Cross*. If, as someone has stated, Rubens had "fallen in love with his own style and sought to enhance the beauty of his own feeling rather than to accentuate the character of the beauty he was supposed to express," what of it? People have called in question his sincerity. He was a man with a scientific mind and, like his father, somewhat skeptical of religion. Yet the religious paintings of his last period manifest the worship of beauty; and this, after all is said and done, is very closely akin to the beauty of worship.

As for his personal life, let us pass over the weakness of his character and concentrate on the courage he displayed on his sickbed at the end. Before his death he had enough strength left to show his monarch, Philip IV of Spain, one more token of his good will. He sent him from his factory a carload of a hundred and twelve paintings, among which are several examples of his greatest work. The king, in grateful acknowledgment of the courtesy, commissioned a group of new original paintings from the dying artist. Both the king and Rubens knew that the job would never be completed. Rubens was still at work on the first canvas when Death came to snatch the still glowing brush from his hand.

REMBRANDT

Amsterdam, Rijksmuseum: *The Jewish Bride, The Night Watch, The Syndics of the Drapers' Guild.*

Baltimore, Epstein Collection: *Portrait of an Old Man.*

Boston, Gardner Museum: *Christ and His Disciples in the Storm, Self-Portrait, A Young Couple.*

Brooklyn, Museum: *Portrait of Rembrandt's Father, The Rabbi.*

Chicago, Art Institute: *Christ Washing the Disciples' Feet, Portrait of a Young Girl.*

Cincinnati, Institute of Arts: *Young Man Rising from His Chair.*

Detroit, Institute of Arts: *Head of Christ, The Salutation.*

Dresden, Gallery: *Portrait of His Wife, Saskia.*

The Hague, Museum: *Anatomy Lecture.*

Harvard University, Fogg Art Museum: *Portrait of an Old Man.*

Indianapolis, Clowes Collection: *Old Man in a Fur Cap.*

Kansas City, Nelson Gallery: *Portrait of a Boy.*

Leningrad, Museum: *Abraham and the Three Angels.*

London, British Museum: *The Three Trees.*

London, Dulwich Gallery: *Girl at a Window.*

London, National Gallery: *The Adoration of the Shepherds, Portrait of Himself* (at the age of fifty-three), *Portrait of an Old Woman, A Woman Bathing.*

London, Wallace Collection: *The Artist's Son.*

Montreal, Van Horne Collection: *Portrait of a Young Rabbi.*

Munich, Old Pinakothek: *Entombment, Descent from the Cross, Nativity, Sacrifice of Isaac.*

New York, Frick Collection: *Polish Rider, Old Woman with a Bible.*

New York, Metropolitan Museum of Art: *Portrait of Titus, Self-Portrait, Old Woman Paring Her Nails.*

Paris, Louvre: *Philosophers, The Supper at Emmaus, Woman Bathing.*

Rochester, University: *Portrait of a Young Man.*

Toledo, Museum of Art: *Portrait of Himself.*

Washington, National Gallery: *Old Lady with a Bible.*

Washington, Smithsonian Institution: *Man with a Large Hat.*

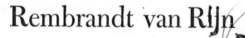

Rembrandt van Rijn

1606–1669

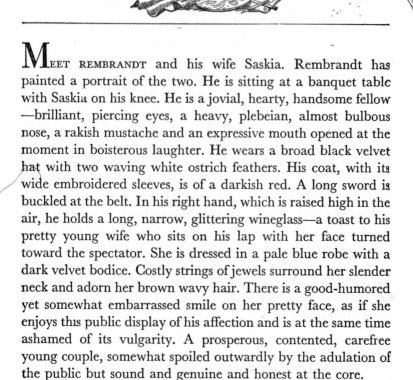

MEET REMBRANDT and his wife Saskia. Rembrandt has
painted a portrait of the two. He is sitting at a banquet table
with Saskia on his knee. He is a jovial, hearty, handsome fellow
—brilliant, piercing eyes, a heavy, plebeian, almost bulbous
nose, a rakish mustache and an expressive mouth opened at the
moment in boisterous laughter. He wears a broad black velvet
hat with two waving white ostrich feathers. His coat, with its
wide embroidered sleeves, is of a darkish red. A long sword is
buckled at the belt. In his right hand, which is raised high in the
air, he holds a long, narrow, glittering wineglass—a toast to his
pretty young wife who sits on his lap with her face turned
toward the spectator. She is dressed in a pale blue robe with a
dark velvet bodice. Costly strings of jewels surround her slender
neck and adorn her brown wavy hair. There is a good-humored
yet somewhat embarrassed smile on her pretty face, as if she
enjoys this public display of his affection and is at the same time
ashamed of its vulgarity. A prosperous, contented, carefree
young couple, somewhat spoiled outwardly by the adulation of
the public but sound and genuine and honest at the core.

Such are the successful young artist and his wife shortly after their marriage. They are as yet unaware of the dark days that lie ahead of them. For the moment they are wrapped up completely in their mutual happiness.

And they have every reason to be happy. Rembrandt is by far the most popular portrait painter at Amsterdam. He gets many more commissions than he can attend to, and for each of these commissions he can dictate his own price. His earnings amount to twelve thousand gulden (equivalent in purchasing power to about twenty-five thousand dollars) a year, and his expenses are even greater than his earnings. For he loves to live, this son of the miller of Leyden, and he loves to see others live. His extravagance is equaled only by his generosity. His money melts away like snow under the sunlight of his good nature. Jewels for his wife, banquets for his friends and unsecured loans to all those who ask for them. Strange that a man of the North should have been so tropical in his character and in his genius.

For his genius, like his generosity, was warm, boisterous, effervescent, rich. Brightness of color, strong contrasts of light and shadow, deep reds, strong purples and brilliant blues— these were among his chief characteristics. And, above all, a sweeping and impetuous technique. Many of the figures in his group paintings seem to have sprung into life with a single stroke of the brush. Rembrandt was one of the most rapid as well as one of the most perfect of painters. And he painted incessantly. Though many of his works have been lost, we still have at the present time no less than five hundred of his pictures, nearly three hundred of his etchings and more than fifteen hundred of his drawings. His genius was a Niagara. He poured forth his masterpieces with a stintless abundance and apparently with an effortless skill.

II

HIS FATHER, the prosperous half owner of a mill, had tried to make a scholar out of Rembrandt. Accordingly, in 1620 he had the fourteen-year-old boy enrolled as a Latin student at the University of Leyden. Rembrandt, however, implored his father to let him become an artist. And so, reluctantly, the old miller consented to transfer his son back from Latin into life. Rembrandt studied for a number of years under the painters Van Swanenbruch and Lastman, amazed them both with his precocity and at twenty-six settled in Amsterdam and plunged into the stimulating life and thought of the seventeenth-century "hub of the universe."

Amsterdam at that time was regarded as the most interesting city in Europe, and within a few years Rembrandt came to be known as the most interesting man in Amsterdam. The world was at his feet, and he delighted it with his art and entertained it with his bounty.

He met Saskia, married her and adored her. He painted her portrait over and over again. And he painted his own portrait again and again. Not out of vanity—for Rembrandt, with all his faults, was not a vain creature—but out of the sheer gusto of living. Self-expression was the very breath of his life, and self-portraiture was merely the most intimate mode of his self-expression. In painting himself he never flattered himself. He was pitiless in exposing the weakness as well as the strength of his character. And the same was true of the other portraits he painted. His paintings are all human, all-too-human, and that is why to this day they are able to arouse so sympathetic a response within us. We recognize them at once as our friends. For *their* thoughts are *our* thoughts, *their* failings *our* failings, *their* hopes *our* hopes. Rembrandt was one of the first European artists to bring painting down from the skies and to establish it as a mirror of the imperfection and the glory of the earth.

Not only in his portraits, but in his biblical and in his mythological subjects, Rembrandt aimed at the human rather than the divine touch. His Christs and his Madonnas, as well as his pagan gods and goddesses, have nothing of the remote, idealized and ethereal atmosphere about them. They are human. They represent the aspirations, the struggles, the dreams, the achievements, the hopes, the disappointments, the sufferings and, above all, the eternal faith and courage of mankind. In the paintings of Rembrandt Jesus is not the Son of God but the Son of Man.

III

THUS FAR, however, Rembrandt had found it rather pleasant to be counted among the sons of men. The world was good to him. In his paintings the note of joy predominated over the undertone of sorrow. But this undertone of sorrow was now becoming more and more audible in his life if not in his work. Saskia gave birth to three children, and two of them died in their infancy. And then, only eight years after their marriage, Saskia herself took sick and died.

This tragedy marked the end of Rembrandt's fortune. Like a rocket his light had shot up, and now suddenly it had gone out, and he was left in mid-air in the darkness. In the same year in which he had lost his wife he also lost the patronage of his clients. And the manner in which he lost this patronage possessed its comic as well as its tragic side. The wealthy burghers of Amsterdam, whose sense of dignity was greater than their sense of humor, had commissioned Rembrandt to paint them in their military glory. This painting, which is now known as the famous *Night Patrol*, aroused the ire of the sitters. And the reason for their displeasure was that the painting was too good. Instead of lining them all up and giving each one of them an equal place in the light, Rembrandt had grouped them in such a way as to produce an artistic unit. Result—a masterpiece of composition and a company of disgruntled patrons. Some of them appear in full light. Others are painted partly in the light and partly in the shadow. Still others are shown only in profile. All of them, they complained, had paid an equal sum for their portrait. Why, then, had Rembrandt failed to give them an equal prominence in the general ensemble? To which criticism Rembrandt replied that he was an artist and not a census taker. It was his business to create beauty and not to count heads. This reply was good sense but bad business. His commissions began to fall off. He now painted more and more for himself. He was no longer obliged to cater to the vanities and the whims of the rich. His art for the first time became the expression of his own untrammeled personality. Rembrandt had won his freedom—and lost his livelihood.

IV

FROM THAT TIME ON his downfall was rapid. A lover of life, and particularly of family life, he took unto himself another woman, Hendrickje Stoffels. But he did not make her his wife. For Saskia had written into her will a clause to the effect that if he married again he was to lose the guardianship of their only living child, Titus. The woman who now came into his house as his mistress was in every way worthy of him. But the burghers of Amsterdam, and especially the relatives of Saskia, found in this liaison an added excuse to torment him. From passive neglect they went on to active persecution. They bespattered his character, they took away his house, and finally they forced him into bankruptcy. He was compelled to move into a small and unsanitary tenement in the Jewish Ghetto.

But his art kept on rising to greater and greater heights. In his happier moments he had painted the vanity of the rich. Now he depicted the humility of the poor—the Dutch peasants and fisherfolk at their toil and the Jewish rabbis and scholars at their prayers. Characteristic of this period is his *Blind Tobit*, an etching that shows a weak and pathetic old man whose outstretched arms are groping toward the door. He has just heard his son knocking. In his eagerness to welcome his son he has overturned the spinning wheel. His movements, as he tries to feel his way toward the door, are at once bold and timid. It is easy to see that his blindness is recent. For the objects in the room are as yet unfamiliar to his touch. He does not yet know the direct way to the door. His uncertain right arm is going astray. It will not come anywhere near the doorknob—a pathetic picture of helplessness and failure. "This etching," writes Charles Blanc, "is the finest print in the world . . . Even if one concealed the head of Tobit, his whole body, his arms, his legs, would still be those of a blind man."

When Rembrandt etched his *Blind Tobit* his own eyesight had begun to fail him. In order to maintain his mastery of detail he was now obliged to paint his portraits larger than life. The fine points of his art were beginning, slowly but definitely, to desert him.

And yet it was at this time that he produced what many of his critics regard as his greatest masterpiece—the famous painting of the *Cloth Merchants*, better known as *The Syndics*.

It was due to the endeavors of the few friends who were still faithful to him that Rembrandt secured the commission to paint *The Syndics*. He was fifty-five at the time—prematurely old in body but just arriving at the full maturity of his genius.

The picture of the syndics represents five officials of the Clothmakers' Company and their servant. These are the only figures in the picture but not the only people in the room, as is obvious from the express on of the six faces that we can see. They are all evidently discussing a matter of common interest. The central figure is presiding at the table, with the book of accounts open before him. He is trying to explain something to one of the members in the hall (but not in the picture). All the other faces are turned in the direction of the invisible troublemaker. Some of the faces look serious, others amused, still others scornful, as if they are impatient at the unnecessary interruption. The eyes, that look out from under the black steeple hats, are full of shrewdness, of humor, of good-natured understanding. The glow of health shines upon all the faces, even that of the elderly gentleman with the grayish hair whose hand rests firmly upon the knob of his armchair. This chair, as well as the paneled wooden background, is of a deep mahogany hue. But this color is subordinated to the brightness of the tablecloth in the foreground—the richest of imaginable reds which kindles into scarlet on the left, at the spot where the light falls directly upon it. The whole picture breathes with the luxurious warmth of well-being and prosperity. The businessmen of Amsterdam, immortalized by the most unbusinesslike of its citizens.

The money that he made on the painting was soon swallowed up in the whirlpool of his debts. His pictures, which only a few years earlier had fetched fancy prices, were now being offered at auction. And—such is the fickleness of the unappreciative public—they found few bidders. His son Titus opened an art shop in partnership with Hendrickje Stoffels. But even through this medium they could not dispose of his paintings. Rembrandt was suffering from the bitter fate of those who are unfortunate enough to become famous too early in life. He lived to witness the death and the burial of his own reputation. Within his own lifetime he had become an ancient and forgotten classic.

We have one of the self-portraits which he etched at this period. He sits drawing at a window. Gone are the embroidered cloak, the dangling sword, the jaunty mustache, the rakish hat and the mischievous twinkle in the eye. He is now dressed in an old and wrinkled working blouse. His thinning hair is covered with a plain broad-brimmed and square-topped hat. His face is sad, sallow and bloated with suffering. Time and trouble have left their mark upon it. Yet the lines about the mouth are strong, determined, confident. Come what may, he will fight on to the end!

And fight on he did. But to no avail. Blow after blow fell upon him in rapid succession. Hendrickje fell seriously ill. Her life was despaired of. Anxious hours at her bedside, anxious worry as to how he was going to pay the doctors. She recovered, but only for a short space. Again she took to her bed, and this time there was no recovery.

In order to pay for the burial of his mistress he was obliged to sell the vault in which he had buried his wife. But the end was not yet. On September 4, 1668, his one remaining son, Titus, died. The young man's death followed his marriage by only a few months.

Rembrandt lived long enough to see the birth of a daughter to Magdalena, the widow of Titus. They christened her Titia, in memory of her dead father.

Bereavement, poverty, sorrow, neglect—and then the great silence. The gods were through with their sport of him. At last they took pity on him and closed his eyes.

But they played one final joke at his expense. They dishonored him in death as they had neglected him in life. This man, who had left to the world his hundreds of priceless treasures, was buried at the beggarly price of thirteen florins (about five dollars and twenty cents)!

EL GRECO

Great Paintings by El Greco

Boston, Museum of Fine Arts: *Portrait of Fray F. H. Palavicino*.

London, National Gallery: *St Jerome*, *Agony in the Garden*.

Munich, Gallery: *Spanish Girl*.

New York, Metropolitan Museum of Art: *Cardinal Niño de Guevara*, *Toledo in a Storm*.

Paris, Collection of Comtesse de la Béraudière: *Pietà*.

Paris, Louvre: *Altar Piece*, *Portrait of Philip IV*.

Toledo, Cathedral: *Parting of Christ's Raiment before Crucifixion*.

Toledo, San Tomé: *The Burial of Count Orgaz*.

Domenico Theotocopuli
Called El Greco
1548–1625

SOME SAY El Greco was mad. Others give him the benefit of the doubt and assert that his work was the result not of an unbalanced mind but simply of poor eyesight. They maintain that he saw everything in distortion because he suffered from astigmatism. Still others believe that El Greco is without a doubt the greatest of all the artists Madness, infirmity or genius? This question has been the subject of constant debate from the time he settled down to paint in Toledo till the present day.

El Greco is the Spanish for *the Greek*. His real name was Domenico Theotocopuli, and he was born on the island of Crete. It was here, according to the ancient legend, that Theseus slew the Minotaur. It was here that archaeologists have discovered some of the strangest architecture and statuary and pottery, dating from the period of the early Mycenean civilization. Crete was always an island of mystery, and Domenico brought this mystery with him wherever he traveled. His entire life is shrouded in uncertainty. All that we have is a handful of authentic facts about him. The date of his birth is doubtful. We merely know that he was born some time between 1541 and 1548. How he spent the first twenty-five years of his life is another mystery. About 1570, however, a letter written by Clovio to Cardinal Farnese Viterbo mentions a young man from Candia, Crete, a "disciple of Titian, who has lately arrived at Rome." Clovio calls him a painter of rare talent. "Among other things he has painted a portrait of himself which causes wonderment to all the artists in Rome." Clovio begs the cardinal to lodge the young man in the Farnese Palace, "until he can find other accommodation."

The second established fact in El Greco's life comes to light in a letter written in 1576 by a certain Giuseppe Martínez. "Domenico Greco," writes Martínez, "has settled in the famous and ancient city of Toledo, introducing such an extravagant style that to this day nothing has been seen to equal it; attempting to discuss it would cause confusion in the soundest minds."

A third reference to El Greco records a quarrel he had with the Chapter of the Toledo Cathedral over the price of an altarpiece they had commissioned him to paint, shortly after his arrival in Spain. The quarrel had to be settled in court. The Chapter appointed a committee consisting of the church architect, the church sculptor and the church painter to appraise the work. El Greco was represented by a similar committee. The Greco committee reported, after a month's deliberation, that the merit of the painting in question "was so great . . . it could not be priced or valued." But they set the purchase price of the painting at a sum equal to about eight hundred and seventy-five dollars. The committee acting for the cathedral answered, however, that "such valuation is excessive and out of the bounds of reason." A certain silversmith, Alego de Montoya, was appointed to be the judge. After considerable deliberation he went on record as saying that the painting was one of the best he had ever seen and that if it were to be valued in accordance with its true merit the sum would be so great that no one would be able to pay for it. He added, however, that "in view of the nature of the times and the amounts paid generally for the paintings of great artists," he would set the price at three thousand five hundred reals—about three hundred and fifty American dollars.

The painting is today considered one of the world's masterpieces. It is the *Espolio*, or *Christ Despoiled of His Raiment on Calvary*.

The few incidents in the life of El Greco that have come to light seem to be bound up with quarrels. There is the record of a quarrel he had in 1580 with no less a personage than the King of Spain. He had been commissioned by Philip to paint for the Escorial Palace the legend of the martyrdom of St Maurice. At first El Greco complained that he was unable to undertake the job because it would require a great deal of the very costly paint known as ultramarine blue. Philip advanced the price of the paint, and the work was executed. But when the painting was completed Philip refused to have it hung in the Escorial after all. He commanded the artist to hide it away in shame. One person connected with the court, a Father Siguenza, wrote of this picture, "It did not satisfy His Majesty. And this is not astonishing, because it pleased hardly anyone, although they say it is a work of high art and its author a very learned man from whose hands have come many excellent pictures."

All through his life, it eems, El Greco was the center of debate. He was abused by his enemies and misunderstood by his friends. He lived in Toledo for thirty-eight years until his death—a complete enigma to his contemporaries. Did he have a wife? There is no record of a marriage. There does exist, however, a record of a son, George Manuel, who became a minor architect. Some of Greco's biographers claim that the marriage record has been lost; others, that the son was by a mistress who appears in several of his portraits. No one knows whether he had any other children. Several of his studies of girls have been declared to be the likenesses of a daughter. One painting deals with a family group that has been called his own. All these statements, however, are mere conjectures.

What did Greco look like? A self-portrait which he painted when he was a young man, and which Clovio mentions in his letter, has been lost. Some have surmised that certain people who appear in several of his masterpieces are in reality self-portraits. One figure with the same characteristics does recur in his paintings—a face with a long striking profile and nervous tapering hands, a strong nose, a thin, somewhat cruel mouth, a high forehead and dark, restless eyes. Is this the picture of El Greco? Perhaps, but there is no evidence to prove it.

His death is shrouded in the same secrecy as his life. He left no will. But the date of his death was entered in the city registry —April 7, 1614. "On the 7th died Domenico Greco. He left no will. He received the sacraments. He was interred in Santo Domingo el Antiguo."

But his body was moved shortly after that date. It is not known for certain where his bones rest today.

II

FROM these few isolated facts how can we reconstruct the man? Even though the facts are pale and insignificant, we have every reason to believe that the man was quite the contrary. Indeed, by all indications, El Greco was one of the strangest and most fascinating men that ever lived. And it is not ironical that such a powerful personality should have left behind him so scanty a record of himself. There is a strong suspicion that he deliberately led a life of secrecy in the land of his adoption and that he deliberately effaced all personal records that would serve as clues by which posterity might be able to rediscover him. That is, all clues save one—his painting. All his important pictures were signed by him in bold Greek letters. It was as if he had said, "The world shall know me by my paintings alone. They are sufficient to keep my fame secure." This is supreme egotism. And yet it is the truth. The man has come down to us as a legendary curiosity called *El Greco*, but the work has a definite personality of its own. With a diabolical cleverness the man had veiled himself in mystery. Even his contemporaries couldn't get close enough to him to understand him. Pacheco, the father-in-law of Velasquez, mentions that "the Greek was a student of everything, a philosopher, a wit, a sculptor and an architect as well as a painter." He called him in all things "as singular as in his painting." Above all, he was a severe critic of his own as well as of other people's work. On one occasion he remarked blandly to Pacheco that "Michelangelo was a good man, but he did not know how to paint." He meant by that, apparently, that Michelangelo was primarily a sculptor and that he lacked the sensibility of a colorist. Such criticism shocked the conservative Pacheco, to whom all the masters of the Italian Renaissance were gods. Giuseppe Martínez, in the letter we have already mentioned, wrote of the painter, "His nature was extravagant like his painting. It is not known with certainty what he did with his works, for he used to say that no price was good enough for them . . . He earned many ducats, but spent them in too great pomp and display in his house, to the extent of keeping paid musicians to entertain him at meal times. He was a famous architect, and very eloquent in his speeches. He had few disciples, as none cared to follow his capricious and extravagant style, which was suitable only for himself."

III

HE LIVED IN SPAIN the last thirty-eight years of his life. But at no time did he merge with Spanish society. He held himself coldly aloof. He was proud of his Greek nationality, and he looked down upon the countrymen of his adopted land. If he lived a life of loneliness socially, he was even more alone spiritually. Other painters belonged to schools, had predecessors, had followers. Apart from his early Italian pictures, some of which might be mistaken for the work of Bassani, El Greco showed the imprint of no artistic family tree. He had no direct followers.

So disdainful of things Spanish was this father of Spanish painting that he didn't bother to learn the national language. When he flew into a blind rage before company—an occurrence which was frequent—he shouted sounds in his native Greek that no one present could understand. When he arrived at Toledo (in 1576) the mayor of the city asked him a number of routine questions about himself. He replied abruptly: "I don't consider myself obligated to state why I came to this city, or for that matter to answer any other question put to me."

Yes, the only clues El Greco left of himself are his paintings. And these tell volumes about him. Many of the paintings that we now regard as masterpieces were hidden away in dusty cellars for hundreds of years. It wasn't until the twentieth century that El Greco was rediscovered. It was only at the birth of modern art and Cézanne that El Greco found his true contemporaries. In the seventeenth century he was a stranger. Perhaps that is why he drew a veil around himself, preferring to let his pictures speak to another generation that perhaps might be able to understand them.

What about these paintings? They read like a detective story in color and design. The Prado in Madrid, the San Tomé at Toledo, the National Gallery in London, the Metropolitan Museum in New York—all these contain the magnificent fragments of an El Greco picture puzzle. Put the fragments together, and you have before you an amazing chapter in the history of art.

Born in Crete, which was Byzantine in culture, El Greco was Byzantine to the core. This Byzantine culture from the East had found its way in the wake of the Arab invasions to the shores of Spain. The Arabs had remained for seven centuries and left there the imprint of their arabesques. When the Christians rose to power in Spain and drove out the infidel they inherited from him the fruits of the Orient. Spain was Oriental. And this means that she was partly Semitic, partly Egyptian and partly Mohammedan, in addition to being passionately Christian, in her psychology. Her characteristic art, even before the time of El Greco, had dealt with dark long faces, bare feet, hot brown eyes and the beards of prophets. All this was an immigrant art. When court pictures were desired by the Spanish monarch he sent for artists from the Netherlands, Germany and Italy. The center of the Spanish national life was Madrid, where the king lived. But El Greco came to Toledo. This was the perfect city for him. It was a Venice in cold colors. It stood on rocks of a reddish brown against a background of a lonely ultramarine sky. There was power to its landscape, a unique, rugged expressiveness. It was a city of silence and contemplation. Few of its houses opened on the streets; they had been built around courtyards in complete and sacred domestic privacy. "A strange proud city, this! It was a paradox of mysticism and filth, of crusading splendor and vulgarity, of poetry and gutter oaths." Amazing that a foreigner like El Greco should interpret the spirit of this city so accurately and so splendidly; amazing that a Greek should become the father of modern Spanish painting. He was a sort of latter-day Aeneas who brought the seeds of a new vision to a new country. And, judging by the mad poetry of this vision, his pilgrimage must have taken him, like Dante, through the abodes of the damned.

IV

EL GRECO's first masterpiece at Toledo was the *Espolio* over which, as we have already noted, he had quarreled with the cathedral Chapter. His second outstanding work was the *Martyrdom of St Maurice*. The legend of the martyrdom around which this picture was painted is as follows: Maurice and his Theban legion were Christian converts living in the Roman Empire. As loyal subjects of the *Emperor*, they were obliged to salute the pagan gods of Rome; as loyal subjects of Christ, they refused to do this. They therefore decided to kill themselves for their faith.

The painting is composed of three episodes in the drama. In the foreground Maurice is shown explaining the situation to five of his staff officers. On the right and in the middle background of the canvas Maurice stands stoically and watches his soldiers as they offer their heads one by one to the executioner's block. One naked man is lying full length on the block. The others wait patiently for their turn in a long line that twists in serpentine fashion to the very depths of the canvas. In the right-hand corner angels are waiting to receive the souls of Maurice and his fellow martyrs. The painting is executed on a tremendous scale. It is fifteen feet high and ten feet wide—reminiscent of Michelangelo's *Last Judgment*. The colors are light in tone—royal blue, pale rose and lemon yellow for the military cloaks of the martyrs, and greens, yellows and pinks for the angels. In the execution scene there are waves upon waves of naked flesh that remind one of Michelangelo at his best. There is the same dynamic portrayal of the limbs of men in agony. Yet the intensity of the suffering is softened by a note of lyrical quiet and religious resignation that almost raises the tragedy to a paean of joy. No wonder El Greco had remarked that Michelangelo was good at modeling but that he didn't know how to paint. The Italian could express the torture of pain in bas-relief. But he was unable to express the ecstasy of religion in color. A sculptor, yes. But a painter? Certainly not. So argued El Greco, and he did much to prove his argument in his *Martyrdom of St Maurice*.

El Greco had the great genius of a colorist. He turned the dark moody browns and the rigid silvers and greens of his

Byzantine heritage into the canary yellow and ultramarine blues of his own original imagination. He combined the modeling of a Signorelli with the color of a Renoir. This unity of design and color has been the ultimate goal of painters for the last thousand years. And the colorists, the female species of the world of art, have always fought violently against the masculine devotees of the sharp line and the sculptured relief. Perhaps only three painters in the entire history of art have happily wedded the two sexes—Giotto, El Greco, Cézanne.

The third of the El Greco masterpieces at Toledo hangs in the Cathedral of San Tomé. It is the *Burial of Count Orgaz*. The count had been a very pious nobleman of Toledo. According to the legend, when he was about to be buried in the family vault his two patron saints, St Stephen and St Augustine, descended from heaven in a blaze of glory, to the amazement of all the assembled Castilian grandees, and took a leading part in the ceremony. The painting of this scene by El Greco is about as haunting as one can imagine. There are twenty Spanish noblemen witnessing the lowering of the count into his grave. These spectators are grouped in a solid wall behind St Stephen and St Augustine, who tenderly support the head and the knees of the sagging body. The figures are all lifelike and life size. They seem to have walked into the Church of San Tomé just a few minutes earlier in order to perform the service. There is an atmosphere of silence and a lyrical mysticism of gravity that overwhelm the spectator when he approaches the picture. Each noble head that watches the interment is the study of a complete personality. No two expressions are the same. Yet the entire picture represents a single and harmonious effect—a profound feeling of astonishment, veneration, awe. A perfect blending of the finite and the infinite, the real and the unreal, the mastery of life and the mystery of death. A thousand and one concrete details to produce an abstract thought. The ruff collars and the lace sleeves of these great men of Castile are painted with the exquisite perfection of a Rubens or a Velasquez. The thin, delicately drawn faces and the pale, tapering, agitated hands express the powerful spiritual quality of the scene before us. For all the realistic brushwork and photographic design, it is the spirit of mysticism that guided the hand of the painter. The pallor of death on the count's face is delicately contrasted with the living tints upon the face of St Augustine as he bends over the body. It has been said that there is the poetry of Rembrandt in the countenance of this saint. The upper half of the canvas contains a group of angels. They are depicted in the act of carrying the soul of the count to heaven, where the Christ and the Virgin, surrounded by the prophets, are waiting to receive it.

Such, in bare outline, is the canvas. It will baffle art lovers to the end of time. For all its intimate portraiture, it is executed on a scale that is reminiscent of Michelangelo. But though Italian in conception, this picture is thoroughly Spanish in spirit. It represents a Spanish burial scene. The faces of all the spectators are the faces of Spanish grandees. Yet this typically Spanish work was painted by a Greek. And there is an added mystery to the picture. In the foreground, at the left, there is a kneeling page who seems to be the narrator of the story. His eyes are directed toward the front, facing the spectator, and one of his hands points to the scene of the burial. A document peeps out from one of his pockets. On the document the artist has signed his name in Greek letters—Domenico Theotocopuli. Next to the name he has written a date—1578. The boy and the date have been the subject of a great deal of controversy. The date can not have applied to the painting of the picture. For the picture was commissioned not in 1578 but eight years later, in 1586. Some critics have assigned the date to the boy. El Greco had a son who, the offspring of free love, was born in 1578. And at the time the picture was painted he was just the high age of the little page boy.

V

AFTER the *Burial of Count Orgaz* El Greco returned to his practice of painting on a small scale. Great anatomist though he was, he began to experiment and to elongate the drawing of his limbs to the point of exaggeration and caricature. His great imaginative genius sought for new forms and new artistic limits to express his own unconventional ideas. He seized upon the hand as the best medium for expressing the character and the emotion latent in a human being. No feature of the face, no other member of the body, perhaps, is more difficult to paint. The treatment of the hands is a test whereby you can separate the aristocratic artist from the plebeian. It has been said of the hands painted by El Greco that they are "directly in touch with the brain; not limbs, but merely nerves laid bare." They are delicate and white—as white as the ruff collars of their owners. And they have "muscle tone." Without this muscle tone, this imperceptible charge of energy that always runs through the hand except in death, no artist can invest his portraits with the appearance and the "touch" of life. In the paintings of El Greco the hand is the mirror of the man.

Most of he great masters have erred, as some of the El Greco enthusiasts have pointed out, in the strict anatomical representation of the human hand. When they paint a gesture they represent the fingers as pivoting on the fore knuckles, when they should have represented the pivot in its rightful place—the back knuckles below the finger web. El Greco has never erred in this respect.

If El Greco was an *observant* anatomist, he was also a *grotesque* anatomist. In the final period of his art his legs and his torsos are out of all proportion to his heads. And it is the work of this period that is most popularly associated with El Greco. Basically Oriental even in its most realistic period, the art of El Greco in his old age reverted more and more to a Byzantine mumbo jumbo, with its thin-headed people who possessed legs looking like seven-league stilts. Occasionally he threw in a patch of wild, rocky, uncontrollable landscape rising vertically within very narrow limits against a lightning-charged sky. He seems to have gone slightly mad with the visions of his old age. But there should be no doubt about his genius even then. He did at this period a Toledo landscape in a storm that is a witch's cauldron of imagery. It contains all the poetry of the storm scenes in Shakespeare's *King Lear*. The painting is amazingly three-dimensional, with a virile personality of lightning flashes, livid clouds and flaring greens. This is an ultrasophisticated art. Some of the figures of his human beings at this time are nothing more than linear symbols. The flesh of El Greco's imagination had melted away in the intense heat of his insane genius and left only the skeleton of a fancy. When friends visited the artist they listened to him as he flew into a series of blind rages, and they came away convinced that he was incurably mad. El Greco's soul pushed out from its flesh and stamped itself in the ectoplasm of his personality on canvas. The figures, the landscapes, are out of all sympathy with reality. El Greco strove for a science of personality in art—a language of linear design and geometric license. People say that he suffered from astigmatism and painted what he thought he saw. If he was suffering from astigmatism at all, it was an astigmatism not of the eye but of the spirit. The spirit was a lonely one, existing in the poor, dreary light of its own solitude until it had become near-sighted and dim with self-worship. Yet the loneliness of this spirit was the reason for its strength. El Greco had learned to know himself so thoroughly that he caught something of the infinite that was his. He saw perhaps the mysterious preliminary sketches of the universe in the various shapes he called men. He was a truly amazing and exasperating genius. "What he did well, no one did better; and what he did badly, was never done worse."

VELASQUEZ

Boston, Gardner Museum: *Portrait of Philip IV.*

Boston, Museum of Fine Arts: *Portrait of Don Baltasar with a Dwarf, Portrait of a Man.*

Detroit, Institute of Arts: *Portrait of a Man.*

London, Apsley House: *Water Carrier.*

London, National Gallery: *Christ at the Column, Venus and Cupid.*

London, Wallace Collection: *A Boar Hunt, Lady with a Fan.*

Madrid, Prado: *Aesop, The Crucifixion, The Dwarf, The Forge of Vulcan, The Maids of Honor, The Surrender of Breda, The Spinners, The Topers, Several Portraits of Philip IV*

Montreal, Van Horne Collection: *Portrait of a Young Man.*

New York, Hispanic Society: *Portrait of Duke Olivarez, Portrait of Admiral Pareja.*

New York, Metropolitan Museum of Art: *Christ and the Pilgrims of Emmaus, Portrait of a Man.*

Chicago, Art Institute: *The Kitchen Maid, Job.*

Chicago, Epstein Collection: *Isabel of Bourbon.*

Paris, Louvre: *Portrait of the Infanta Margarita.*

Rome, Doria Pamphili Gallery: *Pope Innocent X.*

San Francisco, Legion of Honor Gallery: *Portrait of Himself.*

Diego Rodríguez de Silva y Velasquez

1599–1660

VELASQUEZ was a rare phenomenon—an artist who was never at war with life. His days were spent in tranquillity. He was contented with his lot. He found his station in the society of his day, and he liked it. He saw nothing wrong with his position at the Spanish court, in which the artists, the barbers and the clowns sat together at one of the bottom tables. Descended, as he believed, both on his father's and on his mother's side from the lesser nobility, he never resented the fact that the king refused to regard him as a nobleman by right of birth. His even temper enabled him to live a life of undisturbed calm. He was one of the happiest of men in the entire history of art. If we want to find drama in Velasquez, we must look at his paintings rather than his life. He regarded and recorded the sufferings of humanity like a spectator who watches a shipwreck from a sheltered vantage point upon the shore. Velasquez was one of the most objective of painters.

[*129*]

II

DIEGO RODRÍGUEZ DE SILVA Y VELASQUEZ was born in the early part of June 1599 at the city of Seville, the commercial center of Spain and the golden treasury of Spanish art. Brought up on "the milk of the fear of the Lord," he acquired an education in secular philosophy, sacred art and stoical self-restraint. From earliest childhood, however, he grew up with a profound belief in his own ability. As a youngster he filled his notebooks with sketches. His quick intelligence told him that he had an eye to observe things and a hand to record them. He asked his father to let him become an artist, and his father consented.

Accordingly, at the age of twelve Velasquez entered the studio of Herrera, who was then at the height of his career. This painter, wrongly regarded as the "Michelangelo of Seville," had won his following through his picturesque personality rather than through the picturesqueness of his art. Velasquez soon found that he had very little to learn from his master. He left Herrera and went to another teacher—Pacheco.

This painter taught his young apprentice to observe nature keenly and to reproduce it faithfully. He was not a great artist. Indeed, some people regarded him as no artist at all. In an epigram which is more cruel than clever a contemporary critic held up one of his paintings, the *Crucifixion*, to eternal ridicule. "This picture," he said, "proves that it was not the Roman soldiers but the Spanish painter who crucified Jesus." This criticism, however, like most critical epigrams, was an unfair and distorted summary of his ability. For Pacheco was a competent if uninspired painter. And, what was even more important for Velasquez, he was an excellent teacher. He possessed the one quality necessary to a man who is called upon to instruct pupils of superior talent. He was remarkably free from dogmatism. Instead of compelling his pupils to copy his methods he allowed each of them to develop in his own way. In a textbook which he wrote on the *Art of Painting* he made the following wise observation: "All that is here said, and might still be said and proved, by no means claims to tie down . . . those who are striving to reach the summit of the Art . . . There may still be other methods, possibly easier and better. I write only what I myself have practiced, without wishing to impose burdens and yokes on good heads."

This freedom from pedantry was one of the chief reasons why Velasquez remained a patient and painstaking disciple of Pacheco for a number of years. But there was another and perhaps even more important reason. Pacheco had a beautiful daughter, Juana. In due time Pacheco's favorite pupil became his son-in-law. Velasquez and Juana were married in 1618.

III

AT TWENTY-THREE Velasquez had already become the father of two little girls, Francisca and Ignacia. To support his growing family he had to stick close to his easel. The subjects that he selected for his early paintings were the realistic scenes of everyday life, the so-called *bodogones*, or kitchen and tavern scenes, for which the Spaniards of that period showed a great fancy. It was an age of realism, of joyous living and loving, of picaresque adventures and an honest appraisal of the world, without glorification on the one hand or condemnation on the other. Velasquez fell readily into the spirit of the time. In his pictures of the *Water Carrier*, the *Steward*, the *Vintager*, the *Musician* and the *Old Woman Preparing an Omelette* he represented neither a hymn to the holiness of poverty nor a sermon against its injustice. He merely painted a lifelike scene, in somber colors because the subject matter was somber, and without any social message, because Velasquez was an artist and not a reformer. At this, the formative period of his life, Velasquez had de-

veloped an observant eye rather than an imaginative mind. He
selected only those subjects which he best understood. His
paintings showed the beauty of the commonplace. "I would
rather," he remarked to one of his critics, "be the first of the
vulgar painters than the second of the refined ones." Yet later
on, as we shall see, he was to become the first of the refined
as well as of the vulgar painters.

IV

WHEN PHILIP IV came to the Spanish throne Velasquez decided
to seek his fortune at the capital city of Madrid. The naturalistic movement in Seville had spent its force, and a wave of
sentimentalism had taken its place. Velasquez was no senti-
mentalist. He had a level head on those Andalusian shoulders
of his. He had heard that the young king was a lover of art. Let
the king see and appreciate a *real* artist, said Velasquez to himself as he set out to present his credentials to the court.

These credentials, especially the recommendation of his
father-in-law, Pacheco, produced the desired effect. Velasquez
gained an audience at the palace, made a good impression on
the king and secured a commission to paint his portrait.

So pleased was Philip IV with this "first real" portrait of himself that he ordered all his other portraits to be removed from
the walls and promised that thenceforth Velasquez alone should
be allowed to paint His Royal Majesty. He invited Velasquez
into the palace, raised him to the exalted status of a clown and
began to heap commissions and remunerations upon his obedi-
ent head.

A new phase had now begun in the development of his art.
The dark, heavy colors of his *bodogone* pictures were beginning to
give way to the more delicate tones of the genteel life about him.
The coarse outlines of the toilers and the topers of Andalusia were
being replaced by the elegant figures of the grandees of Madrid.

Yet even in these paintings Velasquez retained his natural simplicity. He painted his royal personages without any of the trappings of royalty. They stand at ease, against an unobtrusive background—a gray wall, a table, a curtain—just ordinary human beings whom the accident of birth has invested with extraordinary powers. The pictures seem to breathe and talk. The faces are animated. Velasquez surprises his sitters while they are in the process of thinking. His portraits are, in the truest sense, *living* pictures.

It was not long before Velasquez was hailed as the leading portraitist in Spain. Some of the other artists, indeed, began to insinuate that he was a portraitist and nothing else. They accused him of debasing a noble art to mere picture daubing. "Portraiture," wrote one of them, Vicente Carducho, "is the lowest branch of art . . . No great painter has ever been a portraitist alone . . . All that Velasquez can do is to paint the human head." To this taunt Velasquez replied tartly: "This gentleman pays me too much honor. For he ought to know that nobody can really paint the human head."

At about this time Velasquez had an opportunity to prove that he could paint something besides portraits. The king had announced a competition for a painting that would commemorate the expulsion of the Moors from Spain. Several artists, including the critics of Velasquez as well as Velasquez himself, entered the competition. The committee unanimously selected the Velasquez painting as the best. This picture was sufficient to establish Velasquez not only as the leading portraitist but as the outstanding artist of the Spanish court. From now on he was immune against the attack of his rivals.

V

THE PAINTING of the *Expulsion of the Moors* has unfortunately been lost. Another of his commemorative pictures, however, has been preserved, and it is regarded by many experts as "the greatest historical painting in the world." This famous painting, *The Lances*, represents the delivery of the keys of the captured city of Breda to its Spanish conqueror, the Marquis of Spinola. He places his right hand upon the shoulder of his vanquished opponent. The background is a broad expanse of flat country bounded by the ocean. With less than a dozen figures, a couple of horses and a small group of heads Velasquez creates the illusion of two vast armies. The sunlight that illumines the picture is centered between the Spanish and the Dutch commanders. The full brightness of the sun falls upon the triumphant yet kindly face of the conqueror, while the sad features of the conquered general are half concealed in the shadows—a stroke of artistic genius and of merciful generosity. The most striking detail in the picture, however, is the row of lances on the extreme right—tall, thin, upright, like a forest of slender beeches on a windless day.

VI

AND NOW BEGAN the most fruitful period in the life of Velasquez. He received commission after commission to paint the king, the queen, the infante, the infanta, the nobles of the court and the worthies of Madrid. In his personal appearance he represented the courtier rather than the artist. Let us look at him as he reveals himself in the portrait now hung at the Valencia Museum. A handsome, pale face, eyes that look directly out from the canvas and seem to penetrate to your very soul, a straight, slightly heavy nose, dark hair brushed far down across the high forehead, an upturned black mustache, a sensitive mouth and a strong chin. He is dressed in black with a starched white collarette. A man who is able to take orders and to execute them, an artist who has made it his life's business to stoop in order that he may conquer. He is still obliged to sit at the table with the jesters and the dwarfs. All of them are looked upon with an equally indulgent contempt. They are merely the entertainers of the king. The clowns amuse him with their jokes, and the artist diverts him with his pictures. Well, such is the way of the world. It is the world which gives you bread and butter, a heap of abuse, an occasional pat on the back—and leisure to paint. Not a bad world, when all is said and done. Not the best of all *desirable* worlds, perhaps, but most likely the best of all *possible* worlds. A world in which success is based upon the four cornerstones of flattery, obedience, hard work and contentment with your lot.

Velasquez was one of the most contented men of his age. He accepted his position at the palace as a matter of course. He painted quietly, diligently, brilliantly. His colors were still dark, with occasional flashes of sunlight that transformed his canvases into miracles of magic. He painted the courtiers at Madrid; he traveled to Italy and painted Pope Innocent X, a triumph of magnificent ugliness which Sir Joshua Reynolds characterized as "the finest piece of portrait painting in Rome"; and he exhibited his pictures in the cloister of the Pantheon, receiving the unanimous verdict of the critics that "all the other work seemed painting, this alone truth."

Velasquez had now learned to paint the truth, to transmute his colors into the flesh and blood of life. He returned to Madrid and entered upon the period of his mature genius. He was now a master of the simple detail. He used none of the tricks which the other artists employed in the fabrication of their pictures. Instead he attained his effects with an economy of pigment and with a few swift, simple strokes of the brush. His purpose was to achieve not an idealization but an honest representation of nature and of the human soul.

It was at this period that he produced those pathetically exquisite pictures of the human soul in its distorted form. In keeping with the custom of the day, the Spanish court had in its retinue a large number of buffoons, monstrosities, insane people, idiots and dwarfs. They served as a laughingstock to the king. But not to Velasquez. He saw the pity of their disfigured bodies and the beauty of their ugliness. And what he saw he translated upon his canvas. These portraits of the dwarfs of Madrid are among the most inspired masterpieces of Velasquez. He painted them in his spare moments—broken pieces of clay thrown carelessly aside by the bungling hands of Destiny, misshapen bodies and sorrowful faces, stifled hopes, unfulfilled ambitions, unrealized dreams, living commentaries upon the cynical cruelty of life. One of the most characteristic of these paintings is that of El Primo, the Scholar. This pygmy, dressed in a velvet suit, is sitting upon the ground. His fine head stands out from the background of a huge black hat which is tilted downward, courtier fashion, upon the left side of the high, intelligent forehead. The eyes are the eyes of a man who observes keenly and feels deeply, a thinker who has achieved serenity through suffering. His diminutive right leg is stretched out in pathetic contrast to an enormous open book which he holds upon his knee and which completely conceals the other puny leg. He is in the act of turning one of the pages of the book. On the ground beside him there are two other books, together with an open notebook and an inkhorn. The background of the picture is a jagged mountain range. The strength of the mountains and the weakness of the dwarf. A vigorous mind and a crippled body. An ironical study in contrasts. The study of a philosopher artist who possessed the grace of pity as well as the magic of paint, a man who knew how to evaluate the sardonic laughter of the gods.

The other dwarf paintings of Velasquez are similar studies in distortion—sad, smiling commentaries on the curious inconsistencies of life. His own life, too, was a curious inconsistency. Here he was, the greatest painter in Spain, held on a footing with these human derelicts whom he was immortalizing with his portraits. He too, like the dwarfs, was merely an animated toy hired for the amusement of the king. Perhaps, in painting the dwarfs, he was symbolizing his own disagreement with the inequity of fate and the inadequacy of the standards whereby man is accustomed to measure his fellow men. Whatever his inner conviction about his own inferior status at the court, however, he was outwardly content. He accepted his insults and his rewards, just as the dwarfs accepted their own destiny, with a philosophical resignation that enabled him to work in peace.

VII

ON ONE OCCASION, indeed, he made an effort to rise above his lowly position at the court. In 1658 he tried to claim legally that he was of noble blood. The king's council, after an investigation of several months, disal'owed the claim. "Velasquez is a good painter," was the council's verdict, "but unfortunately is a man of common clay."

And so Velasquez was content to remain a good painter. He went ahead with his realistic interpretations of life, his paintings of pygmies and princes and his "retouchings of things human till they rose to meet the stars." At this, the last period of his life, he combined the two best phases of his genius into one. He became the first painter of the lowly as well as of the exalted conditions of humanity. These two aspects of his genius found their most perfect expression in the two paintings, *The Spinners* and *The Maids of Honor*.

The Spinners (*Las Hirlanderas*) represents a tapestry workshop in which five women are busy at their handicraft. These women are divided into three groups. On the extreme left an old woman sits spinning at a wheel, and a young girl behind her draws aside the heavy red curtain that screens the window. The glittering rays of the sun, coming in from a room just beyond the workshop, fall upon the white sleeve of the girl, the headcloth of the old woman, the spindle, the stool and various objects that lie scattered on the floor. In the center of the picture a young girl, facing directly front as she cards her wool, is silhouetted against the glare of the sunlight that pours in from the other room. On the extreme right two girls are at work. One of them has just entered through a dark door and is about to place a basket on the ground. The other, with her back turned toward the spectator, is busy disentangling a skein of wool. It is upon this figure that the entire picture is focused. The girl is barefoot. Her body, outlined underneath her white chemise and her green petticoat, is strong, supple, superb. The sleeve on her left arm is rolled back to the shoulder; and the arm, stretched out to its full magnificent length as the fingers untangle the wool, directs the eye of the spectator straight to the alcove in the background. In this alcove, which is raised two steps above the floor of the workshop, a rich tapestry has been hung. Three ladies in elegant dresses, potential customers perhaps, are examining the tapestry. The three figures are bathed in the sunlight which floods into the alcove from an unseen window on the left. Animation, motion, rhythm, realism, strength. The entire picture dances and pulses with life.

Equally full of light and of life is *The Maids of Honor* (*Las Meninas*). In *The Spinners* Velasquez has taken us on a visit to the workshop of the poor. In *The Maids of Honor* he ushers us into the palace of the king. This is not a picture but a scene in motion. The little princess, Margarita, occupies the center. She wears a grayish white dress that balloons out like a hoop skirt from the waist down to the floor. She has just entered the room with her two *meninas*, or maids of honor. The one on her right is kneeling to offer her a flagon. The other, on her left, is in the act of making a graceful bow. Just beyond this maid stand two dwarfs, and in front of them lies a huge mastiff, half asleep. There are several other figures in the room—a lady in waiting, a guardsman, another court officer standing in the glittering

light of an open door and, on the extreme left, Velasquez himself, with brush in hand and a huge canvas in front of him,
occupied in painting a portrait of the king and the queen. These
two royal personages are seen only in reflection through a mirror
which hangs on the back wall, facing the spectator. The whole
is a fleeting moment in the life of the palace captured and
handed down to future generations by the inspired brush of
Velasquez. The painting is so great because the subject is so
simple—a father and a mother looking upon their child and her
attendants. It is a masterpiece of spontaneity. "There you are,"
we can hear the artist saying. "I have caught you unawares.
I have painted you in your least regal and most human mood.
I have succeeded, I believe, in placing upon the canvas the
ever-old, ever-new child-drama of the ages."

The center of the interest is the child. But from her the interest radiates outward and upward throughout the room. The
light plays in rhythmic waves upon plane after plane of the
high and shadow-haunted room, the face of the princess, the
open door in the background, the edge of the easel upon which
Velasquez is painting, the mirror that reflects the faces of the
king and the queen, and the long, narrow panels on the walls,
until finally it gathers into a glittering pool of splendor upon
the ceiling. As one of his biographers, C. Gasquoine Hartley,
has justly remarked, "It is the light that is the principal person
in the picture."

VIII

AT LAST, when Velasquez was sixty years old, the king bestowed
upon him the patent of the Spanish *hidalguía*. And thus the
greatest artist in Spain was, by royal decree, reduced to the
status of a nobleman. Unfortunately this royal decree was unable to raise the noblemen to the status of a Velasquez. In this
funny little world of ours the kings can give titles to genius but
they can't give genius to titles.

And so Velasquez, in his old age, became a blue blood instead of a red blood. But the color of his genius remained unchanged, and his paintings continued on the same supreme level of universal human understanding. He went on depicting the soul of Man, whether garbed in the flesh of a prince or of a pauper. The figures of his later as well as of his earlier paintings, whatever their social or their economic condition, are all invested with the selfsame grandeur of their common humanity. Velasquez may almost be called the Walt Whitman of the seventeenth-century painters.

Like Walt Whitman, Velasquez was so universally sympathetic because he was so sincerely religious. From his earliest to his last years, whenever he could spare the time, he depicted sacred scenes in secular surroundings, divinity in unexpected places, immortal souls in humble shepherds and fisherfolk and hermits.

It was one of these hermit pictures that he was painting just before he died. St Anthony visits St Paul in his lonely cave. They are hungry. St Paul raises his hands in prayer, and a raven comes flying toward them bringing bread in its beak. Bread for hungry bodies, beauty for hungry souls. This, in a sentence, sums up the personality and the genius of Velasquez.

IX

HE DIED, at the height of his power, in his sixty-first year. His wife followed him only a week later.

The king gave him a splendid burial and then allowed the royal council to rob his children of a thousand ducats due them for their father's work.

HOGARTH

Boston, Museum of Fine Arts: *Countess Kingston and Her Son, Earl Kingston and His Son.*

Detroit, Institute of Arts: *Portrait of a Lady.*

London, Dulwich Gallery: *Fishing Party.*

London, National Gallery: *Calais Gate, The Graham Children, The Harlot's Progress, Marriage à la Mode, Portrait of Himself, The Shrimp Girl.*

London, Sir John Soane's Museum: *The Election, The Rake's Progress.*

London, Tate Gallery: *Scene from The Beggar's Opera, Sophonisba.*

New York, Frick Collection: *Mary Edwards.*

New York, Metropolitan Museum of Art: *Peg Woffington, The Price Family, The Kidderminster Wedding.*

St Louis, City Art Museum: *Lord and Lady Grey as Children.*

Washington, Corcoran Gallery: *Portrait of a Woman.*

Washington, Smithsonian Institution: *Portrait of Mrs Price.*

William Hogarth

1697–1764

Never was a period in the life of a nation better suited to the brush of an artist than the eighteenth century in "Merrie England." To be sure, Hogarth would have been the master cartoonist of any age in which he lived. Yet the British society of the Restoration was the atmosphere par excellence for this puckish little photographer of laughter who restored the art of satire from the black night into which it had descended ever since the days of Juvenal.

Hogarth's father was a literary hack writer. His salary was precarious. He was well acquainted with Grub Street and Misery Mall. He knew the social set of Gin Lane, and he knew his fairs at Southwark. In addition to all that, he knew that his son William had an uncommon genius for drawing; and he apprenticed him, after an elementary education, to Ellis Gamble, the silver-plate engraver at the sign of the "Golden Angel."

"I had a good eye," Hogarth in his old age wrote of his youth. "Mimicry, common to all children, was remarkable in me. Shows of all sorts gave me uncommon pleasure." As a matter of fact, the entire world was to Hogarth a huge setting for a Punch and Judy show; and all the actors in it, puppets dangling on the strings of fate. Such a world was a shocking revelation to most of his English compatriots, who had been brought up on the dignified notion that the human race, and particularly the Anglo-Saxon race, was meant for better things. The solemn Englishman didn't like to be classified as a wooden-faced puppet at a children's entertainment—the occasion of humor and ridicule to everybody but himself. To Hogarth the riddle of human existence didn't even have the dignity of light opera. It was a sawdust street scene staged in a little tinderbox. And all the howls and bickerings of the crowd were no louder than the momentary puff of the sputtering little flame.

As a lad Hogarth didn't go through a course in academic art. He didn't have the patience to learn the technique of formal design. His fingers galloped into caricature. Natural humor knows no "acceptable" creed of etiquette. And Hogarth's humor was unacceptable in the most glorious sense. He became an illustrator for novelists. He engraved on copper. And in 1733, at the age of thirty-six, he drew forth the first bright gem from the treasure chest of his genius.

II

HE MADE a series of plates entitled *A Harlot's Progress*—five etchings which represent the decline and death of a country girl who comes to London from rural England and who loses her virginity in the process of assimilating herself to urban life. Richard Steele had written a paper, in the *Spectator* of 1712, defending this class of girl who so innocently supplied the London brothels with most of their unfortunate recruits. When Hogarth, twenty years later, revived this tear-stained theme he neither stooped to point the moral nor stiffened to pass judgment on the result. He merely painted the harrowing story in a very businesslike manner. Most of the contemporary artists in England made a living out of their portrait work. But Hogarth had decided to seek for his livelihood in some other field of art. "I wished," he wrote, "to compose pictures on canvas similar to representations on the stage." He would endeavor to treat his subject in the manner of a dramatic writer. He wished to refer to himself not as an artist but as an author. "My picture is my stage, and men and women my players, who by means of certain actions and gestures are to exhibit a dumb show." It was the business of Hogarth to paint and not to preach. Yet, in spite of himself, his stories not only satisfy the eye but stimulate the mind. There are books in running brooks, sermons in stones and philosophy in the etchings of Hogarth.

The first plate in *A Harlot's Progress* is an eloquent prologue to the birth of sin. The young girl of seventeen has driven up to London with her father. She has just alighted from the carriage in the courtyard of an inn. An obese, pock-marked procuress interrogates her and persuades her to accept a job as her waiting maid. On the steps of the inn stands a fat and prosperous-looking man—the owner of a chain of prostitution houses. He is ready to lay his greedy hands upon her. A dapper young pimp is leering lasciviously at his side.

In the following picture the girl has already lost her chastity. She has become the mistress of a rich Jew. One look at her face shows us that she has already become privy to the primrose paths of debauchery and deceit. She sits in her drawing room entertaining her affluent client at breakfast. But just a few moments before her mate had appeared on the scene she had been entertaining another gentleman. How to get rid of her lover without causing a scene? The picture depicts the young lady with an ingenuity that certainly is not part of her country-girl heritage. With an apparently careless thrust of her knee she dashes to the floor the tray of food that the servant has just placed before her. In the midst of the confusion the lover gets up from behind a chair where he has been hiding and tiptoes out of the room in his stocking feet.

In the next scene the Jew has abandoned her. She has become a "gangster's moll." Her price has fallen even more rapidly than her virtue. She has drifted from the salons of the rich into the gutter. Her income is derived from highwaymen; her financial losses are occasioned by the unanticipated hangings of some of her assets. What is the logical result of this kind of life but Bridewell Prison? She beats hemp; misery is written in loud lines on her face. Disease and death follow swiftly. In the final scene her last mortal remains are stowed away in a wooden coffin in a funeral parlor. There are groups of mourners seated in various attitudes about the room. Most of them are poor wretches like herself. Half of them are laughing outwardly; all are laughing inwardly; some of them make idiotic grimaces. One miserable hag pulls off the lid of the coffin and leers at the corpse. A few people pretend to cry with exaggerated gestures of buffoonery. There isn't in the entire room a genuine tear, a single heartbeat of sincerity. The minister sits gingerly in his chair with a professional attitude of hypocritical grief on his face. His lady clasps her hands and simpers.

This is indeed a grotesque funeral scene. Charles Lamb has found in its very incongruity the essential of its great pathos. Since tears are very often too shallow a medium in which to express the profound truths of sorrow, Hogarth plumbs deeper than the mere lip service of grief. Rarely has the absence of the human heart been better expressed than in this funeral scene. The heartlessness of the mourners in the presence of death, the inability of the miserable wretches to feel true sorrow, is as startling a revelation as if it were scientifically demonstrated that the human body is constitutionally incapable of lodging a soul. Such a discovery would do much more than offend our morality; it would knock from its props the emotional balance of our very identity. That is precisely what the Hogarth picture does to us. The mourners haven't even the heart to be sincere in their manifestations of insincerity. A man who expresses genuine laughter can be moved on the proper occasion to genuine tears. But the grinning, the smirking, the guffaws of these wretches are external gestures that have no relation to any inner feeling. Yet all of them are aware that the end of this prostitute is bound to be their own end. The only individual in the room who is not at all conscious of the tragedy in its midst is the little son of the dead woman who, completely oblivious to his surroundings, sits at the foot of the coffin in a mourner's cloak and plays merrily with his top. His childish regard for his top is the one genuine sentiment expressed in that little room of death. He is the only one with a heart that feels. He is the sole redeeming grace in that group of the unredeemed. Here is enough pathos to open a floodgate of tears.

Just before he published these pictures Hogarth had eloped with the daughter of an English nobleman. Sir James Thornhill disowned them. But Lady Thornhill was more lenient. She bought *A Harlot's Progress* and hung the etchings in the dining room. When the old man saw them he asked her who the artist was. "Your son-in-law," she replied. Whereupon Sir James opened his door to "the man who can furnish representations like these."

III

HOGARTH BECAME FAMOUS as the result of this series. He followed it up with a sequel called *A Rake's Progress*. Tom Rakewell, at the age of nineteen, inherits his father's fortune. He comes home from Oxford and has himself measured for mourning clothes. The floor is cluttered with bundles of leases and bonds. Money· bags peep from drawers. The servants ransack chests and strong· boxes, running nimble fingers throughout the treasure.

In the following scene Tom is dressed in the latest fashion

He stands in the drawing room, surrounded by milliners, wig-makers, tailors and art dealers ready to serve him. The music master waits for him to take his lesson at the harpsichord, while a pompous musician toots a few notes on a French horn. A fencing master from Paris flourishes his sword foppishly through the air, while a gymnastic master from London leans on his quarterstaff and scowls.

Plate three finds Tom in a Drury Lane tavern at three in the morning. His mind is soggy with drink. A "daughter of joy" settles into his lap, places his hat on her head and picks his pockets. Other prostitutes are seated at various tables, acquainting a number of gentlemen with their charms. One plump little harlot strips herself and goes into a dance. Another courtesan puts a candle to a map that hangs on the wall behind her and sets the "world" on fire. A tipsy gentleman twangs the strings of a harp to the accompaniment of a middle-aged woman who yodels a street song. Such is chapter three in the progress of Tom Rakewell.

From Drury Lane Tom progresses along St James Street to the Court of Queen Caroline, where her majesty's birthday is being celebrated. But as he tries to join the merrymakers he is seized by a constable. He has squandered all his father's money and now he finds himself in debt. A young girl, whom he has ruined in his more prosperous days, now rushes loyally to his side, pleads with the constable and saves him from prison. By way of gratitude Tom marries a one-eyed widow who possesses a bulging bankbook and the face of a witch.

Plate four finds the bride and the bridegroom united at the altar. She beams upon him toothlessly, with a look of lust and ugly craftiness in her eyes, while he flirts nonchalantly with her maid in waiting. The church is a dilapidated building whose structure, half covered with cobwebs, grins with cracks. The poor, faithful girl that Tom had ruined attempts to run up to the altar, with her baby at her breast, and to stop the marriage proceedings. But the sexton interferes with a strong and holy arm.

From the bliss of this marriage Tom descends to the pleasures of the gaming house. Plate five represents him sitting in a gambling den, surrounded by cutthroats highway robbers and other picaresque gentlemen of London. He is dissipating his wife's fortune at the turn of the wheel. Finally Tom finds himself in the Fleet Street prison—again having been arrested for debt. This time he enjoys the added happiness of having his wife at his side. From her toothless mouth she is pouring a cataract of abuse.

The change on poor Tom's face, as he passes from one to another of these adventures, is a masterpiece of subtle realism. At the start, when he first comes fresh from Oxford into his father's house, he is the picture of merry but uncontaminated innocence. From then on the cynicism of life disfigures his features with blow after blow. At the end of all this punishment what is there left for poor Tom but Bedlam? The final scene depicts him as a raving lunatic, chained down to the floor. The girl whom he has ruined, but who is still faithful, pleads with him on her knees. But in vain. He writhes on his belly and foams at the mouth. The final plate is a horrible picture of the shipwreck of human reason.

IV

A Harlot's Progress found its way into many British houses of the eighteenth century. The consequences of vice were so vividly delineated in the story of the wayward girl that Puritan mothers kept the series of pictures in the living room as a constant reminder to their children. But the progress of Tom Rakewell never attained the same notoriety. It was quite proper to hang out the dirty linen of a poor country girl. But when Hogarth went searching for obscene smells in the mansions of high society, high society accused him of overstepping his bounds. The rich and the well-born didn't relish the painful moral that Hogarth had drawn from the consequences of inherited wealth. They judged Hogarth as a moralist, not as a painter. It was not until some years after his death that Charles Lamb succeeded in opening the eyes of high society.

Charles Lamb has compared the madhouse scene of poor Tom with the mad scenes in Shakespeare's *King Lear*. The disintegration of the ne'er-do-well spirit in Hogarth's *Rake* has seldom been matched. Hogarth is a master of the mirthless grin. Why bother with the moral of Tom's slow decay? The point is that he started life as a human being and ended it as something quite different. He has lost his moral sensibilities, the badge of his humanity. If the world is a madhouse, then no one has ever painted it in a truer spirit than Hogarth. Lunatics are "perfect meat" for the satirist. They are the ideal subjects for tragedy. Death, physical suffering, unrequited love—these, too, are tragic. But the profoundest tragedy of human experience is the loss of the human mind. In Shakespeare the capstone on the edifice of grief, the final misadventure in the miserable lives of his great tragic characters, Lear, Lady Macbeth and Ophelia, is to be found in their madness. The actions of these groping, witless spirits are far beyond the sanity of tears. Only the bitterest laughter of the keenest satirist can justify the noble sorrow. The greatest satirists are the greatest tragedians. Satire was Hogarth's particular forte. Henry Fielding, the novelist, wrote of his friend, "I esteem the ingenious Mr Hogarth as one of the most useful satirists any age has produced."

V

HOGARTH CONTINUED to record English society. For a while he tried his hand at "the grand style of historical painting," with which contemporary artists were so engrossed. He painted *A*

Good Samaritan with figures seven feet high, and he presented it
to charity. No one else would take it. Somehow or other he was
never able to paint in the academic parlor manner of the times.
His personality was never contented with a whimper when it
had a chance to season its suffering with laughter. Hogarth had
a hearty disdain for the demimonde world of painting, especially
in France. He looked down with equal contempt upon the
British art dealers who imported "shiploads of dead Christs,
Holy Families, Madonnas . . . If a man, naturally a judge of
painting, should cast his eye on one of their sham virtuoso pieces,
he would be very apt to say, 'Mr Bubbleman, that Grand Venus
(as you are apt to call it) has not beauty enough for the character of an English cookmaid.' "

And so he went back to his satire. He painted a picture called
The Sleeping Congregation. The preacher addresses his parishion-
ers in a lazy soporific drawl. The congregation dozes off—all
but the clerk, who sits solemnly at the foot of the pulpit, sup-
presses a yawn and glances sideways greedily at a sleeping girl
in a near-by pew of the overheated church. The girl has un-
buttoned her sweater and bared a generous area of her bosom.
Her hands have dropped inadvertently upon her prayer book
in her lap, and they rest at the section of the text commencing
with the words, *Of Matrimony.*

And he painted a picture of *The Distressed Poet*—a poor, starving wretch in a Grub Street garret, who rises shivering in the
dawn to compose for a wealthy patron a poem on the Vanity
of Riches. The poet has finished the prologue of his composition,
and he racks his brain for new ideas. Behind him, on the wall,
hangs a map inscribed with the heading—*A View of the Gold
Mines of Peru.* The wind whistles through a broken windowpane.
A baby awakes from its crib and starts to howl. A dog ransacks a
plate which contains the family's miserable meal. A milkmaid
opens the door and shouts vituperatively that the milk bill must
be paid at once. In the background sits the poet's wife, "the

sweetest woman Hogarth ever drew," knitting clothes for her husband, a smile of infinite patience on her face. What sad, autobiographic memories this painting must have brought to the poet, Oliver Goldsmith, who didn't even have the consolation of a wife!

VI

IN 1745, when Hogarth was forty-six years old, he painted his masterpiece. His long life of keen observation, and his talent for hitting his target cleanly and mercilessly with the barbs of satire, finally bore its full harvest in a series of pictures entitled *Marriage à la Mode*. A written description of this series, even though it fails to do justice to it, may nevertheless be more effective than any other possible commentary. The series represents, as Hogarth put it, "A Variety of Modern Occurrences in High-Life."

Scene one is the marriage contract. An old fat earl, with a gouty foot swathed in bandages, addresses himself enthusiastically to a sallow-faced, bespectacled London merchant, who is holding in his hand a paper endorsing "The Marriage Settlement of the Right Honorable Lord Viscount Squanderfield." The earl has at his feet a chart showing the Squanderfield family tree, and he points to it as he discusses his pedigree with animation. A third gentleman stands between the two contracting parties. He holds out in his hand a mortgage paper for the earl's signature. But look at the pair of lovebirds who are about to be united in this romantic manner! The daughter of the merchant and the son of the earl have seated themselves discreetly at the rear of the room. The young lady, clothed in her bridal dress, nonchalantly twirls between listless fingers a dainty handkerchief on which she has strung the wedding ring. She bends slightly to her right and cocks her ear to the honeyed whispers of the best man, Counselor Silvertongue. The bridegroom to be,

as effete a young fop as you would ever care to behold, sits next
to her. He wears a magnificently powdered wig tied at the back
with a brilliant ribbon. He holds a half-open box of snuff in his
hand and stares into space with a look of exquisite idiocy in his
eyes. In front of the loving couple sit a male dog and his bitch
in a coupling chain—a magnificently sly caricature of the grand
couple behind them. The only human being worth anything
in the entire room is an old lawyer who, standing with his back
to the group, gazes with a look of cynical contempt out of the
window at the ruins of a building across the street. The drawing
room is a subtle caricature of the Georgian style of the period.
On the wall hangs a large portrait, painted in the French manner, of one of the earl's ancestors, who strides within the frame
like a colossus. Beneath him a cannon explodes. Above him a
comet rises. His head is covered with an elegant Queen Anne
periwig, and he wields a thunderbolt of Jupiter in one hand and
a Queen Anne sword in the other. Nothing seems to daunt him.
The ceiling is covered with a mural of Pharaoh in the Red Sea.
A bronze gorgon in a sconce looks down upon the marriage
transaction with horror.

The second scene takes place some time after the firms of the
merchant and the earl have cemented their merger with the
bodies of their children. The deal has not been an unqualified
success. We are escorted into the young couple's drawing room.
By a clock on the mantelpiece we see that it is past one in the
afternoon. But the household is not yet recovered from the
effects of a party that has taken place on the previous night.
The lights are still burning low in the chandeliers. The furniture
has been thrown all over the room, and a footman yawns and
arranges it back into its proper place. Playing cards are scattered
on the rugs. Two violins and sheets of music are lying aimlessly
on the floor. The lady of the house, our little lovebird of the
previous scene, is just awaking from the effects of the festivities.
She sits at a tea table by the fireside and stretches her arms

[*153*]

sleepily. She is wearing a morning jacket about her shoulders
and a nightcap on her head. As she yawns she casts a sidelong
glance at her husband who slumps like a half-empty sack on a
chair beside her. Evidently he has tottered home early this
morning from some independent debauch. His velvet coat and
waistcoat have been thrown open. His wig is in disorder about
his face. His ribbon has been lost. His sword is broken and lies
on the floor beside him. His hat sits tipsily on his head. His
hands are thrust limply into his undershirt. A woman's garment
dangles loosely from one of his pockets, and a lap dog is busy
snuffing at it. He is in a semistupor, and his face wears a look of
nausea mixed with the cynicism and the disgust that have set
in as a reaction to a life of prolonged debauchery. Neither he
nor his wife have taken any notice of the steward who, after
several attempts to rouse them, walks stiffly and with upturned
nose out of the room—a list of overdue bills in his hand. Out of
a pocket peeps a book entitled *Regeneration*.

The third episode is rather confused. It is not quite clear what
Hogarth wishes to bring out in detail, though the general impli-
cations are evident. The husband has brought a girl, whom he
has ruined, to the office of a quack doctor. Here, amidst an
assortment of skulls, stuffed alligators, mummies, cogwheels
for setting collarbones and the model of a gallows, the doctor
gives his advice on the health of the girl.

Meanwhile Lady Squanderfield leads a life of her own. Scene
four shows a typical episode in this life. She is holding a musical
soiree in her boudoir for a group of intimate friends. She sits
at her toilet table in a yellow dressing gown. A Swiss valet
curls her hair. She is all attention to Counselor Silvertongue,
who was the best man in the first scene. That worthy gentleman
reclines nonchalantly on the lady's sofa and converses with
her in a tone of easy familiarity. Just how far he has insinuated
himself into her bedroom graces is certified by the fact that
on the wall, side by side with *Jupiter and Io, Lot and His*

Daughters and the *Rape of Ganymede*, hangs a portrait of Counselor Silvertongue himself.

The rest of the company are shown in various attitudes as they listen to the singing of an Italian primadonna who is accompanied by a German flute player. Neither virtuoso is flattered by the artist. Hogarth was provincial to the core and he hated all things exotic, whether they were art connoisseurs or concert musicians. The singer has an awkward, swinish physiognomy; the flute player is lean and dark. He looks like a henchman of Satan. As for the audience? One pinch-faced lady listens to the music in ludicrous ecstasy, swaying back and forth in a trance, with her hands outstretched, while a black boy servant, in the process of handing her a cup of coffee, looks into her face in wide-eyed astonishment. Another "listener" is a gentleman who is profoundly and mercifully asleep. But two of the Lady Squanderfield's friends listen to the music with admirably contrasted expressions of "superlative connoisseurship." One of them, a fan dangling from a clasp around his wrist, clutches his cup of coffee as if it were a nugget of gold and screws his lips into a loud professional smack, signifying his veteran enjoyment of the music. Next to him is a skinny, simpering little man of property, with ladylike hair and dainty demeanor, one pretty hand tucked professionally beneath his brocaded coat, the other holding the demitasse to his mouth. He sips his drink and his music leisurely, puckering up his lips to distill every last drop of the melody over the rarefied taste buds of his own appreciative genius. What other sort of men would attend a concert in a lady's boudoir!

We may just as well pass rapidly over the fifth and the sixth episodes in this tragicomedy. The husband finally catches his lady in bed with Counselor Silvertongue. A brief quarrel, and then a sword duel. The husband is stabbed in the encounter and totters weakly on his buckling legs. His wife, overcome with remorse, gets down on her knees and screams in terror as

Counselor Silvertongue escapes through the window in his undress uniform.

The final episode is brief and to the point. Counselor Silvertongue is apprehended for the murder and hanged. The wife takes a bottle of laudanum. And her father, the benevolent merchant who has contracted the marriage in the first place, supports the dying girl tenderly with one hand while with the other he removes the gold wedding ring from her finger and thrusts it in his pocket.

Books in running brooks, sermons in stones and bad in everything. Marriage without love, and love without marriage. A sad and sordid story, this brief and ridiculous and moneygrubbing little dream called human existence. Such was the substance of Hogarth's artistic creed.

VII

HOGARTH CONTINUED to paint his cynical pictures of human character, with its tragedy, its cheerlessness, its stupidity, its savagery, its emptiness, its grief and its occasional glimpses of nobility. He painted a portrait of his friend, the great actor, David Garrick, as he appeared in the role of Richard III; he painted the portrait of Sarah Malcolm, a notorious murderess, two days before she went to the gallows; he painted Lord Lovat, a patriotic old rebel who gave up his life to King George because of his devotion to the Stuart cause. When he took a trip to France he yielded to his prejudice against all things foreign and represented the Frenchmen as lean, half-starved and tattered scarecrows as contrasted with the sleek and well-fed Britishers. Yet even with his compatriots he was always the cynic. He described the departure of a division of British guards to Scotland in all their glory. But he did not omit the detail of an officer kissing a milkmaid as he takes leave of her, while a private pours her milk into his hat, and of a soldier nudging a pastry cook to pay attention to the foregoing episode and absconding with his wares as the cook looks on and grins at the funny spectacle. One drunken grenadier in the gutter turns his face away from a cup of water offered to him by a friend and holds out his hand to a prostitute who offers him a tankard of gin, while a half-shriveled infant in her arms imitates his gesture. And so on.

He satirized political elections, painting a harrowing picture of a battered pensioner, minus a leg, a left arm and a right hand, standing at the head of a line of voters at the polls. Behind him, sitting in a wheel chair, is an idiot wearing a bib; and next in line is a dying patient in a stretcher carried by a nurse and a beggar without a nose. A blind man, a boy with a gaping mouth and a cripple bring up the rear. In the background an electioneering crowd has formed. It storms and rages and destroys everything in its way. In the midst of the mob a coach, bearing the label "Britannia" has broken down, while the coachman and the footman sit heedlessly beside it on a couple of boxes and play cards. No country will ever break down in the manner of this coach, however, as long as it gives its satirists full freedom to express themselves.

Hogarth was a whole audience of people laughing at the play of human life. He sat in the pit and wasn't the least bit ashamed to stamp his feet and to shout his approval or disapproval at the antics of the stagehands and the actors and the spectators, including himself. And when the time came for him to leave the theater (in 1764), after he had sat through the performance for sixty-seven years, he left his seat with the feeling that the drama, in spite of its many imperfections, was on the whole worthily written and bravely played. And as he moved out of the theater and went home to his sleep David Garrick stepped to the footlights to say a final word about his severest critic and dearest friend:

> *Farewell, great painter of mankind,*
> *Who reached the noblest point of art.*

When pictured morals charm the mind,
And through the eye correct the heart.

If genius fire thee, Reader, stay:
If nature touch thee, drop a tear;
If neither move thee, turn away,
For Hogarth's honored dust lies here.

REYNOLDS

Great Paintings by Reynolds

Albany, Art Society: *Portrait of Sir John Hamilton.*

Atlanta, High Museum: *Portrait of Richard Brinsley Sheridan.*

Baltimore, Museum of Art: *Duke and Duchess of Marlborough.*

Baltimore, Peabody Institute: *Portrait of Himself.*

Boston, Museum of Fine Arts: *Portrait of Mrs Palk, Portrait of Louisa Pyne.*

Brooklyn, Museum: *Portrait of Christopher Baek.*

Chicago, Art Institute: *Lady Sarah Bunbury.*

Cleveland, Museum of Art: *Mrs Collier as Lesbia.*

Detroit, Institute of Arts: *Mrs Chalmers.*

Indianapolis, Tarkington Collection: *Portrait of Mary.*

London, Dulwich Gallery: *Mrs Siddons as the Tragic Muse.*

London, National Gallery: *The Age of Innocence, Angels' Heads, Lady Cockburn and Her Children, The Dilett... , Th Gra s, Por rait o Hims lf.*

London, Tate Gallery: *Admiral Keppel, The Infant Samuel, Dr Samuel Johnson.*

London, Wallace Collection: *Miss Emily Pott as Thaïs, Mrs Hoare and Her Infant Son, Nelly O'Brien.*

New York, Frick Collection: *Portrait of Lady Skipwith.*

New York, Metropolitan Museum of Art: *Lady Carew, Mrs Arnold, Sir Edward Hughes.*

New York, Public Library: *Mrs Billington as St Cecilia.*

Philadelphia, Museum of Art: *Master Bunbury.*

Pittsburgh, Carnegie Institute: *Mrs Dawkins.*

Toledo, Museum of Art: *Mrs Watson.*

Washington, National Gallery: *Lady Betty Delme and Her Children, Lady Caroline Howard.*

Worcester, Art Museum: *Portrait of Captain Bligh.*

Sir Joshua Reynolds

1723–1792

LIKE A SUNDIAL, Reynolds recorded only the serene hours of the period in which he lived. His tolerant brush portrayed what was best in the features of his clients, and his gracious manner brought out what was noblest in their hearts.

His painting was tranquil because his life was tranquil. His character had never become fermented with the bitterness of suffering. He underwent no early hardships. He was successful from the start.

His father, a poor schoolmaster of Plympton, the West Country of England, presented the world with a quiverful of eleven children. The most acceptable of these gifts was his third son, Joshua, who first saw the light on July 16, 1723.

He received all his education at his father's school. His knowledge in his mature life was wide rather than deep. From earliest childhood his brush had interested him more than his pen. Under the tutorial supervision of his father he learned his three Rs, acquired a smattering of Latin and neglected his spelling and his grammar. Throughout his life his numerous lectures and his letters contained ample evidence of this defect in his education.

His carelessness about the grammar of the English language, however, did not extend to the grammar of his art. Here he worked assiduously from beginning to end. He began his own crude and unassisted studies in the intricacies of drawing almost as soon as he had learned to write. In the kitchen of his home, in the classroom, in church—wherever he could lay his hand upon a bit of paper and a pencil—he made sketches of the people about him. In his constant eagerness to draw he neglected his studies. His father soon realized that Joshua would be no scholar like himself.

However, as Joshua grew older his father had to decide about his son's career. For a time he was divided between the professions of painter and apothecary. The first might give the boy satisfaction, but the second would provide him with a living. The boy, on being consulted about the matter, replied that he would rather be a good painter than a rich apothecary. And so his father scraped together £60; Joshua's married sister, Mrs Johnson, contributed an additional £60; and Joshua was apprenticed to the leading portrait painter of London, Thomas Hudson.

Hudson was not so much a painter as a manufacturer of faces on canvas. Stiff, formal, uninspired, yet technically correct, he turned out his portraits by the hundred, doing the faces himself and leaving the bodies and the draperies to be painted in by his apprentices. It was this sort of work that Reynolds learned to do at Hudson's studio. And during the short period that Reynolds worked under Hudson there came forth from that man's studio a number of strange pictures—portraits with dead faces and living garments. From the very beginning the pupil was a better artist than the master. Indeed, after an apprenticeship of only two years, Reynolds felt that he had nothing more to learn from Hudson.

And so, in 1743, the hopeful young artist of twenty returned from London and set up a studio in his native town. Here he received a sufficient number of sittings to start him on the road to financial security. Young as he was, he possessed the aesthetic daring of the innovator. He did away with the funereal stiffness of the Hudson portraiture and painted his sitters in their natural and lifelike attitudes. One of his earliest portraits, for example, represents a father carrying one of his youngsters pickaback—a surprising and delightful departure from the old-style portrait painting of England.

And, fortunately for Reynolds, this proved to be a *profitable* departure. When his father died on Christmas Day of 1746 it was with an easy conscience. He had made no mistake in turning his young son into a painter instead of an apothecary. The brush and the palette, as well as the mortar and the pestle, seemed to possess the magic virtue of transmuting labor into gold.

II

REYNOLDS made much money and many friends. And he worked hard. Every morning, after a long walk, he sat down to his easel at seven o'clock. And he kept steadily at work until late in the afternoon—painting, studying, drawing, mixing pigments into new, rich colors and always trying to perfect himself in his art. He came at this time under the influence of a very original but rather obscure painter by the name of William Gandy. "A picture," this artist had once remarked, "ought to have a richness in its texture as if the colors had been composed of cream and cheese." Reynolds adopted the idea and the spirit of these words. He infused into his pictures a "creamy richness," a mellow grandeur of white and red and brown and yellow and blue. This peculiarity of color distinguishes the portraits of Reynolds from all the work of his contemporaries. His canvases look as if they had been painted in a cathedral, in the warm yet subdued sunlight that streams in through a stained-glass window.

It was not only from Gandy that Reynolds learned the "subdued gusto" of his color effects. At about the same time that he became interested in the work of Gandy he also found an opportunity to study at first hand the paintings of the Italian masters. This opportunity came to him tnrough a lucky friendship he had struck up with a young naval officer, George Keppel, commander of the Centurion. When Keppel was entrusted with a diplomatic mission to the countries of the Mediterranean he invited Reynolds to sail with him as his guest. Reynolds left England on May 11, 1749, executed on the way a masterly portrait of Keppel in action as a sea fighter, stopped in various countries to study and to paint and finally arrived in Rome toward the end of the year.

And then began a systematic pilgrimage to the various shrines of Italian art—Rome, Florence, Assisi, Bologna, Mantua, Ferrara, Venice. He studied and copied and absorbed into his very lifeblood the classical manner of Carracci, Borghese, Raphael, Tintoretto, Correggio and Titian—and, above all, Michelangelo. "I think Michelangelo," he said, "superior to the whole world."

For three years he studied these masters; and then, to quote the felicitous expression of John Ruskin, "he rose from their feet to share their throne." He returned to England, by way of Paris, on October 16, 1752. He took a studio in London and sat down, after the manner of the Greek poet Sophocles, to paint men not as they were but as they ought to be. "It is my aim and duty," he remarked, "to discover only the perfections of those I paint."

III

THE UNCONVENTIONAL BACKGROUNDS and the realistic postures of his figures became the fashion of the day. His studio was besieged by sitters from morning till night. Within a single year, we are told, he received no less than one hundred and eighty-four commissions. His quarters became too small for his growing popularity; and so, at the age of thirty, he rented a large house on Great Newport Street, where an admiring procession of clients came flocking to his painting room in a seemingly endless stream.

And these were no ordinary clients. Many of them were members of the first nobility. Sneer as we may at this undemocratic atmosphere in which Reynolds found himself so perfectly at home, we must remember that Reynolds lived in an undemocratic age. To him there was no disgrace in courting the favors of the great. He was honest both in his art and in his social approach toward his clients. In bringing out their best features he did not mean to flatter them. He did the same with the beggars that he painted. It was merely that he saw the goodness rather than the evil of a man's character. In his speech there was always a tone of respect, never of adulation. He addressed the nobility as an equal, not as an inferior. He never called them *Lord This* or *Lady That*, but merely sir or madam. And, in spite of their pomposity, the lords and the ladies of London enjoyed his dignified and businesslike independence. They enriched his pockets, and they honored him with their invitations—invitations which he readily accepted because he loved the society of people in general and not merely Society with a capital S.

And from the very first he was a great social success. In spite of his disfigurement—as the result of a riding accident he had sustained a cut which gave to his upper lip the faint suggestion of a harelip—he was one of the most lionized men of his day. The leaders of London society vied with one another for the privilege of entertaining him. He got to know them all, but none of them intimately. Some of his recent biographers have accused him of "indiscretions" with various of the London ladies. That these biographers are mistaken is evident even from a cursory examination of his female portraits. They are ethereal, cold, stately, far above and beyond the sensual world of flesh and blood. His men, on the other hand, are creatures idealized, to be sure, but *living*

[*165*]

creatures with red blood flowing in their veins. He understood his men, but he did not understand his women. His male portraits are the work of a man who loves to eat and drink with his fellow men. His female portraits, however, are the work of a celibate.

The evidence of his portraits is amply corroborated by the evidence, or rather the lack of evidence, of his contemporaries. The Londoners of the period loved their gossip, and yet not one of them ever breathed a word of scandal against him. His later biographers have based their accusations upon a fancied intimacy which they believe to have existed between Reynolds and two of his admirers—Angelica Kaufmann and Fanny Burney. Let us glance at these two "love affairs" of Joshua Reynolds.

Angelica Kaufmann was a beautiful woman and competent artist. Reynolds admired her beauty and praised her work. She was married to a scoundrel who had formerly served her as her valet; and Reynolds, together with several of her other friends, helped her to get rid of this unpalatable husband of hers. Angelica, we are told, was not sparing of her glances. Among those whom she had tried to ensnare were the obscure painter, Dance, and the famous poet, Goethe. It was an age of free living and frank loving. The men and the women of the eighteenth century were not ashamed of their amours. A liaison between Reynolds and Angelica would have served as a fascinating and quite permissible subject for conversation among their friends. Yet no record of any such conversation exists, in spite of the fact that the Boswells and the other faithful commentators of the day have given us an almost photographic reproduction of the intimate lives of Reynolds and his circle.

As for the supposed liaison between Reynolds and Fanny Burney, the very thought of it is rather absurd. Fanny had just published her novel, *Evelina*, a book whose success was somewhat similar to that of *Gone with the Wind*. The critics were united in their verdict that "never was such a masterpiece as *Evelina*." (Who ever hears of it nowadays?) The leading minds of the period, Sheridan, Gibbon, Burke, Garrick, and even the momentous mouthpiece of public taste and thought, the great Samuel Johnson himself, had forgotten all about *Tom Jones* and *Clarissa Harlowe* and *Tristram Shandy* in their Niagara of enthusiasm for Fanny Burney's *Evelina*. The social matchmakers of the period had hit upon the plan to unite Joshua Reynolds and Fanny Burney, thus bringing about "a perfect marriage between two of the most important arts, painting and literature."

The two met and smiled and exchanged compliments but did not unite—either legally or otherwise. And for a very good reason. Fanny Burney was twenty-six, and Joshua Reynolds was fifty-five. However desirous Fanny might have been of whispering soft nothings into his ear, she couldn't have done so. For Reynolds was quite deaf by this time. He was obliged to use an ear trumpet when people spoke to him. Moreover, Fanny had no taste for Reynolds as a lover. We have her own statement to prove it. When her sister hinted at a possible marriage between the two Fanny sent her the following rejoinder: "How, my dearest Sissy," she wrote, "can you have any such wishes about Joshua Reynolds and myself. A man who has had two shakes of the palsy! (Reynolds had suffered two paralytic strokes.) What misery should I undergo, if I were only his niece, from the terror of a fatal repetition of such a shock!"

Reynolds might have been a happier man and perhaps, too, a greater artist had he been a more adequate lover. But Romance and Reynolds were never on intimate terms. Those of his biographers who, either through sentimentalism or through malice, have been trying to turn him into a Don Juan have merely succeeded in setting up a phantom structure without a concrete foundation. Reynolds was an experienced habitué of the salon, but he was no connoisseur of the boudoir.

[*167*]

IV

REYNOLDS was now one of the wealthiest men in London. And he loved to display his wealth. He moved into an imposing mansion, he bought a magnificent gilded coach, he had the liveries of his servants laced with silver and he gave lavish and—it must be confessed—somewhat vulgar entertainments to his ever-growing circle of friends. His prosperity had come too rapidly. He had had no opportunity to train himself in that most difficult of the social graces—the refined manipulation of superfluous wealth. He suffered from the inevitable awkwardness of the newly rich.

Yet, in spite of his external gaucheries, his character was sound at the core. His purse was always open to the needs of his fellow artists. And his mind was equally open to the ideas expressed by the more educated of his friends. Having neglected his education in his earlier days and unable now, in the busy days of his professional engagements, to spare much time for reading, he turned his social activities into an unofficial school for learning. He surrounded himself with the leading statesmen and scholars and writers of the day—Edmund Burke, Goldsmith, Sterne, Sheridan, Garrick and Johnson. Reynolds especially prized the friendship of Samuel Johnson. "This man," he said, "qualified my mind to think justly. The observations he made on poetry, on life, on everything about us, I applied to our art, with what success others must judge."

As for Oliver Goldsmith, Reynolds regarded him almost with the tenderness of a brother. And Goldsmith returned this tenderness in like measure. It was to Reynolds that he dedicated his favorite poem—*The Deserted Village*. "The only dedication I ever made," wrote Goldsmith, "was to my brother, because I loved hi n bett r tha most men. He is since dead; permit me to ir cribe this poe m to o 1." r l F ey ol retul tied this touch-

ing compliment with an equally touching dedication of his own
—a portrait of Goldsmith. This is the only painting of Reynolds
in which the subject is pictured realistically, without any attempt at embellishment. And because of this unflattering candor
the portrait of Goldsmith is one of the finest paintings in the
entire gallery of Reynolds' masterpieces. It is a face in which
there is a little vanity, much tenderness and an infinity of com-
passion—a homely, hopeful and lovable face, the face of a man
who has struggled with want and hunger and neglect, a poet
who has learned sympathy through suffering and who, in the
midst of his own distress, is ready to give away his last shilling
to a needy friend—poor, impractical, foolish, wise, childlike,
noble, inspired Noll Goldsmith, the dunce who has failed in the
business of making a living, the genius who has taught humanity
the art of life.

Such were some of the men in whose company Reynolds spent
the best hours of his leisure. He entertained them at his home,
he took journeys with them to various parts of England and to
the continent, he helped them over their financial difficulties
and he absorbed their wit and their wisdom at the famous meet-
ings of the Monday Night Club. Reynolds was the clubman par
excellence. He loved to bask in the warmth of human fellowship.
In addition to his membership at the Monday Night Club, he
was a leader in the activities of the Dilettante Society, an organ-
ization of aristocrats who were united in their taste for "good
art, good fellowship and good living." Among the most magnificent of Reynolds' paintings are his two group portraits of the
members of this society. These members, as represented by
Reynolds, are leisurely enjoying their wine and their dessert and
exchanging their ideas about classical vases, precious stones,
medieval manuscripts and famous paintings. As a prerequisite
to the three standard requirements of the Dilettante Club there
was, as we can readily see from the portraits, a fourth standard
—good breeding. The aristocracy of character, as well as the

aristocracy of birth, is stamped upon the faces of the members.
The aim and duty of Reynolds, as you will recall, was "to discover only the perfections of those I paint."

But Reynolds had another aim and duty—to improve the art
of his fellow painters. To improve the art and to encourage the
artists. With this purpose in view he was the founder, as well as
the lifetime president, of the Royal Academy of Fine Arts.
Thanks to this institution, London for the first time in its history
was becoming recognized as one of the art capitals of the world.
As one of the duties of the presidency, Reynolds was called upon
to deliver a series of *Discourses* upon the progress, the technique
and the future of painting. In these Discourses, interesting
though they are, Reynolds the professor contradicts Reynolds
the artist. He talks grandly and he paints simply. He advocates
the melodramatic and he produces the dramatic. Reynolds was
a better worker than teacher. Those who watched him at his
studio absorbed an excellent technique, but those who listened
to his lectures merely acquired a false theory. To quote Ruskin
once more, "Reynolds seemed born to teach all error by his
precept, and all excellence by his example."

V

TO THE END OF HIS DAYS Reynolds remained a student rather
than a teacher. He was always experimenting with color effects
—frequently at the expense of his portraits. His one great weakness was his inability to discover the secret of permanent colors.
When he first painted his pictures they were able to stand comparison with the best paintings of Velasquez and Tintoretto and
Rubens. Now, however, the colors have faded on many of them,
the glazing has rubbed off and the faces are becoming pallid
and unearthly, so that the pictures, like their originals, are nothing but ghostly memories of their former living glory. This,
however, does not hold true of all his paintings. In quite a

number of instances his experiments were successful, and the pigments have retained their lifelike freshness to the present day. And, interestingly enough, the older he grew the more skillful he became not only in the mixture of his color but also in the texture of his design. His last years brought no diminution in his genius. His art never suffered from the sunset of an outlived inspiration. On the contrary, like good wine, it improved with age. In spite of his failing eyesight and his enfeebled hand his last pictures were his best.

VI

HIS LAST YEARS, like the earlier periods of his life, were an uneventful flow of untroubled success. He received the degree of Doctor of Laws from Oxford University, he was knighted by King George III and—a distinction which he prized as much as any other—he was elected mayor of his native town of Plympton. "Every man," writes Johnson, "has a wish to appear considerable in his native place." The honor conferred upon Reynolds by his own townspeople marked the fulfillment of his dearest wish.

And thus we see him in his uneventful but cheerful old age— a florid, roundish, lively, blunt and friendly little fellow of about five feet and five inches. He is entertaining his cronies at dinner. The table has been prepared for eight guests. But seven others have dropped in unexpectedly, and Sir Joshua is not the man to turn anyone away. The servants have managed to crowd them all into the cramped space around the festive board. There is no formality at Sir Joshua's dinners. Everyone calls for whatever he wants—bread, wine, meat, beer, desserts. There is a ripple of animated conversation. And in the midst of it all, jovial, unruffled, composed, sits Sir Joshua, turning his ear trumpet now to one and now to another of his guests. And these guests, so much at their ease in this house of their unconventional host, are the cream of London society—lords, lawyers, clergymen, physicians, painters, statesmen, musicians and poets.

VII

HIS ROBUST STRENGTH began to give way at last. The first warning came in his sixty-sixth year (July 1789), when he felt a slight uneasiness in his left eye. Two weeks later, as he was working on one of his portraits, the vision of that eye became suddenly veiled. Within ten weeks the use of his left eye was gone.

He kept at his work, however, finishing a number of portraits which he had undertaken to paint. At night he went on with his social life, but in a more subdued manner. Sometimes, in his leisure moments, he amused himself with a canary. This bird was so tame that it would perch upon his finger. He talked to it; and the canary, as if it understood, would answer with a flourish of trills. One day it flew out of the window. "There goes my youth," said Reynolds with a melancholy smile.

But he kept on with his work. In the fall of 1790 he was still painting. In December he delivered his last Discourse at the Academy. He concluded this Discourse with a eulogy upon the one artist whom above all others he had worshiped throughout his life. "I reflect, not without vanity," he said, "that these Discourses bear testimony of my admiration of that truly divine man, and I should desire that the last words I should pronounce in this Academy, and from this place, might be the name of Michelangelo."

Throughout the following summer he still took an occasional long walk without any sign of fatigue. But in October he developed a serious tumor in his sightless eye. The end was now a matter of weeks. It came on a Thursday evening in February 1792.

His mind was tranquil to the end. For he knew that his brush had made two generations of his countrymen immortal.

TURNER

Great Paintings by Turner

Boston, Museum of Fine Arts: *The Falls of the Rhine, The Slave Ship.*

Chicago, Art Institute: *Dutch Fishing Boats.*

Cincinnati, Hanna Collection: *Coblentz.*

Cleveland, Museum of Art: *Carthage, Queen Mab's Grotto.*

Harvard University, Fogg Art Museum: *Waterfall, Ruined Castle, Mountains.*

London, National Gallery: *Calais Pier, Crossing the Brook, Death of Nelson, Dido Building Carthage, Edinburgh from Calton Hill, Evening Star, The Fighting Téméraire, Frosty Morning, Snow Storm, Sunrise through the Mist, Wilkie's Burial.*

London, Tate Gallery: *Hastings, Norham Castle.*

London, Wallace Collection: *Rainbow.*

New York, Frick Collection: *Arrival of the Packet Boat, Mortlake, Early Morning.*

New York, Metropolitan Museum of Art: *The Whale Ship, Grand Canal, Venice.*

New York, Public Library: *Fingal's Cave, Staffa, The Wreck.*

Philadelphia, Widener Collection: *Coal Heavers in the Moonlight, Venice.*

Washington, Corcoran Gallery: *Dutch Men of War.*

Washington, Smithsonian Institution: *Edinburgh—Sunlight and Air.*

Kansas City, Nelson Gallery: *Fish Market.*

Joseph Mallord William Turner

1775–1851

J OSEPH MALLORD WILLIAM TURNER, England's foremost painter, was the son of a barber. Unlike the barber of Seville, Turner the elder had no talent for singing. Indeed, he had no particular talent for anything. He kept his shop in the theatrical district of London and powdered the wigs of the classical grandees of Drury Lane. His son Joseph was born (1775) into an England that knew very little painting of the first quality. Sheridan was dashing off his immortal comedies; Goldsmith was drinking his ale and writing his plays and his poems; Johnson was turning his bitter spleen into brilliant epigrams; and Garrick was electrifying his audiences with his impersonations of Hamlet and Othello. But as for painting, very few Englishmen of that period cared anything about it.

Yet, strangely enough, the stubborn son of the Drury Lane barber insisted on becoming a painter. Even as a youngster of thirteen he began to exhibit some of his crude sketches in the windows of his father's shop. He was a restless boy, with wide pale eyes and a heavy Semitic nose. He was built close to the ground; his bones were thickset; he looked like an adolescent monkey. He was shy, taciturn and desperately anxious to make good. He entered the Royal Academy after submitting a couple of test drawings in chalk. But he learned very little, either at the Academy or anywhere else. He wasn't the kind to learn. His mind was as heavy as his body, and his speech was halting and uncouth. He was the insignificant son of an insignificant father and of a host of insignificant ancestors. But somewhere down the line he had inherited clever fingers. That was his fortune.

II

ONE DAY, when he was ready for love, he met the sister of a school chum and became attached to her. They were soon engaged. Then he left her to get a job, and he promised to write often. Some of the letters were intercepted by the girl's unsympathetic mother. Others of the promised letters were never written. The girl lost complete track of him, and her love grew cold. She betrothed herself to a much older man. On the eve of her marriage Turner charged back to her like a bull out of nowhere. Always hampered by his inability to express himself, either in his speech or in his writing, he had provoked a terrible misunderstanding. He loved her desperately, and he had come back to claim her at last—but too late. The girl could not sacrifice her honor. She married her betrothed, and Turner went home in sadness, to remain a bachelor for the rest of his life.

III

HE SPENT most of his time with a fellow student at the Academy, Tom Girtin. Together they painted landscapes in water color for a supper and a bed. Water color was an atrophied art at this time. Bright, rich tints were unknown. The technique of flooding the paper with paint would have been considered as scandalous as the habit of stuffing one's self with food at an afternoon tea.

The water colorist sketched an outline in India ink and shaded it with low tints of brown, yellow, green and red. What he produced was little more than a monochrome. The effect of such a painting depended upon the design. The tints were merely added like a semitransparent dress to give the curves underneath a greater appeal.

An artist in water colors was in some respects no more than an engraver. And Turner, who followed the accepted canons, spent most of his early years in the industry of engraving. He engraved from copies and sketches and notes and sometimes from life. He developed a supreme technique as an etcher. And he acquired an equally skillful technique as a money-maker. He began to make a good living at an early age, and at twenty-one he was instructing several classes in art. One of his pupils was the poet William Blake, who afterward complained that he had never learned anything in Turner's classes. The young master, though he had perfected his own skill in etching, was unable to communicate it to his pupils. For Turner and the English grammar were never on good speaking terms. He was amazingly unintellectual. His words were uncouth, his voice was heavy and his manner unimpressive. His personality, like his speech, was slovenly. He was like a lump of clay that had been only half finished by the sculptor. There was magic in his fingers and beauty in his eye. All the rest of him remained formless, unpolished, incomplete. He could no more deliver a lecture about the beauty of the canvases that he painted than a jeweler can write a poem about the beauty of the jewels that he cuts. His pupils were left pretty much to themselves to solve their own problems. And they learned ever so much more from watching his work than they did from listening to his talk.

His work progressed rapidly. At twenty-six he had already exhibited at the Academy, and his exhibitions were well received. An art critic of the time wrote of him as follows: "A new artist has started up—one Turner. He had before exhibited stained drawings, but now he paints landscapes in oils. He beats Loutherbourg and every other artist all to nothing. A painter of my acquaintance and a good judge declares his painting as magic; that it is worth every landscape painter's while to make a pilgrimage to see and study his works."

Within a year Turner was elected a full-fledged member of the Academy and Tom Girtin died of consumption. Tom was the only rival of Turner's art, and with his untimely death Turner had the field to himself. Powdered wigs went out of fashion when the British government put a tax on them to carry on the war with America, and together with the powdered wigs Barber Turner went out of business. Thereafter he served his son faithfully as a domestic servant. He cooked the meals, strained the canvases, showed the people around the studio and threw in a little extra advice for his son as to how to squeeze and to save his halfpennies in the best barbershop tradition. Turner continued with his landscapes, achieving remarkable success with them. His artistic habits were strange. When he saw a picture he didn't like he would stick a wafer upon it to show its faults. He spit in his powder instead of wetting it with water. He stood for hours in the country and on the seashore, taking notes as if he were going to write a description of the scene instead of painting it. At about this time he drew a very striking study of a sea storm entitled *Calais Pier*. This was the first of the Turner sea studies. And it has a special interest for several reasons. England was surfeited with the portraits of Reynolds and Gainsborough. And now here was an artist who depicted nature, and nature alone, in its wildest, most savage form. The sea is angry. The clouds spurt lightning. However, there is one serious defect in the picture. As John Ruskin has observed, neither the men in the boats, nor the women watching on the pier, nor even the boats themselves, are the least bit wet. This is a serious error of treatment in an otherwise most impressive scene. The waves lash in fury, but the men in the lifeboat are immaculately dry. The reason, as some apologists for Turner have explained, is that no one in England thought of painting realistically—never had. And Turner, though he took a subject from nature, merely followed the tradition. He attempted to idealize a realistic scene. The man who couldn't express himself in words was nevertheless in his art a poet. Never did he render a strictly naturalistic interpretation of any of his nature themes. England at that period was steeped in the portraiture tradition. And even the portraits were unrealistic. Whatever light fell on a picture came from the lighting effects of the gloomy studio. If a landscape was fitted into the background of the portrait, it was always an artificial landscape in which the grass was never painted green and the leaves of the trees were always painted black. "In the *Calais Pier*," writes W. L. Wyllie in his biography on Turner, "the light and shade is just that of Turner's own studio in Harley Street; the inky clouds throw black shadows just as a table or a sofa would in a room; the pale blue sky is not reflected anywhere, either in the tumbling water or on the tarry side of the fishing boat." The picture, in short, is what today we would call a Hollywood version of a couple of ships at sea—photographs of baby ships in a baby tank and magnified by Hollywood wizardry into a realistic illusion. Turner, indeed, was a wizard in his own right. In his Harley Street dark room his magic fingers worked effects which by a thousand little secret tricks could move his audience to awe and wonder and fear.

When Turner was thirty Nelson fought his heroic sea battle at Trafalgar. Turner was inspired to paint a shipwreck in commemoration of the event. Once again knowledge and artifice rather than realism combine to make a wonderful and terrible illusion of reality. Turner became a sort of patron saint of the old sea salts. He was asked to do a large study of the battleship Victory at Trafalgar. With his sublime neglect of literal representation and historical truth he went ahead with the painting and before many days had the entire admiralty down upon his neck. Nelson's flag captain took a look at it and remarked, "It is more like a street scene than a battle, and the ships are more like houses than men-o'-war." One tough old sailor said: "I can't make English of it, sir, I can't make English of it." And a leading art critic observed: "To say what time of the day, or what particular incident in the Victory's proceeding is meant to be referred to, we do not pretend. For the telegraphic message is going up, which was hoisted at about 11:40 A.M.; the mizzen topmast is falling, which went about 1 P.M.; a strong light is reflected upon the Victory's bow and sides from the burning Achille, which ship did not catch fire until 4:30 P.M. nor explode until 5:45 P.M.; the fore topmast, or rather, if our memory is correct, the foremast of the British three decker is falling, which never fell at all, and the Redoubtable is sinking under the bows of the Victory, although the French ship did not sink until the night of the 22nd, and then under the stern of the Swiftsure."

IV

IN SPITE of his habit of fictionizing, and to the great annoyance of the people who hired him to paint the truth, Turner received a chair at the Royal Academy as Professor of Perspective. Perhaps it would be more correct to say that he obtained this position *because* of his habit of fictionizing, for the art of perspective is the art of illusion and trickery. It was as if he had been appointed Professor of Egg Juggling in a magicians' school.

As we have already remarked, Turner had no talents whatsoever as a teacher. "He had every disadvantage: humble birth, little or no education, ungainly manners, eccentricity and a shy, retiring nature." In appearance he was "the very model of a master carpenter, with lobster-red face, twinkling, staring gray eyes, white tie, blue coat with brass buttons, crabshell turned-up boots, large fuffy hat and enormous umbrella." He was a vc thipei of the ccuntrys de. I atire in al it roc ls, all its manifestations, was carefully jotted down in his notebook and woven into his pictures. Once on a visit to a friend he stood in the doorway of the house and watched a thunderstorm that was in progress outside. He called quickiy for his host to join him. "Isn't it wonderful? Isn't it sublime?" After a while he took out an envelope and began to jot down a number of notes on the back. When the storm had passed he said, "There, Hawkey, in two years you will see this again and call it *Hannibal Crossing the Alps*." And sure enough, he actually painted that picture.

It was his custom to append a few lines of poetry to his canvases. The poetry was his own. For forty years he kept writing a single poem that rambled on and on and never seemed to die. He called it *The Fallacies of Hope*. A more appropriate title would have been *The Fallacies of One Who Thinks He Is a Poet*. This poem had no particular theme and was unintelligible for the greater part. In his spare time Turner would write down whatever verses occurred to him in that curious incoherent way of expressing himself. The poem included every topical and historical incident imaginable, to say nothing of the many incidents that were unimaginable. The whole thing was wonderfully obscure. But every time a new painting was turned out by the author a few lines from this poem were quoted at the bottom.

Turner made thousands of paintings and sketches. A friend of his suggested that he prepare a complete series of plates for his paintings and give them to the public in book form. Turner agreed to do this and hired a group of expert illustrators for the job. He quarreled with them incessantly. He divided all his subjects under the headings of *Elegant* and *Pastoral*. But when the overworked illustrators asked him for more pay the reply that Turner gave them was neither elegant nor pastoral. One by one his workers left him. Turner continued on his way alone, sketching in the drizzling rain.

Heretofore his colors had been the kind you see on a cloudy day. He had obediently followed the somber, traditional etching effects. He was the man with the soggy umbrella. But one day this umbrella blossomed into a parasol. He painted a classical study of *Dido Building Carthage*. In this painting the sun sets squarely in the middle and glares right into the eyes of the spectator. Tall Renaissance columns shine resplendently. The canvas looks as if it had been painted under the blue skies of Southern France rather than in the foggy atmosphere of London.

Turner was now definitely launched upon a career of prodigal art. Certainly his country, his ancestry and his home life were not conducive to it. The elder Turner was a crafty and thrifty fellow, hardly the father for an artist. He possessed a servile sort of faithfulness, but he was at bottom a cantankerous, ugly, slovenly and misanthropic old man. He was Davie Balfour's Uncle Ebenezer come to life. Once Turner had invited a friend to dinner at his studio, and the friend at the last moment had received an invitation to dine at the house of a lord. He called on Turner and invited him to accompany him to the nobleman's dinner instead of playing host, as originally planned. Turner hesitated and finally said, "Well, if I must, I suppose I must, but——" Whereupon his father stuck his head out of the kitchen and shouted, "Go, Billy, go. The mutton needn't be cooked, Billy."

V

WHEN any of his pictures turned up at a public auction the artist would send a personal friend to bid briskly and to keep it from selling at too low a price. Yet he was not always the business-man. There were times when he displayed a generosity that amazed even the most intimate of his friends. On one occasion he painted a picture with an unusually brilliant sky. The picture was hung in an exhibition next to a painting of Sir Thomas Lawrence and completely deluged it with its color. Noting Sir Thomas' despair, he took a brushful of black smudge and smeared it over the sky just before the exhibition opened. His friends were amazed and asked him why he did this. Turner replied: "It's all right; it will all wash off after the exhibition. And poor Lawrence was so unhappy."

These outbursts of generosity, however, were exceptional. Like his old father, Turner was a confirmed misanthrope. He shunned the society of his fellow men. He lived in lonely squalor to the end of his days. He ate and slept and painted behind the "dirty, blistered door" of his house on Queen Anne Street. A contemporary art collector describes a visit he made to Turner's studio when the latter was about fifty-five years old. "I arrived at the house with the black, crusted windows; I pulled the bell which answered with a querulous, melancholy tinkle. After a long, inhospitable pause an old woman with a diseased face . . . descended and tardily opened the door." At first she wouldn't let the visitor enter. But he wedged his foot in between the door and the threshold. "In a moment Turner was out upon me with the promptitude of a spider whose web has been invaded by another arachnid . . . When I stated that I had come to buy he shouted, 'Don't want to sell.' " But when the collector flourished twenty thousand dollars' worth of bank notes Turner listened to reason.

On another occasion a group of merchants came to Turner and offered a thousand pounds for one of the canvases. Turner took the canvas off the table and proceeded to pack it.

Suddenly he asked, "Well, would you like to have it?"

"Yes, yes," they answered impetuously.

"I daresay you would!" he returned with a dry, sarcastic little chuckle as he put it away. He was quite indifferent to the opinions of his fellows, to the sordidness of his surroundings and at times even to the fate of his canvases. He allowed the oil from the paper that had been sealed over the skylight of his studio to drop on many of the paintings hung below. The room was cold and damp. And the damp ruined many of the paintings as they lay unfinished by the palette. As for the sofa and the rest of the furniture, one friend remarked, "It seemed dangerous to rest your future peace upon it." A bottle of sherry with a broken cork stood in the dust of the corner. Ugly cats, with their tails clipped off, meandered in and out of the room from a smashed window and often put their heads through the canvases. In this studio over thirty thousand pictures and engravings rotted against their dirty frames or lay piled up under the table.

As Turner reached his sixties his style, as well as his life, became less and less conventional. In most of his landscapes the foregrounds were sketchy, unsubstantial and often carelessly if not poorly painted. But the foreground, whether it was a tree or a group of figures, merely served to set off or to drive back into their proper perspective the important areas of the canvas, which to Turner were the middle and the far background. The middle and upper half of the landscapes were always painted with an incredible beauty. The illusion of vast spaces and three-dimensional perspectives is almost uncanny, not only in his large paintings but in the smallest of his sketches. In an area measuring only five inches by three he is able to suggest innumerable square miles of open country—rivers, valleys, mountains, forests, lakes. Every fold in the ground is brought out in clearest detail, down to the last line. In the bulk of his masterpieces there is a combination of the sublime and the ridiculous. A sublime background against a ridiculous tree, for instance. The Turner tree is as awkward as the Turner body. It is the work of a conventional painter drawing with no originality, no art, no life. It serves its purpose, however. It is a scarecrow guarding the entrance to Eden—ugliness serving as a sentinel to beauty, weakness as an introduction to strength. Turner was an artist to an incredible degree. He was a *pure* artist. He knew exactly what effects would appeal directly to the aesthetic sense. He harmonized realistic forms and colors into fantastic dreams. This was an ability that he could not develop to his own characteristic extreme until he was past sixty and had thrown all caution to the wind. It was only when he learned to weave together the magnificent combinations of color into his own inimitable dreams that he released the wild horses of his genius over the new and purely aesthetic plains of art. His later paintings are a blaze of color. His light and shadow structure is unscientific, incorrect—and incredibly beautiful. It is recorded that once, as Professor of Perspective, he gave a lecture to a class on the rules of light and shadow which was so incoherent in form as to reveal clearly that the great master seemed to have no scientific knowledge of what he was talking about. If he was successful in his own perspective, it was because his genius spoke to him intuitively and because his remarkable powers of observation enabled him to copy what he saw faithfully. But as long as he was committed to the course of painting along the traditional lines his genius was hampered. As long as he was forced to use the English language his speech, as we have seen, was stammering, incoherent, confused. But suppose he had discovered a new language—a language without words and grammar and sentence structure! Turner discovered such a language when he broke with the formal rhetoric of art. Great hazy blobs of color, squashed, picturesque anatomy—and, over everything, a mood. He suddenly became supremely eloquent in his own newly found Tarzan language of painting. He had struck beauty through a detour instead of traveling along the accepted highways. Or, better still, he had arrived at the appointed place in an airship through the clouds instead of traveling on his hands and knees.

It is significant that John Ruskin, who worshiped aestheticism almost above sense, became a frantic devotee of Turner's art and spent almost his entire life writing eulogies about it. Indeed, he was ready to construct a new God, a new religion, a new scheme of rationalization and a new human race to make this world a better place for Turner's art to live in. Turner once remarked about Ruskin, "He knows a great deal more about my pictures than I do. He puts things into my head and points out meanings in them I never intended."

Turner went on painting and arousing the enthusiasm of Ruskin with his "diaphanous spectres of mist and moonbeams called ships," and with his maelstroms of sky and sea. Not all of Turner's critics were as receptive as the passionate young Platonist. One of Ruskin's fellow critics had this to say of Turner's picture entitled *Snowstorm:* "This should be entitled *A Typhoon Bursting in a Simoon over the Whirlpool of Maelstrom, Norway; with a Ship on Fire, an Eclipse and the Effect of a Lunar Rainbow.*" Another critic called it "soapsuds and whitewash" and let it go at that. "Soapsuds and whitewash," mumbled Turner to himself. "I wonder what *they* think the sea is like!" Turner *knew* the scenes he painted. Even in his old age he clung to his habit of observing things closely and jotting them down in copious notes before painting them. At sixty-seven he had gone to sea in a snowstorm. He had begged the sailors to lash him to the bottom of the boat so that he might observe the tempest and the roaring waves rushing over the side. The painting called "soapsuds" was the result of this adventure in observation. He had merely painted what he saw—a tempest. Not the conventional conception of a critic's limited vision but the real and unlimited fury of a battle between the sea and the sky.

Turner was, in a very real sense, a modernist. He was filled with an insatiable curiosity about new developments in the world of painting, politics, love. He had lived in lustier days with several mistresses who had borne him a number of children. One of his *filles de joie* he retained as his faithful maidservant when she became old and pock-marked. She ministered to his simple needs, and he kept on experimenting with his paints. Frequently he visited the Academy, where his work was almost always on exhibition. Here, somewhat the worse for his sherry, as his biographer, W. L. Wyllie, tells us, "he would sit on the top of a flight of steps, or a box, like a shabby Bacchus nodding

at his pictures." He was like an old brown overcoat that life was
ready to cast off from her healthy body. And he was not unwilling to go. For his strength was gradually leaving him. His
strength but not his curiosity. His mind was still awake, vigorous, questioning. He developed an interest in photography.
And he paid several visits to a leading photographer to learn
the art. He came under an assumed name, calling himself a
Master in Chancery. Once the photographer met his visitor at
the Academy, and Turner continued his discussions on the
spectrum. A friend who happened to be present whispered to the
photographer, "Do you know to whom you're speaking? The
great Turner!"

The "great Turner" never visited the photographer's shop
again. Evidently he had developed a persecution mania, or perhaps it was his extreme shyness that made him detest notoriety.
A fellow artist met him in a public bar, at the farthest corner of
the room, looking silently into a glass of wine. The friend rushed
over to him full of enthusiasm and surprise. "I didn't know you
used this house! I shall drop in often now that I've found out
where you quarter." Turner emptied his glass. "Will you?" he
said slowly. "I don't think you will." He put down his glass,
walked out of the bar and was never seen there again.

Throughout his last years he lived the life of a hounded man.
He fled from his house in Queen Anne Street and took a cottage
at Chelsea. He drew out a roll of bank notes as a payment for
the house in advance, since he was unwilling to give a reference.
The landlady, staggered at the sight of so much cash, asked for
his name so she could make out the receipt. "What is *your* name,
madam?" countered Turner.

"Mrs Booth."

"Then I'm *Mr* Booth," he said quickly. "And don't ask any
more questions."

His closest friends in London were unaware that he had left
his house on Queen Anne Street, for rarely had any of them

been admitted into the intimacy of his domestic affairs. His studio had always been a mystery. And the faded housekeeper with the pock-marked face slammed the door to all visitors, merely saying, "Mr Turner does not wish to be seen."

Turner was the loneliest of men. And his heart was never opened, though the sunlight of fame shone down on his head. There are rumors of much drinking, of debauchery, of trips with sailors and low women to the slums, of degeneracy—and silence. The leading artist of England, the painter of the fine landscapes, they say, wallowed until the end in sailors' haunts from Saturday to Monday of every week. Perhaps Turner was a Dr Jekyll and Mr Hyde. Perhaps his life *did* savor of limehouse nights and of abandoned cellars fronting the sea. We must respect the veil that Turner himself has thrown over the more intimate recesses of his enigmatic personality.

VI

IN 1851, just after the seventy-six-year-old artist had secretly retired to his cottage in Chelsea, his friends noticed that he was absent from a meeting of the Academy Council for the first time in half a century. Two weeks later he visited the studio of a friend, sad and broken. The friend begged him to say where he had been and asked him how he was feeling. "You must not ask me," answered Turner. "But whenever I come to town I will always drop in to see you." When the friend tried to cheer him up he laid his hand on his heart and replied, "No, no, there is something here which is all wrong." Then he left.

The housemaid in Queen Anne Street feared that something had happened to her master; he hadn't been home in months. She searched the streets of London frantically. She went through his clothes in the closet and found a letter from the cottage at Chelsea. She rushed down to Chelsea and in a public bar got news of a stranger living there under the name of Mr Booth who answered to Turner's description. She found him in the cottage. He was very ill. He hadn't been out in two months. Yet he could not believe he was going to die. A doctor was summoned and told him to prepare for the end. "Go and get yourself a drink," Turner joked. He asked the maid to put him in a chair and to wheel him to the window. This done, he looked out upon the sunshine and the fields he loved so well. He took a slip of paper and commenced to jot down some notes, just as he had done thousands of times before. A little while later the blind was drawn and the eyes had closed.

He left behind him one of the greatest names in English painting, an estate of a million dollars and a far more important legacy of three hundred and sixty-five oils, one hundred and thirty-five water colors, seventeen hundred sketches in color and nearly twenty thousand drawings. And, to the curiosity of his countless admirers, he left his palette with his soiled gloves and neckerchief thrown carelessly over it—a symbol of his divine genius and his sordid mortality.

GOYA

Great Paintings by Goya

Boston, Museum of Fine Arts:
Portrait of a Young Man,
80 prints from the *Caprices*.

Brussels, Museum: *Girl's Head*.

London, National Gallery:
Dona Isabel, The Bewitched.

Madrid, Academy: *The Bullfight*.

Madrid, Prado: *Charles IV on
Horseback, Charles IV and
His Family, The Execution,
May 3, 1808, The Clothed
Maja, The Nude Maja*.

New York, Bache Collection:
Don Manuel Osorio.

Toledo, Cathedral: *Treason of
Juda*.

Francisco José Goya y Lucientes

1746–1828

SPAIN produced two supreme artists—Velasquez the Serene and Goya the Turbulent. Alike in their genius, they were unlike in everything else. Velasquez was a smiling spectator in the tragicomedy of life. Goya was a boisterous actor. Velasquez, the philosopher, shook his head indulgently and said, "What *fools* these mortals be." Goya, the fighter, brandished his fist threat‑eningly and cried, "What *rascals* these mortals be!" And he him‑ self was not the least of the rascals. Both Velasquez and Goya were Spanish to the core. But the spirit of Velasquez' painting was primarily national, while the spirit of Goya's painting was at all times universal. Velasquez was a citizen of Spain. Goya was a man of the world. Velasquez depicted the life of his com‑ patriots. Goya represented the life of mankind.

Goya was one of the most comprehensive of the world's paint‑ ers. He may well be called the Shakespeare of the brush. His imagination was all embracing. The scope of his genius included portraiture, landscape painting, mythological scenes, realistic stories, symbolical representations, tragedy, comedy, satire, farce, men, gods, devils, witches, the seen and the unseen and—

as was the case with Shakespeare's extravagant genius—an occasional excursion into the obscene.

Physically, this roisterous knight of the dagger and the brush was impressive rather than handsome. Somewhat below the medium height, he had the figure of an athlete. His features were coarse and irregular, but they were alive with the fire of an unsuppressed impetuosity. His deep black eyes would suddenly light up with the impudence of a child about to play a naughty prank. His nose was thick, fleshy, sensuous. His lips were firm, aggressive and unabashed. Yet there lurked about their corners at times a smile of good-natured joviality. His chin was the round, sensitive, smooth chin of a lover. A lover of life, of gaiety, of beauty. He enjoyed three things with equal gusto—to flirt with a wench, to fight a duel and to paint a picture. He was a master in the art of indiscriminate living. How exquisitely the late Douglas Fairbanks might have portrayed this audacious, brawling, philandering, befriending, swashbuckling and dreaming Don Juan of Saragossa!

II

FRANCISCO JOSÉ GOYA Y LUCIENTES, the son of a peasant in the province of Aragon, was born on March 13, 1746—a period when Spanish art was at its low ebb. The red-blooded realism of Velasquez and Ribera had degenerated into the anemic pink-and-white figurines of the uninspired artists of the eighteenth century. These artists had a genius for mediocrity. The world was old and tired. It was sleeping under the snows of one of the winter epochs of history. Nobody suspected, when Goya was roaming over the fields of his native village Fuendetodos, that here was a youngster who would usher in a new spring. Least of all was Goya himself aware of his destiny. To keep his busy hands out of mischief he amused himself by sketching in the fields that bordered upon the road to Saragossa.

One day, in 1760, a monk was walking slowly over this road and reciting his breviary. A shadow lay across his path. Looking up, he saw a young lad drawing pictures with a piece of charcoal upon the wall of a barn. Being somewhat of a connoisseur, the monk stopped to examine the boy's work. He was amazed at the youngster's aptitude. "Take me home to your parents," he said. "I want to speak to them."

When he arrived at the Goya farmhouse he had no difficulty in persuading the parents to entrust their child to his care. It was this anonymous monk who was responsible for the awakening of the latent genius of Goya and for the renaissance of Spanish painting.

III

GOYA was fifteen years old when he entered upon his apprenticeship as an artist. Thanks to the recommendation of his ecclesiastical benefactor, he was admitted into the studio of Don José Lujan Martínez. Here he remained for five years, acquiring an exuberant virtuosity in color and design, a passionate admiration for Velasquez and a hearty contempt for the academic conventionalities of his fellow artists. There was only one of them for whom he had the slightest respect—a painter by the name of Francisco Bayeu. In spite of the fact that Bayeu was twelve years older than Goya the two pupils of Lujan became fast friends.

"Fast" in more senses than one. Goya and Bayeu were the life of the studio—and the talk of the town. Ardent in their work, headstrong in their pleasures and reckless of the consequences of their pranks, they threw themselves heartily into the whirlpool of the Aragonese underworld—singing, dancing, drinking, wenching, quarreling, with an occasional killing thrown in for good measure. Goya was always in the forefront of the street battles. In one of these battles, occasioned by nobody knows what flimsy excuse, three young men belonging to the rival faction were left lifeless on the ground. Somebody warned Goya that the Inquisition intended to arrest him. Hastily packing his belongings, he left Saragossa in the dead of night and made his way to Madrid.

Here his reputation as an artist had preceded him. Bayeu, who had arrived in Madrid shortly before him, introduced him to the German, Mengs, the Superintendent of Fine Arts in Madrid. Mengs, a somewhat better than mediocre painter but somewhat worse than mediocre teacher, was at that time decorating the royal palace at Madrid. From all the pupils who assisted him in this work he exacted a slavish obedience and a faithful imitation of his own unimpressive ideas. He offered to take Goya into his studio as one of his assistants. Goya, whose artistic ideas were superior to those of Mengs, refused the offer.

Goya had come to Madrid not to secure employment but to continue his education. In spite of his supreme confidence in his own ability he felt that he was not quite yet ready to enter upon a professional career. He strongly believed in the formula, *to easy earning through hard learning*. Accordingly he spent his days in studying the artistic treasures of the capital. And his nights in conquering the hearts of the señoritas and the señoras. Whether single or married, a woman was to him equally desirable—and equally accessible. Very few could resist his impetuous wooing. With sword at his side and guitar in his hand he wandered through the streets and sang his way into the hearts of the ladies, whose stealthily written messages fluttered down to him from behind shuttered windows. The women adored him, and the men were insanely jealous of him. And they had every right to be jealous.

Sooner or later this heedless quest for the forbidden adventures of love was bound to cost him dearly. And, indeed, it came near to costing him his life. One early morning he was found in a side street with a deep dagger thrust in his back. In order to protect him from the ubiquitous eye of the Inquisition his friends kept him concealed for a time. And then, when he was well on the way to recovery, they hustled him out of Madrid.

This time Goya set sail for Italy. Here too, as in Madrid, he apprenticed himself to the study of the great masters. He applauded the geometric precision of their design, he extolled the subtlety of their chiaroscuro, he admired the accuracy of their observation, he worshiped the fire of their genius—and he refused to be influenced by any of them. For the greater part of his life his inspiration came from within rather than from without. He was the product of no school. His art was strictly and completely his own.

IV

IN ITALY, as in Saragossa and in Madrid, he lived a life of romantic and perilous adventure. "At one time," relates Señor Cardarera, "Goya carved his name with his knife on the lantern of Michelangelo's cupola"—a neck-breaking achievement—"on a corner of a certain stone which not one of the other artists, German, English or French, who had preceded him in the mad ascent, had succeeded in reaching." And on another occasion, "he made the circuit on the tomb of Cecilia Metella, barely supporting himself upon the narrow projection of the cornice."

These were but preliminaries to a still more dangerous adventure. He met a young girl in Rome, fell in love with her and proposed to marry her against her parents' consent. Warned in time, the parents placed her in a convent. Goya, determined to have his bride, attempted to break into the convent and to carry her off. He was captured and handed over to the police. Kidnaping a nun from the Holy Church was a serious matter. It was only the interposition of the Spanish ambassador that saved him. Chastened, at least temporarily, Goya abandoned his impossible quest and returned to Madrid. Here his earlier escapade had been fortunately forgotten. Once more he met his old friend Bayeu, found that he loved Bayeu's sister, married her and settled down. His student days were over. It was now necessary for him to think of making a living. Again the Superintendent of Fine Arts offered him a job. This time Goya accepted the offer. Having agreed to follow the instructions of his German employer, he took that artist's lifeless mythological figures and breathed into them the spirit of living men and women.

Thus far Goya had done nothing to prove his rank among the genuine artists of the world. He had been regarded merely as a playboy with a clever brush. Now, however, he revealed himself to a dazzled public as an *inspired* playboy. His riotous imagination, his daring design, his interplay of color effect, his humor and his unerring instinct for the dramatic aroused the enthusiasm even of so hidebound a traditionalist as Mengs himself. As for the connoisseurs of Madrid who had been vainly seeking for signs of a new life in their national art, they greeted Goya's work with a veritable ovation. Goya accepted this public recognition of his genius with the same self-assurance with which he had accepted the smiles of his señoritas. Goya never suffered from excessive modesty—or, for that matter, from excessive vanity. He was merely conscious of a superior power within himself. "He knew now (at the age of thirty)," writes M. Charles Yriarte, "that he had only to take his brush in hand in order to become a great painter."

V

For fifty years he wielded his brush, to the delight of his own generation and to the enrichment of the generations to come. He began with genre pictures, stories in color dealing with the manifold activities of the people—bright, vibrating, vigorous scenes of plays, processions, bullfights, bandits, masquerades, courtships, seductions, dances, banquets, picnics, rambles, quarrels, reconciliations—in short, the entire panorama of Spanish life in the eighteenth century. These paintings are not always flawless in design. Some of the bulls, and at times even the human figures, are drawn with exaggerated anatomical proportions. But these exaggerations are always deliberate. They are calculated to produce a definite dramatic effect. When you look at them you have the feeling that if Nature *hasn't* produced such creatures, then Nature *ought* to have produced them. For Goya is a pictorial rather than a photographic painter. He is a realist with an imagination. And his art is so alive, so spirited, so impetuous, that it kindles a sympathetic spark of imagination in the most sluggish of his spectators.

In this first period of his art Goya acknowledged one master, Velasquez. He made a series of etchings in which he reproduced the best of Velasquez' paintings. *Reproduced*, however, is the wrong word. It would be more exact to say that he *re-created* them. For Goya never was an imitator. Like Shakespeare, he put his own original stamp upon whatever ideas came into the mint of his universal personality. In the etchings which Goya published in 1778 he did no injustice to Velasquez. On the contrary, he did him a great service. It is as if he had borrowed a sum of money from a friend and had subsequently repaid him with interest. These etchings are today of incalculable value.

In addition to his genre pictures and his etchings Goya executed at about this time two religious paintings, *Christ on the Cross* and *St Francis Preaching*. These paintings, in spite of their luminous color and their design, are inferior to his other work. For Goya did not quite feel at home in these subjects. His was not a religious nature. These two paintings have every artistic quality save one—reverence.

To his contemporaries, however, Goya's religious pictures were as satisfactory as his other paintings and etchings. The Spanish public acclaimed their virtues and overlooked their faults. They now idolized him as their national painter, and they compelled the Academy of St Marc, in spite of the jealousy of its officers, to admit him as a member. Accordingly, on May 7,

1780, Goya was publicly honored with the official title of "academician by merit."

VI

HAVING PROVED his mastery of the genre painting and the etching and his ability to arouse the enthusiasm of his public with his religious pictures, Goya now turned his hand to another branch of art—portraiture. Here he was successful from the start. To be painted by Goya became the fashion—indeed, the *passion*—of the day. From morning till night his studio was besieged by wealthy and noble clients. This was all the more surprising because he never flattered any of his subjects. He painted them as they were, in all their physical imperfection and with all their moral shortcomings. "Here we are," they seem to say to the spectator, "a bunch of as arrant rascals as you'd ever like to see." This is especially evident in the two portraits of *Maja*, subject unknown but believed to have been the Duchess of Alba, and in the portrait of *King Charles IV and His Family.*

The two *Majas* are two pictures of the same woman, in exactly the same pose and with exactly the same expression on her face. In one of the pictures she is nude, and in the other she is dressed in a long transparent shift of thin white silk which is tightly folded around all the lascivious contours of her body. (It was intimated by some of his contemporaries that Goya painted the clothed Maja for her husband and the nude Maja for himself.) In both of the pictures she lies on a couch, her arms folded under her head which is raised on a pillow, and her body turned three quarters toward the spectator. The right leg is resting lightly upon the left leg. The curves of the body, the half-drowsy voluptuousness of the eyes and the seductive, subtle smile of the lips all seem to be concentrated upon a single thought, "I want to be desired." The picture produces a strange effect. It attracts and at the same time it repels. There is beauty in its ugliness, and there is ugliness in its beauty. The interpretation of the double portrait is written large upon every line and feature—"What rascals ye mortal women be . . . But what *desirable* rascals!"

The other portrait, that of *King Charles and His Family*, is even more indicative of Goya's contempt for the human race. Charles IV had conferred upon Goya the title of First Painter. But Goya, as is evident from this picture, did not confer upon Charles IV the title of First Spaniard. The features of the king and of most of the members of his family are vulgar in the extreme. They look like a family of laborers masquerading in royal robes. The king, with his hooked nose and his self-satisfied smirk; the queen, with her fat naked arms, her double chin and her heavily bebrooched and earringed features puffed up into a halo of pompous insipidity; the princes and the princesses of the Blood, twelve of them, each with a face as innocent of thought as that of the youngest one among them, a suckling child in his nurse's arms—all these were depicted with relentless brush to represent what they actually were, a picture of Royalty in Decadence. Yet the king and the queen were proud of this picture. For they saw in it what they wanted to see—a great imperial family depicted in colossal proportions upon a canvas of enormous size. How Goya must have secretly smiled when he looked upon this finished handiwork of his—a brood of pitiable mortals, with the bodies of titans and the souls of fleas!

VII

WE NOW HAVE about two hundred portraits which are known to have been painted by Goya. Nearly all the celebrated personages of the period submitted, at one time or another, to have their likenesses perpetuated by this relentless realist of the brush. The result—an eloquent commentary on the follies and the foibles of eighteenth-century Spain. But these portraits form only a small part of the pictures with which Goya represented the human comedy of his age. He depicted the restless life of the city in *The Blind Street Singer*, *The Pottery Market*, *The Vegetable Woman*, *The Runners on Stilts*, *The Carnival*, *The May Festival in Madrid*, *The Madhouse* and *The Bullfight*. He immortalized the toils and the joys of the countryfolk in *The Washerwomen at the Pool*, *The Harvesting of the Hay*, *The Attack on the Stagecoach*, *The Widow at the Well*, *The Village Wedding*, *The Water Carriers*, *The Country Dance*, *The Greased Pole* and *The Seasons*. He pictured the horrors of war—for in spite of his turbulent spirit he hated the organized business of slaughter—in a series of devastating satires such as *The Massacre of 1808*, *Forever the Same Savagery*, *The Beds of Death*, *The Hanging*, *The Garrote* (a Spanish mode of strangling with an iron collar and a screw), *Dead Men Tell No Tales*, *I Have Seen the Horrors* and *There Is No One to Help Them*. Stark, honest, realistic, heart-gripping, these painted indictments of man's inhumanity to man. But most characteristic, perhaps, of all the pictures of Goya are his famous *Caprices*.

These *Caprices*, done in etching and in water color, have never been paralleled, either before Goya or after him. They are an entire world seen through a distorted looking glass, half realistic and half fantastic representations of beastlike humans and humanlike beasts, scenes that depict the rapacity, the hypocrisy, the cruelty, the superstition, the licentiousness, the pomposity, the violence, the stupidity and the inevitable destiny of that creature called Man, who starts his life in hope and ends it in disaster. One of these *Caprices*, entitled *Until Death*, represents an old woman whose hands and whose face are already reduced to the semblance of a skeleton and who looks gloatingly into a mirror as she places a gorgeous bonnet upon her stringy hair, while her attendants look on and try their best to conceal their snickers behind their outstretched palms. In another of these *Caprices*, bearing the provocative title, *The Tooth Hunt*, a terrified woman is seen slinking toward the gallows, under the ghostly light of the moon, and tearing out the teeth of a hanged criminal. Her purpose? To use these teeth as a charm against sickness. Still another *Caprice*, entitled *The Rise and the Fall*, portrays the helplessness of Man in the hands of his Fate. A gigantic figure, with the legs of a goat and the face of a devil, has just taken hold of a man by the ankles and swung him aloft toward the sky. The man rejoices in his great good fortune and in his costly robes. There are flames spurting upward from his hands and his head. He is a king among his fellow men! In his ecstatic glee he fails to notice, poor little mortal, that other men, like himself, have just been raised aloft only to be dashed headlong to the ground. This pessimistic *Caprice* bears the following comment: "Destiny is cruel to those who woo it. The labor that it costs to rise to the top goes up in smoke. We rise only to fall." And so on. The *Caprices* of Goya are like an *Inferno* of Dante. But, unlike Dante, Goya depicts not the sufferings of the dead but the tortures of the living. And it would seem that Goya considered the Inferno of life to be even more tragic than the Inferno of death.

VIII

THE *Caprices* of Goya made him persona non grata with the Inquisition. For in many of the *Caprices* he had attacked the practices of this outmoded institution of the Middle Ages. Spain had become an unhealthy place for Goya to live in. Accordingly, in his late seventies, this old-young adventurer packed his brushes and his paints and went to end his days in exile at the French city of Bordeaux. Here he found a number of his compatriots, refugees from the tyranny of the new Spanish king, Ferdinand VII.

Settling down in the Spanish colony of Bordeaux, Goya began to paint anew. His eyesight was now so dim that he was obliged to paint with the help of a magnifying glass. Yet some of the pictures that he executed at this period, especially the miniatures that he painted on bits of ivory, are among the rarest artistic possessions in the world.

While his dimming eyesight held out to the end, his hearing gave way completely. One of his friends describes him sitting at the harpsichord, playing a Spanish tune and bending his ear toward the instrument in a futile effort to catch the beloved song of his homeland.

In the early spring of 1828 he sent a letter to his son Xavier, who had written him from Madrid that he was coming to see him. "Dear Xavier," he said, "I have nothing else to say except that I am overjoyed at the prospect of seeing you, and that I am ill. God grant that I live to embrace you. My joy will then be complete. Farewell."

On the sixteenth of April he passed on to his final journey. He was buried quietly at Bordeaux. It was not until 1900 that the remains of the exiled First Painter of Spain were brought back to Madrid. He was given a splendid funeral at last. His casket was drawn by eight horses adorned with gilt plumes and accompanied by eight lackeys in gold-besprinkled wigs. The entire population of Madrid looked on. Too bad that Goya wasn't alive to paint this last of the *Caprices* of his cynical destiny. It might have been the greatest of his masterpieces.

COROT

Boston, Museum of Fine Arts: *Ville d'Avray*, and many other *Landscapes*.

Brooklyn, Institute: *An Italian Girl*.

Chicago, Art Institute: *The Lovers' Bridge*.

Cincinnati, Taft Museum: *The Heights of Ville d'Avray, Evening Glory*.

Cleveland, Museum of Art: *The Willows*.

Des Moines, Weeks Collection: *The Girl in the Red Bodice*.

Detroit, Ford Collection: *Edge of the Pool*.

London, Wallace Collection: *Landscape*.

Los Angeles, Marbury Collection: *The Seine and the Old Bridge at Limay*.

New York, Stephen C. Clark Collection: *La Rochelle*.

New York, Frick Collection: *Land Card — Morning*.

New York, Metropolitan Museum of Art: A large collection of *Landscapes*.

Northampton, Mass., Smith College Museum of Art: *Town on a Cliff, The Spring*.

Paris, Louvre: *The Belfry of Douai, Dance of the Nymphs, Doorway at Dinan, Lady with the Pearl Necklace, Lady in Blue, Madame Baudot, Morning, The Mill, The Pool, The Roman Forum, Souvenir de Mortefontaine*.

Philadelphia, Pennsylvania Museum of Art: *Gipsy Woman*.

St Paul, Hill Estate: *The Springtime of Life*.

Washington, Phillips Memorial Gallery: *Woman with the Water Jar*.

Jean Baptiste Camille Corot

1796–1875

I<small>T IS THREE O'CLOCK</small> in the morning. The sun is not yet up. The painter sits under a tree. He is short, thickset, alert, with a strong furrowed face, a humorous twinkle in his eyes, a protruding lower lip, wrists and muscles of steel and the heart of a child. He looks upon the gray sheet of the dawn, and he sings. Simple, unaffected, joyous at the very thought of being alive, he sings like the birds to the coming day.

He sings, and he waits. In the gray mist the vague outlines of things can barely be seen. There is a faint perfume in the air. The little thin grasses tremble in the breeze.

And then, the first rays of the sun! The flowers awaken, each with its trembling dewdrop. The birds, still invisible in their forest cathedral, burst into their morning hymn. The fog rises, like the curtain upon a new play, revealing the blade of the silver river, the trees, the cottages and the delicately tinted sky overhead. The scene is now spread out before the painter's eyes . . .

And now the sun is up. The heavens are ablaze. But the light upon the earth is still pale and caressing. At the end of the field a peasant with his cart and his oxen. The tinkle of the sheep bell. A traveler upon a dapple horse rises over the brow of the hill and then disappears in the hollow. The white slender birches seem to march, through the shimmering air, along the banks of the river. White birches, green grass, blue air—fresh, delicate, alive. And the artist, still singing, is painting it all. A peasant leaves his work and stands behind the artist. He watches the painting over the artist's shoulder. "C'est bien beau, m'sieu. You make your pictures talk . . ."

It is noontime. The sun has kindled the world. The air is heavy, drowsy, still. The flowers bend their heads. The birds are hushed. Only a single sound is heard—the hammer of the blacksmith in the village. Ding! Ding! How rhythmically it beats upon the anvil! And now the hammer is silent. The hour of rest. The painter goes to lunch at the farm. A thick slice of bread, butter, cheese, eggs, ham. Ah, but it tastes good! And then, after this wholesome lunch, a brief nap. He dreams of his paintings . . . Later on he will paint his dreams . . .

The sun is marching toward the horizon. The air vibrates, as if shattered by the distant beat of a tom-tom. To work again! The selfsame landscape in a different mood, seen under a different light. What a change of features, of contours, of shades, of harmonies—of thoughts. For, under the brush of this magician, the landscape talks and thinks . . .

And now the sun is sinking in the west. It goes down in a splash of yellow, orange, scarlet, cherry, purple. A pretentious and vulgar display. Not a scene for *this* artist. For *he* prefers Nature in her quieter moods. And so he sits down under a poplar and waits. The flowers look tired. But, unlike the tired people, they do not complain. They are thirsty. But they wait. They know that they will get their cup of dew at night. They are patient, and thank God for that . . .

The last ray of the sun is now dipping beyond the horizon. A streak of gold and rpe fringing the cloud. Ah, his is more like it! Twilight, tenderness, peace. The sun is gone. The sky is veiled with a tinted vapor of pale yellow, the last reflection of the sun. And now, as the afterglow merges into the night, the sky is a delicate texture of greens and turquoises and grays and browns. The waters of the river reflect the soft tones of the sky. Everything is vague, confused—the breathless moment when the visible melts into the invisible. Nature is drowsy. The birds have finished their night prayer. They have gone to sleep. The nymphs have come out of their hiding places and are dancing among the shadows of the trees. Hush! Stop your singing, or you will frighten them and they will hide themselves again. Sunset, stillness, night. A star dives from the sky into the pond. And the water reflects the light in a ripple of silver smiles. Another star, and another—three, six, twenty, a thousand! All is darkness except the stars and the pond—a swarm of gold bees reflected in the water. Night, illusion, dreams. Plans for the next day. New landscapes, new visions, new secrets of Nature to capture and to interpret upon the canvas. But for today the work is done. "My Heavenly Father has put out the lamp, and I must stop. . . ."

Such is a typical day of Corot, the poet painter who succeeded in representing not only the form but the psychology of Nature. Like Bonsels, Corot invested every tree, every flower, every blade of grass with an individual personality and a living soul. The finest tribute ever paid to the art of Corot was the simple statement of the peasant: "M'sieu, you make your pictures talk."

II

THE NAME with which he was christened, Jean Baptiste, was prophetic. For, like John the Baptist, he turned out to be the forerunner of a new religion. The religion of a revitalized art. An art of simplicity, sincerity, conscientiousness. His landscapes are prayers in colors, poems of adoration to the gentler beauties of Nature.

The very life of Corot was a gentle poem of generosity and genius. Yet his life began in a stormy period of the world's history. For 1796, the year of his birth, was the transitional period between the tempest of the French Revolution and the tempestuous holocaust of the Napoleonic Wars. He grew up in a generation of blood and thunder, of ambition and intolerance and hatred and dishonesty and revenge. But his character remained untainted by the savage stupidities of his age. For he was fortunate in the wholesome and the friendly environment of his home. His father was a hairdresser, and his mother was a dressmaker—artists after a fashion, and people of splendid souls. They adored their child, and although they disapproved of his "tinkering with the paintbrush," they were tolerant and allowed him to have his way. Shortly before Corot's birth his father had abandoned his hairdressing business and had become the manager of his wife's dressmaking establishment in the Rue du Bac, one of the more fashionable districts of Paris. The business prospered, and Corot père hoped that his son, too, would become a businessman. He sent him through school and college, and then he secured for him a job as a drapery salesman. Corot stuck to his job for six years and then gave it up for his painting. His father made one more attempt to turn the young artist into a merchant. He offered to set him up in a business of his own with a capital of one hundred thousand francs (about twenty thousand dollars). Corot refused this practical offer. He wanted to paint. His mother tried to bring him to his senses. "Mon Dieu, Camille," she exclaimed, "who would have thought that a son of mine would turn out to be so vulgar!" But Corot still persisted in his desire to paint. Whereupon the parents sent him off on his "crazy adventure" with a good-natured shrug of the shoulders and a generous income of twelve hundred francs a year.

Corot climbed the steep road from Paris to the Ville d'Avray and settled down in a little house among the peasants. Here he remained for the rest of his long life, singing, painting and waiting for his fame. And it was slow in coming, this belated fame of Corot. It was not till 1840, when Corot was already in the fifth decade of his life, that he succeeded in selling his first picture.

III

DURING the formative period of his art he paid two visits to Italy —not, however, to study the technique of the Italian masters but to absorb the beauty of the Italian skies. Throughout his life he acknowledged no other teacher except Nature. He never copied. He always painted direct from life. "Do not follow others," he said. "He who follows is always behind . . . You must interpret Nature with entire simplicity and according to your personal sentiment, altogether detaching yourself from what you know of the old masters or of contemporaries. Only in this way will you do work of real feeling." Listen to the criticism of others, he said, and then let your own feelings be your guide. "Follow your convictions . . . It is better not to exist than to be the echo of other painters."

And so he went on in his own way, listening to none and befriending all. His father had increased his income to two thousand francs. But Corot spent it all—on others. He was the extravagant brother of all the needy young artists in Paris. He fed them, clothed them and even bought a house for one of them. To meet these charities—he never called them charities but tokens of his friendships—he was obliged to borrow from his father large sums of money over and above his allowance. "Someday," he said, "I will sell my paintings and then I will repay you." But his father merely opened his purse strings and smiled. Who ever heard of an artist being able to pay money to a businessman? Of what good were artists, anyhow? To the end of his days, he was convinced, Camille would remain a foolish, unpractical and improvident child.

Unpractical and improvident, yes—to a certain extent. But foolish? Not Corot. He was wise with the wisdom of a great heart. Frugal to the point of abstemiousness, Corot could be "gay on a loaf of bread," to quote his biographer, Everard Meynell. For his bread was seasoned with the spice of joy at the thought that some other poor devil of an artist was at that very moment enjoying a hearty meal at his expense. His greatest pleasure was to lend, without hope of repayment. His little house was like a banking establishment where everybody came to draw, never to deposit. One day a woman arrived at his door in a cab. "She is very well dressed," said his housekeeper. "I can't understand how anyone with such clothes can be in need of charity. If I were you, I would refuse."

"Give her this money," said Corot, handing a number of notes to his housekeeper. "And in the future please remember that the worst kind of misery is misery dressed in silk."

On another occasion a young artist came to his house while Corot was at his work. "I'm at the end of my resources," said the artist. "If you don't give me five hundred francs, I'll blow my brains out."

The manner of the young man's request displeased Corot. "I'm sorry," he mumbled, "but I haven't the five hundred francs."

The young man departed, and Corot continued with his painting. But nothing went right after that. His hand shook as he tried to wield his brush. "No, no," he cried to a friend who happened to be in the studio at the time. "I lied to him. I had the five hundred francs when I spoke to him. This can't go on." And, running to his desk, he wrote: "Cher confrère, come here at once. I have the money, and it is at your disposal." Sealing the letter he sent it off with his housekeeper. "And now," he said, "I will be able to paint a great picture."

His pictures were great because they came out of the goodness of his heart. And, little by little, the public grew to understand the greatness of his pictures as well as the goodness of his heart. They began to buy his canvases, and he gave his earnings to his friends. And so he spent his life in a golden circle of charity, inspiration and jovial good-fellowship. For he was no ascetic, this St Vincent of the brush. He loved his play as well as his work. At night he was generally to be found in the center of a circle of merrymakers. Changing the blue blouse of his studio to a Spanish costume of black and yellow, he sang and he laughed and he danced his way into the heart of his friends. And what friends! There was Daubigny, who painted and played and jested with him through life and who upon his deathbed whispered, "Adieu. I go to heaven to see if friend Corot has found me subjects for landscapes." There was Rousseau, of the massive head and the heavy beard, the artist whose merry face still bore the traces of an early hunger—a hunger to which Corot's generosity had helped to put an end. There was Diaz— Narcisse Virgile Diaz de la Peña—the rich color of whose paintings matched the colorful richness of his name, the man of the crippled leg and the energetic heart, a Spaniard who looked like a pirate and painted like a god, a black-haired John Silver who had begged upon the streets, who was now enjoying the cup of success to the brim and who, upon a tragic day, was to die of a viper's sting. There was Baudelaire, the apostle of Romanticism whose genius verged upon insanity—or, as some of his more malicious critics would have it, whose insanity verged upon genius—Beaudelaire the unpredictable, the man who one day paraded through the lobby of the Hotel Pimodan dressed in a white collar, immaculate tie, snugly fitting gloves and carefully polished shoes and who another day went about with earrings in his ears, a blue wig on his closely shaved head and a jeweled dagger in the girdle of his outlandish costume. And then there was the great Courbet, whose vanity was even greater than his genius. One evening Corot and Courbet were guests at the house of a mutual friend. They were talking about modern art. "And who, Corot," asked Courbet, "who is it that France regards as the greatest of her artists?" And he went on to answer his own question. "Why, me"—and then, suddenly remembering his manners, he added, but without enthusiasm—"and you." Which anecdote recalls a similar story about Victor Hugo, another contemporary of Corot. "Who, in your opinion," asked one of his acquaintances, "is the greatest poet in France?" "Alfred de Musset," replied Hugo with a smile, "is the *second* greatest."

IV

VICTOR HUGO and Alfred de Musset, it is interesting to note, were among the last to recognize the greatness of Corot's art. But Hugo was a dramatist, and De Musset was a romanticist; and Corot was neither dramatic nor romantic. He was just sincere. He painted the world as he found it. He refused to exaggerate the colors of Nature. His pictures are never overdone. Indeed, some of the leading art critics of Paris believed that his pictures were *underdone*. Nieuwerkeke, for example, described Corot as a "miserable creature who smeared canvases with a sponge dipped in mud."

And so the dramatists and the romanticists and the critics remained blind to the finer subtleties of Corot's art. But his fellow artists, men whose eyes had been trained to see, began to acknowledge him as their master. As a result of their constant urging, Corot received (in 1846) the Cross of the Legion of Honor. "Incredible!" exclaimed his father when he heard of this. And when Corot, like the dutiful son that he was, displayed the red ribbon before his parents, his mother cautioned him to be tidier in his dress now that he had been recognized as a great man.

If Corot's decoration failed to make him a tidier, it succeeded in making him a happier, man. For he was now able to sell his paintings at will and to fill his purse for the benefit of his friends.

And now that success had come to him he developed some of the business astuteness of his father. Occasionally he demanded fairly good prices for his pictures—one thousand francs, three thousand francs, ten thousand francs. But he generally priced his pictures in accordance with his needs at the moment and not in accordance with their intrinsic worth. On the whole he rather underestimated his worth. He would have been not a little surprised could he have foreseen, when he sold his *Lac de Garde* for eight hundred francs, that within thirty years this painting would fetch two hundred and thirty-one thousand francs!

V

COROT remained unspoiled by his success, just as he had been unembittered by his failures. He still went laughing and singing through life. Once he was invited to the palace of the emperor. As he marched up the stairway he so completely forgot himself that he sang out at the top of his voice, much to the amusement of the royal gathering.

In the palace of the king, as in his own little studio, he remained his simple self. He hated the ostentatiousness of some of his fellow artists. "This love of luxury," he said, "is killing everybody, and first of all the painters. God has given them talent, and they use it that they may go into the world with pomposity, and give parties, and soirees, and concerts, where they take hold of women by their waists . . . Ah, Messieurs les artistes modernes, God is not pleased with you."

He upbraided his fellow artists for wasting their money on their mistresses. As for himself, "My only mistress is Nature. To her alone I shall remain faithful all my life." He never married.

The world that Corot saw was the world at peace. His genius was attuned to the "still small voice" of creation, rather than to the tempest and the thunder of destruction. During the siege of Paris, in 1870, the Prussians cut down the trees of his beloved Ville d'Avray for firewood. This was one of the great tragedies of his life.

"In the midst of the battles," he wrote, "I took refuge in painting." In painting and in the singing of the birds. "The concert of the birds! Compared to that, and Nature's quietudes, what are the little, unenduring tempests made by man?"

Throughout the tempest of the Franco-Prussian War he remained calm, attending to his own business of creating beauty, befriending and being befriended. Though in his middle seventies at the time, he refused to grow old. He expected, as he said, to reach the age of one hundred and four. He had an insatiable appetite for work. At the age of seventy-seven he still climbed the four flights of stairs to his studio on the Rue Paradis Poissonière. In the winter of the following year one of his dearest friends, D'Aligny, died. There was a blizzard during the funeral at the cemetery of Montparnasse. But the old painter, with the snow whipping into his white hair, refused to leave until the end of the ceremony.

At last his health began to give way. He still went regularly to his studio—not, however, to paint, but to be among his beloved pictures. "If I only had the strength now!" he said to his friend Robaut. "You have no idea of the things I could paint . . . I see what I have never seen before. New tints, new skies, new horizons . . . Ah, if I could show you these immense horizons!"

Three weeks later, on February 22, 1875, he passed on to these new horizons. "In spite of myself," he said just before he died, "I go on hoping . . . I hope with all my heart there will be painting in heaven."

MILLET

Great Paintings by Millet

Baltimore, Walters Collection: *Potato Diggers, Breaking Flax.*

Boston, Museum of Fine Arts: *Girl Spinning, Harvesters Resting, Homestead at Gréville, The Reapers, The Sower, Portrait of Himself.*

Chicago, Art Institute: *Bringing Home the Newborn Calf, The Rail Splitter, The Sheep Shearers.*

Cincinnati, Taft Collection: *Mother and Child.*

Copenhagen, Carlsberg Museum: *Death and the Woodcutter.*

Harvard University, Fogg Art Museum: *The Shepherdess.*

New York, Frick Collection *Woman with a Lamp.*

New York, Metropolitan Museum of Art: *Autumn, The Garden, The Woman with a Rake.*

Northampton, Smith College Museum: *The Farm at Gréville.*

Paris, Louvre: *The Angelus, The Gleaners.*

Paris, Luxembourg: *The Goose Girl, Potato Planters.*

Philadelphia, Pennsylvania Museum of Art: *The Pig Killers.*

St Paul, Hill Estate: *At the Spinning Wheel.*

San Francisco, Museum of Art: *The Man with the Hoe.*

Toledo, Museum of Art: *The Quarriers.*

Jean François Millet

1814–1875

THE TIME—the middle of the nineteenth century; the setting—
Paris. This was the Paris of reaction. The Bourbons had returned to the throne after the fiery fiasco of the Napoleonic upstart. This was the France of pain. Twenty years of financial
misery, dictatorship, military murder. Pain in the pocket for the
masses of people; pain in the body; pain in the spirit. Many of
the art students in Paris had flocked to the masterpieces of
Michelangelo in the Louvre. For they felt a spiritual kinship to
these fellow creatures in marble born of pain. Jean François
Millet was one of the most promising of these art students. And
he was peculiarly sensitive to Michelangelo. When he chanced
upon this titan's painting of a dying man he wrote to a friend,
"I felt myself like him, tormented by death. I pitied him, I
suffered in the same body with the same limbs." Most people
see only ugliness in suffering. They are repelled at the spectacle
of pain. But a few people are raised to the heights of religious
and aesthetic exaltation at the experience of misery. They find
lips of the spirit with which to feed upon the substance of sorrow
and to transform it into beauty. Such a man was Millet, painter

laureate of *The Man with the Hoe, The Sower, The Gleaners, The Angelus*, native of Normandy, child of a peasant and son and heir of poverty. Among the French artists of the nineteenth century he stands out as the patron saint of pessimism, a man who found inspiration in the sadness of human existence.

"You are sitting under a tree," he wrote, "feeling all the ease, all the tranquillity that can possibly be enjoyed; and suddenly you see some poor figure laden with a fagot come toiling out of some little path." This is the fagot of human suffering, carried by the humblest of peasants on his patient quest for the spark that may transmute it into the singing flame of hope. It was in the daily routine tasks of the peasant, for whom the very issue of existence, the very question of life and death was decided by the vagaries of the soil, that Millet found the supreme drama of humanity. The stage for the epic tragedy was the stretch of level, endless, sunsoaked land of Normandy, and the actor was the peasant at work, unceasing, uncomplaining, devout. There was irony and pity in this devotion of the peasant. A spectacle to move an artist to prayers and tears. "Ah, my child," the village priest had told Jean François when he was very young, "you have a heart which will give you a great deal of trouble; you don't know how much you will suffer." And Jean François fulfilled the prophecy.

II

EARLY in Jean François' life there had been a tragic shipwreck on the Normandy cliffs at Gruchy. It was All Saints' Day; Jean François and his parents were at their worship in the little village church. A sailor, drenched to the skin and with bits of sea ice clinging to his face, rushed suddenly up to the altar and cried out that a ship had hit the rocks. They all hurried down to the seashore. They saw men and mastheads sliding up and down the mountainous waves. They heard desperate calls for help.

They got down on their knees and prayed as the wind lashed down upon them. Jean never forgot the faces of those men and women as they knelt in prayer. Often, in his later years, he voiced the sentiment of Michelangelo that the birthdays of human beings should be regarded not as days of joy but as days of mourning. Once he greeted the New Year with the toast, "Here is another year finishing tonight. How sad! I wish all of us as few years as possible!" The critics took his paintings to task for the absence of joy in them. Joy? He knew none. He was a peasant. He had been brought up by a simple, stoic grand-mother, by a father who died at an early age of overwork, by a mother who died in sorrow because her son Jean François, who was away painting at Barbizon, couldn't afford the railroad fare to her bedside. "The joyful aspect of life never appears to me. I do not know what it is. I have never seen it. The most cheerful things I know are calm and silence."

Mon Dieu, but the winter months in Barbizon were cold! Millet spent most of his adult life in this "province for painters." He lived in a small barn heated by a wood stove. Twenty-seven years! He had a patient, uncomplaining wife to support. "Grand old woman," he said of her tenderly. And children, "the little toads," with mouths to feed. How hard the winter was to bear when your paintings weren't selling, when you were forever on the brink of starvation. Yet he wouldn't sacrifice the winter for the spring. To be unable to behold the sadness of the fields and the woods in winter would be too great a loss for the artist. He was not a philosopher. He did not wish to do away with the bitterness of life or to find a formula that would make him stoical or indifferent. Pain is perhaps what gives the artist the strongest power of expression. "Art is not a diversion," he said. "It is a conflict, a complication of wheels in which one is crushed."

III

As A YOUNG MAN he had sketched a few charcoal pieces at night
after a hard day's toil in the fields of his native home. These
sketches had excited the admiration of a third-rate artist who
lived in the vicinity. From then on Millet was aware that a
farmer's career was not for him. Art was his business, his mission,
his very religion. The friendly artist interceded with a committee
in Paris to vote him a scholarship. Millet left his home and went
to the capital. But as soon as he got there a great longing for
the countryside seized him. He had arrived in "black, muddy,
smoky Paris," as he called it, one snowy evening in January.
The traffic of the carriages, the street lights deluged with fog,
the narrow lanes and the dirty hovels sent the tears rushing to
his eyes. To check a sudden burst of sobbing he threw over his
face handfuls of water from a street fountain. That made him
feel better. After all, he was here on a religious pilgrimage. The
last words of his grandmother, a stern, stately, chaste Catholic
with the soul of a Puritan, now came back to him. "I would
rather see you dead, my child, than rebellious and unfaithful to
God's commandments . . . Remember, you are a Christian before you are an artist."

It is precisely this quality in Millet's art that the critics have
seized upon. They say that he was more of a Christian than an
artist. Take, for example, his well-known study of *The Gleaners*.
Three peasant women are gleaning in the fields, mechanically,
wearily, under a hot, blazing midsummer sun that scorches the
land with its devastating rays. In the background a group of
harvesters pile up the golden grain. A farmer, mounted on a
wagon, supervises their work. Two of the women gleaners,
dressed respectively in red and blue kerchiefs, are bent over,
fumbling with their fingers in a dumb, uncomplaining way for
the stubble. A third woman stands up to ease the strain, perhaps

to wonder, for a moment, what cruel law it is that has condemned her to such suffering and toil. But after this momentary
flash of insight, after this partial kindling of the divine fire which
promises to turn this clay into something human, it is apparent
that she will take her place beside the others and bend her back
once more. "In the sweat of thy brow shalt thou earn thy
bread."

When Millet painted *The Gleaners* he was forty-three. For
many years he had sent his pictures to the salons of Paris, only
to be rejected again and again. His work was not palatable to
the aristocrats. They would have nothing to do with a man who
held the plow and tramped over the soil and the manure of
Barbizon. When Millet had joined the art class in Paris the
sophisticated, urbane pupils had sneered at his manners. A few
of them, more outspoken than the rest, had become acquainted
with the strength of his fist. Partly in derision, partly in admiration, they had nicknamed him the Wild Man of the Woods.
And the Wild Man of the Woods he remained throughout his
life. "I will never be made to bow," he said. "I will never have
the art of the Parisian drawing rooms forced upon me. A peasant
I was born, a peasant I will die."

And so he had settled with his wife and his children in a
rambling hut in Barbizon, at the edge of the great forest. He
dug and painted in his garden and brought up his family on the
barest level of subsistence. He knew the peasants that he
painted. He was their brother and a close intimate of sorrow and
despair. In spite of the fact that his living expenses were almost
negligible, he was unable to meet them. At one time he wrote:
"I really don't know how I'm to fulfill my obligations and go
on living." There were days when he didn't have two francs in
his pockets. It was with a great deal of tenderness that he
painted *The Gleaners*. He was quite familiar with the hardships of
the French peasant. Yet the public greeted this painting with a
chorus of derision. Referring to the figures of the three gleaners,

one critic remarked: "These are homely scarecrows set up in a field: M. Millet's ugliness and vulgarity have no relief." To this outburst Millet could have replied that even in things homely there is a goodness which is beyond the comprehension of a blind critic. Some of the critics called in question the technical aspects as well as the spiritual quality of the painting. The field in which the gleaners are working is bathed in a presumably hot, intense August sunlight. Yet the tonal finish is a murky, dull, ashen blue which suggests a haze. One of his defenders, however, explained this, pointing out that "the August sun sheds a powerful warmth upon the canvas. You will not find any of these capricious rays which gambol like holiday schoolboys in pictures by others. This is a grave sunshine which ripens wheat and makes men sweat and does not waste its time in frolics." Millet was a poet of the somber colors—of the woods, the twilight, the shadows. "If you were to see how beautiful the forest is!" he said. "I run there sometimes at the end of the day when my work is over and come back every time crushed. The calmness and the grandeur are appalling; so much so, that I find myself really frightened. I don't know what those rascals of trees say to one another, but that is because we don't talk the same language." Yet the language of his paint, at times, came mighty close to an understanding of the language of Nature.

When *The Gleaners* appeared he was accused of being an agitator. The bourgeoisie believed that he was trying to make the peasants class-conscious, that he was encouraging a social revolution through his personal hatred of the propertied classes. Hatred? "The mission of art is a mission of love, not of hate," he replied. Was he concerned about the emancipation of the peasant from the soil? He himself was a peasant of the peasants. The idea of the eternity, the timelessness, the divinity of man in his chosen occupation, made him desirous of painting the peasant not as he might be but as he actually was—doomed, preordained to till the soil forever without any dream of, or desire for, a social change. Politics, revolution, socialism? "What has art to do with those things? Art will never come except from some small, disregarded corner where an isolated and inspired man is studying the mysteries of nature."

But the critics refused to see. "The three ugly fates of pauperism"—that is what they nicknamed the three gleaners—"the battle cry of Jacobinism and Revolution." "My critics," Millet replied, "are, I imagine, people of taste and instruction; but I cannot put myself into their skins. I have never seen anything in my life except the fields, and I try to tell simply, and as best I can, what I have seen." Theatrical, that is what his painting is, they charged. He strove after melodrama. But melodrama was the farthest thing from the mind of Millet. "The Luxembourg Gallery has given me an antipathy to the theater," he replied. "I have always had a marked dislike for the exaggerations, the falsities and the simperings of actresses and actors." Well, then, at any rate—insisted the critics—he bubbled over with cheap sentimentality; he gushed with the brush! This accusation, like the others, Millet emphatically denied. His own God was Michelangelo, and Michelangelo had once remarked to the Prince of Holland, "Good painting will never draw a tear." How, then, did *The Gleaners* come to be painted? What is the essence of Millet's art?

"Remember, Jean François, you are a Christian before you are an artist." That is what his grandmother had told him just before he had set out for the art schools of Paris. "Up, up, my little François," were the first words he had ever remembered from her. "If you only knew what a long time the birds have been singing the glory of God." And the last words she had ever breathed remained clearly etched upon his memory. "Paint, paint for eternity, and think that the trumpet which will call you to Judgment is always on the eve of sounding."

Jean François Millet was a man of religion. In him there was no message of protest, no plea for social readjustment. "In the sweat of thy brow shalt thou earn thy bread." An immovable fate that never will change. He was brought up on the Bible. He saw, in the incessant struggle of man with the soil, a significance not social, not political, but primarily religious. He was a simple and solitary man of God. His entire object was to show the beauty of life in the sad grind of hard labor. Millet loved life for its very sadness. It was the winter in his soul that made him love it thus. His character had been nourished on the Scriptures and on the winds that lashed the seacoast of his native Gruchy.

The Scriptures, the sea storms, and the poetry of Virgil and Homer. He read these two ancient singers assiduously. They were closer to him spiritually than most of his contemporaries. The men and the women that he painted in *The Gleaners* were not merely subjects for social tracts or mute and inglorious clodhoppers, poor, mistreated, miserable creatures of common clay. They were, like the soldiers of Virgil and Homer, heroic characters in a great poem, the greatest of all poems—the Epic of Life.

IV

FROM BARBIZON Millet wrote to his Paris friends that their life of festivity could not compare with the experience of one who lived, like him, in a little thatched hut. When he took his evening walks he would run his eye over the dilapidated roofs of the rambling country cottages; the chimneys releasing their smoke into the quiet air; the evening stars shining down from the clouds after a splendid sunset; and below, the outlines of human forms returning slowly from the fields . . . And in 1859, two years after *The Gleaners*, he dipped into the memories of these experiences and painted *The Angelus*. Here is a description of the painting, from the graphic pen of Paul Gsell:

"In the middle of the fields a young peasant and his wife have just finished their day's work. Some sacks of potatoes are loaded upon a wheelbarrow. The mists of the twilight are stealing over the field. Away on the horizon is a village. The steeple of the church and a few cottage roofs are discernible through the gathering gloom. Suddenly the far-off music of the Angelus comes floating on the tranquil air. Silent and motionless, the two occupants of the scene stand lost in religious contemplation. The man, baring his head, stands awkwardly holding his hat in his big, toilworn hands; the woman clasps hers reverently together and both of them bow their heads. How poor and uncouth is their appearance! To look at them, you would think they were both compounded of the soil that clings about their wooden clogs. Nevertheless, in the stillness of the twilight, darkly silhouetted against the fading splendor of the sunset, their forms dominate the scene. The world of nature is melting away into the deepening shadows of the night and ceases to overwhelm them with its immensity. They are no longer two poor, lonely folk, but two souls whose prayer fills the infinite."

This painting, not long after Millet's death, was sold for a quarter of a million dollars. But in 1859, when the artist had just completed it, he had reached the very depths of poverty. "We have only enough fuel to last us for two or three days," he wrote, "and we don't know how we are going to get any more; for they won't let us have any without money . . ." The idea of suicide haunted him. But he put it away from him; instead he drew the sketch of an artist lying dead at the foot of his easel and of a woman crying out in terror, "Suicide marks dishonor!"

This was one of the few rebellious periods of his life. When he had been unable to raise the fare for the visit to his dying mother he had thrown up his hands in despair. "I am nailed to a rock and condemned to hard labor without end!" And now, when poverty once more crushed him helplessly down, he departed for once from his usual objectivity and painted the bitterness of his despair in *The Man with the Hoe.*

He clearly anticipated the sensation that this picture would create. "*The Man with the Hoe,*" he wrote to a friend, "will get me into hot water with a number of people who don't like to be asked to contemplate a different world from the one they're used to, who hate being disturbed out of their serenity." Rarely has a picture occasioned a greater storm of abuse on the one hand, or a more fanatical outburst of praise on the other, than this portrayal of a harassed and hopeless toiler of the fields who pauses for a moment to lean on his hoe. "Bowed down with the weight of centuries," wrote Edwin Markham in the poem inspired by this picture, "the emptiness of ages in his face." The mind of the man has been killed by the generations of hard labor imposed on him and all his class. There is a vacant, meaningless stare in his eyes. All character in his face has been snuffed out. He has been dragged down to the level of the beast. "Certain wild animals," said La Bruyère, speaking of such men, "may be seen scattered over the country, male and female, black, livid, and burnt up by the sun, bound to the earth, in which they poke and fumble with invincible obstinacy; yet they have a kind of articulate speech, and when they rise upon their feet—lo—they show a human countenance, and indeed are men."

Critics shuddered at the painful realism of the work. No one before had ever dared to shake this fellow from his obscurity—this peasant with the hoe, back bent, skull elongated like a pear by the long, ceaseless toil, vague, glazed eyes untouched by any thought—dumb, stolid beast of the plowshare. "Millet must have looked some time before he found such a type," wrote one of the critics in scorn. "Such types are not commonly met with even in idiot asylums. Imagine a monster with an imbecile grin upon his face, planted all awry like a scarecrow in the middle of the field. No gleam of intelligence gives a human touch to this brutish thing thus taking his rest. Is it work or is it murder he has been doing? Is he turning up the ground or digging a grave?"

People saw socialistic propaganda in the picture. *The Man*

with the Hoe was typical of the great masses of agricultural work-ers who had toiled in the fields of France for ten centuries with-out a murmur. And now had an artist arisen to give them a voice?

Yes and no. For once Millet had put a sermon into his paint-ing. The Man with the Hoe is a patient servant doing God's work in His cathedral of land and sky. "Is the work these men do the sort of futile labor that some folks would have us be-lieve?" he challenged. "To me at any rate it conveys the true dignity, the real poetry of the human race." Yes, poetry, but *tragic* poetry. The tilling of the fields, the painting of pictures, the writing of hymns—these noble works have to be done. But why such bitter sorrow in the doing?

V

BUT SORROW did not remain with Millet forever. At last he was able to thrust the wolf from the door. *The Sower, The Gleaners* and *The Angelus* had converted a small but influential group of people to the religion of his art. These people were neither baffled nor frightened by his realism. A brother artist, Theodore Rousseau, was one of the first to recognize the genius of this painter of the world's patient sadness. When Millet was going through his struggles Rousseau had bought one of his paintings for a few hundred francs, and to avoid embarrassing him he had pretended that a wealthy American had been the purchaser. Another friend had raised, by means of a raffle, a sufficient sum of money to pay his rent and butcher's bills. Alexandre Dumas wrote glowing articles about his work, and finally a wealthy collector agreed to advance him a thousand francs a month in return for Millet's entire output for a period of three years. During this time he produced a series of pictures dealing with the everyday scenes of domestic life. In one of these pictures a little girl is learning to take her first steps. Her mother has pushed her gently in the direction of her father, who is a few feet away. He has thrown down the spade and stretched out his arms to receive the child. In another of the pictures a peasant woman holds her infant on her lap and blows on a spoonful of soup which is too hot for the child to swallow. Her hand encircles the child and presses it gently toward the spoon. In a third picture a mother holds a sick baby close to her breast. Abandoned toys lie scattered all around. The father stands awkwardly, a look of anxiety in his face, afraid to approach the bed, for he feels that he is too clumsy to be entrusted with so fragile a thing as a sick child.

Millet was himself the tenderest of fathers. "Yes," his friend Rousseau remarked, "Millet works hard for those that belong to him. He exhausts himself like a tree that produces too much blossom and fruit; he wears himself out to keep his children alive." On one occasion Rousseau sent Millet's children a basket of toys and sweets. The happy father wrote of the "frenzied enthusiasm" with which his little "toads" had opened the present. "Imagine beings who lack the power to express themselves with their tongues and whose most vehement and spontaneous excitement can command only shrieks and stamps, and you will have but a faint idea of what it was like."

During the day, whenever the sounds of the children at play came to their father's ears while he was at work in his studio, he would rush up to them, kiss them and tell them anecdotes. While he worked his door was never closed. Yet all the children, even the very youngest, lowered their voices and walked on tiptoe whenever they chanced to pass it. "Sh—Papa is working," they would caution any visitor who was careless about showing the same respect. At night they would all sit around the supper table with tumbled hair and merry faces. Millet, like a patriarch in some ancient saga, sang songs of his childhood on the farm at Gruchy. He wore a noble beard. "His bushy hair fell about his shoulders like a mane, and his ample forehead told of the vigor of his mind," writes Paul Gsell. A contemporary artist called him "a Jupiter in hobnailed boots."

Complete public recognition came to this patriarch painter in 1867, when he was fifty-three. He won a gold medal from the Academy of Arts. One year later he received the sweetest gift from the hand of Fate—and the cruelest blow. He was awarded the decoration of the Legion of Honor and he lost his dearest friend, Rousseau. Stricken with paralysis, this "more than brother" died in his arms.

For six more years he created beauty, and then he too went to his Sabbatical rest. And it was a welcome rest. His soul had been moved to despair by the turbulent events of his last seven years. Louis Napoleon and Bismarck had concocted between them a needless war. The French had been beaten decisively. Paris had been starved into surrender. The workers had risen in revolt and had been massacred by the military. These events overwhelmed Millet, who had been brought up to believe in the Bible as literal truth. "O sword of Satan," he cried, "wilt thou never be sheathed?"

It was a crimson sunset that preceded the evening of his life. Cruelty, suffering, death. A few days before the end, in the season of Christmas, a stag pursued by bloodhounds had taken refuge in his garden, where it died from its wounds. "Poor, dumb animal," said Millet. "His death is indeed a symbol. It tells me that my end is also near."

Millet's end came on a midwinter day in 1875.

VI

DURING THE DARK PERIOD of his poverty Millet had seemed to himself, as he said, like a man "who sings true but with a weak voice . . . and who is hardly ever heard." But the voice grew strong, until one day it became the mighty cry of the soil—the elemental, primordial earth out of which everything springs, to which everything returns. The soil—the Eternal Creator, the Eternal Destroyer. As Michelangelo once said, "All of us are merely lumps of clay brought slowly into life," and—Millet would have added—crumbling slowly into death.

The art of Millet is the true art of simple grandeur. It depicts a solemn, epic struggle—the conflict of Man with the earth from which he has sprung. His helplessness in the face of its cruelty, his adoration in the presence of its mystery. There is a grim humor to all this, the spectacle of Man struggling with his fate. It is a sardonic jest on the lips of the gods that the poet and the painter have been endowed with eyes to behold Man in this piteous struggle and with hands to translate this struggle into beauty. A bitter gift, this flower of art that grows out of the seeds of suffering. But, yet, a sublime gift. For, as the artist translates sorrow into beauty, he transmutes beauty into hope. And, to paraphrase an old aphorism, *while there's hope, there's life.*

It is with prophetic as well as with poetic justice that Millet has been called "the Dante of the Yokels, the Michelangelo of the Clowns."

VAN GOGH

Great Paintings by Van Gogh

Boston, Museum of Fine Arts: *The Postman.*

Chicago, Art Institute: *The Midday Sun, Montmartre, Still Life, Van Gogh's Bedroom.*

Detroit, Institute of Arts: *Portrait of Himself in a Straw Hat.*

Kansas City, Nelson Gallery: *The Olive Grove.*

London, Courtauld Institute: *Portrait of Himself.*

Moscow, Museum of Modern Art: *Cottages at Auvers, Landscape after Rain, The Prison Yard, The Red Vineyard, Shrubs.*

New York, Lewisohn Collection: *L'Arlésienne.*

New York, Metropolitan Museum of Art: *Landscape.*

Paris, Louvre: *La Guingette, Restaurant de la Sirène.*

Philadelphia, Johnson Collection: *The Flower Vase.*

Philadelphia, Tyson Collection: *Sunflowers.*

St Louis, City Art Museum: *The Staircase.*

Toledo, Museum of Art: *The Wheat Field.*

Washington, Phillips Memorial Gallery: *The Garden at Arles.*

Vincent van Gogh

1853–1890

Vincent van gogh was born in Dutch Brabant eight years before our Civil War. At the age of sixteen he had completed his school education and was headed for a business career. He became an assistant to one of the leading art dealers of Europe—a certain Goupil, who had galleries at The Hague, in Brussels, London, Paris, Berlin and New York. Vincent packed the photographic reproductions of famous paintings and occasionally tried to sell the originals to wealthy patrons of art. But he was signally unsuccessful as a salesman. He was by nature shy and most unbusinesslike. He wore his clothes poorly and carried about him the manners of an uncouth Dutch peasant. He didn't know how to get along with people. He was too honest, too outspoken. One day he committed an unpardonable blunder. He quarreled with his employer and told him strange things—for example, that he hated business, that bargaining for pictures was a sin, that making money in art was legalized cheating. The employer gave him a month's salary in advance and told him never to show his face again.

II

VINCENT went to England and secured a job as a teacher of French in a small London boarding school. He was fairly well educated, and he loved children. His parents were relieved to find him in what they supposed would be a congenial situation for him. And for a time Vincent himself felt contented, in spite of his meager salary. The pupils of this boarding school came from the slums of London. They were dumped into the school by irresponsible parents who never even considered whether they could pay the bill. At the end of each semester the vicar who headed the school sent Vincent to the parents to collect the money. The young man walked through muddy streets, he knocked on rickety doors, he entered ill-smelling tenements. He prepared to make his demands to pinched and hungry men and women. But when he saw the sorrow in their eyes, the lines of suffering around their mouths, he turned on his heel and left without a word. He returned to the vicar empty-handed. That worthy gentleman flew into a rage. What business had this young tutor to be victimized by his own foolish sentiment? He told Vincent van Gogh to get out. And Vincent went.

III

HE RETURNED to his parents. They were disheartened and disillusioned about him. What was to become of this good-for-nothing oldest son of theirs? The poor fellow couldn't hold onto a single job. They shook their heads sadly. However, a third opportunity presented itself to Vincent. He went to work in a bookstore. Afternoons, when he got through with his work, he browsed through the old Dordecht museum and feasted his eyes on the masterpieces of art. This at last seemed to be the life he was fitted for—a life of pictures and books. His employer, too, felt that this lonely young book clerk, with his ingrowing soul, might possibly succeed if given a chance at some profession. Accordingly he asked one of his clergyman customers to write a letter to Vincent's parents urging them to send their boy to college. Once again the hopes of the parents were aroused. Vincent went to Amsterdam and, taking up his lodging with an uncle, began to prepare for the entrance examination. He studied Latin and Greek under a Jewish rabbi—studied so assiduously that he had a nervous breakdown and was unable to take the examination. During his convalescence he amused himself by frequenting a number of churches and dreaming while the services were being held. On Sundays he would attend six or seven religious houses of every denomination, including the Hebrew synagogue. Once, under the stress of a great spiritual emotion, when the collector's plate was passed around he threw in his silver watch. At another time he threw in his gloves. He was seized with a desire to go out and preach the gospel. He suddenly imagined himself Christlike. Having read about the sordid lives of the miners in the Belgian coal fields, he decided to save the souls of these miners. Forgetting that his own suffering family was depending upon him for financial support, he rushed to the aid of the sufferers in Belgium. His father, an intensely religious man, swallowed his disappointment and gave Vincent his blessing. His mother sent him a trunkful of knitted clothes and words of love.

Vincent prayed among the miners and brought a little light into their eyes. He lived in the house of a barber and spoke simple messages with forceful gesticulations of his hands. He had no theological training at all, but that did not matter. He dressed the wounds of the men and the women who were injured in the accidents at the bottom of the mines, and when a typhoid epidemic broke out he moved into an empty hut in the coal fields in order to be nearer to his stricken fellows. He gave his money and his clothing and his food in this crusade against typhoid. The local baker and his wife wrote to his parents that he had broken down in health, that he was killing himself. "The young man is unlike anybody we have ever seen." They begged his parents to come and fetch him home before it was too late. The father took the first train to Belgium and pleaded with his son to return with him. At first Vincent refused. But when the baker gave him a solemn promise that he would carry on the work Van Gogh finally consented.

IV

VINCENT was now twenty-eight and the loneliest of men. He began to paint—who knows by what impulse!—completing sketches he had drawn of the Belgian miners. He had slight technical knowledge. He drew like a boy of twelve, covering the paper with awkward scrawls. He had a younger brother, Theo, who liked his work and began to encourage him. What an impression the people in the Belgian coal fields must have made on Vincent! Theo told him to paint the pictures of the people he knew best—those humble, dirty, sad, inarticulate waste products of humanity. Vincent had before him a vision of Millet's *Reaper*. It was his guiding inspiration. He told his brother Theo that he would rather see "a homely woman by Israels or Millet or an old woman by Edward Frère" than a picture of Phryne or Venus. "For of what use is such a beautiful body as that of Phryne? The animals have it, too, perhaps even more than men, but the soul as it lives in the people painted by Israels, or Millet, or Frère, that is what animals never have."

While Vincent was pondering over the mystery of the soul he met a cousin from Amsterdam and entered upon his first serious love affair. The woman was a widow with a child. She was older than Van Gogh and utterly indifferent to his attentions. Moreover her father was hostile to the suit of a man of thirty who had drifted all his life and who apparently possessed no capacity for

making a living. He shut his daughter up in her room and refused to give Vincent access to her. In desperation Vincent put
his outstretched hand into the flame of a candle. "Let me see
her only for as long as I can hold my hand in this flame," he
pleaded. The father blew out the candle and sent Vincent about
his business.

"In order to work and to become an artist," he wrote to
Theo, "one needs love." But it was not merely physical love
that he cherished. It was love from someone who could understand him well enough to free him from his great loneliness.
For he was forced to grope alone. He left his parents and set
himself up in a studio in The Hague, where he became the
friend and the pupil of Mauve. The friendship ended unhappily,
however. Mauve suggested that Vincent should copy some plaster casts in order to perfect his technique. But Vincent would
not think of imitating others. He would paint his visions in his
own crude way or not at all. He threw down Mauve's plaster
casts and rushed out of the studio.

And then, for a time, he found love. "I have met her at last,"
he wrote to Theo. "She is not young, not beautiful. She is rather
tall and strongly built. Her hands are not the hands of a lady,
like those of K (his cousin), but the hands of one who works
hard . . . She stood at the washtub. We talked about everything,
about her life, about her cares, about her misery, about her
health. . . . Is it a sin to love, to need love, not to be able to live
without love? To me, a life without love is a sinful and immoral
thing." Vincent was seeking for a new symbol of beauty, not the
joyous beauty of Venus but the sorrowful beauty of a "half-
faded woman, on whose face is written as it were: *Life in its
reality has left its mark here.*" Had he not, perhaps, within him a
spark of that divine power to regenerate a Mary Magdalene?

For a time this Magdalene returned his love, and then they
went their separate ways. He returned to his studio and to his
lonely quest for the unattainable. He worked fourteen hours a

day in his studio. Theo had received a position in Goupil's art business, and he sent Vincent a monthly allowance with which to buy his paint and to pay his models. When a child modeled for him he would give it an apple. Old men were sure to receive plugs of tobacco. He worked in a sloppy blue blouse. His beard was never shaved; his red hair was never combed. His eyes were heavy and inflamed with overwork. He made a study of water colors and analyzed cartoons in the newspapers. In the cartoon he found the life and personality he had been looking for. The cartoon was racy folklore in line and color. He sent his drawings to Theo, hoping that his brother might be able to interest Goupil in them. But to no avail. Terseeg, an authority on art, advised him to quit, since he was doomed to fail. People abhorred the rough, lazy scrawl of Van Gogh's brush in which misery was written large. They wanted pretty little portraits to hang in their parlors, exquisitely finished landscapes—not cartoons of grief. On one occasion an artist asked a young lady of fashion who was looking at a Van Gogh canvas, "What do you think of his art?" "I am glad you call it art, Mr Gabriel," answered the young lady.

V

STILL ON HIS QUEST, Van Gogh met a woman who had been deserted by her lover. She was about to have a child. "I could not afford to pay her the full wages of a model," Vincent wrote to his brother, "but that did not prevent me from paying her rent; and, thank God, I have been able thus far to protect her from cold and hunger by sharing my bread with her . . . She is slightly pock-marked, and so she is not beautiful any longer . . . That is just the reason why she is useful to me." He mentions rather naïvely that the woman has certain peculiarities that make her repulsive to others. "First, the language she uses; then, her temper. However, Theo, I intend to marry this woman, to whom I am attached and who is attached to me. I want to go through the joys and sorrows of domestic life, in order to paint them from my own experience. . . . One feels best what love is when sitting near a sickbed, sometimes without a cent of money in one's pocket. It is no gathering of strawberries in the spring."

With the money Vincent received every month from his brother he nursed the woman along in her pregnancy and sent her finally to a maternity hospital in Leyden. He was past thirty and far too disillusioned with life to love the woman passionately. What he felt for her was something far stronger than passion. Between them was the sensitive bond of mutual, if mute, under-standing. He too, like her, was an outcast struggling through life alone. This poor, stupid, uncomplaining woman was a fit mate for him. "I intend to marry this woman, Theo . . . Nobody cared for her or wanted her; she was alone and forsaken; and I have taken her up and have given her all the love, all the tender-ness, all the care that was in me." He asked Theo whether this would bring about a change in their friendship. Would Theo mind the unconventionality of the situation? Theo replied that such a marriage would be a great blow to the family, that finan-cially it would be impossible, that morally it would be a catas-trophe. And Vincent answered simply that as far as the moral issue was concerned, the child the woman had given birth to "takes away all the stain from her. I respect a woman who is a mother." By way of answer to this, Theo sent Vincent a hundred and fifty francs. And Vincent washed the baby and cared for the mother. As the child grew older it climbed on the artist's knee and watched him paint with large curious eyes.

Van Gogh was happy in his work. But nobody bought it, and his wife began to resent their poverty. And so they starved and shivered and quarreled and brawled. Finally his wife packed up with her child and returned to her house of prostitution. Vincent went to the hospital where he was treated for a venereal disease that he had contracted from the woman he had tried to

[*241*]

save. For weeks he lay in bed and screamed in agony. Somewhere in his studio stood a simple sketch of a woman—naked, lean and middle aged, who squatted in silence with her head buried in her hands. A few strands of thin, matty hair ran down her spare back. The veins stood out on her legs. Underneath this portrait of his wife was the title in a single word—*Sorrow*.

VI

"YES, I think it is the tragedy, the history of great men," Vincent wrote Theo. "They not only meet obstacles during their life, but usually they are dead by the time their work is publicly recognized." Vincent was still undergoing his formative process as an artist. He had become more and more convinced that the great message in painting was not design but color. And this color must on no account be the *handmaid* of design; it must be the *design itself*. Nor must the color be static; it must be vibrant and dynamic. Once, seeing a landscape that he wished to paint but being out of funds for the lavish pigment he was in the habit of using, he took some kitchen dye and grindings from a coffee-pot. With these he painted the scene in all its natural hues.

Nowhere, however, could he dispose of his paintings. "At times I sit on the dunes, where I sketch with a faint feeling in my stomach because I can't get enough to eat," he wrote Theo. His brother continued to send him money without a murmur. Once, in a sardonic mood, Vincent wrote him that in the artists' section where he lived there wasn't a single painter who could afford to pay the taxes on his studio. "Twice the tax assessors have come to my house," he writes, "but I showed them my four kitchen chairs and rough deal table. Since then they have left me alone." At another time he wrote to Theo: "As to my clothes, I wear what has been given me; I have worn clothes from father and from you which sometimes do not fit as they ought, because of the difference in our sizes."

At this period he painted *De Ardappeleters*—the picture of a peasant's hut in which the family is shown eating a meal of potatoes. The painting is somber and full of a Rembrandtesque spirit. But, as a rule, Vincent sought for other effects. He sat in the sand dunes and sketched in the heat of the noonday sun. "To paint the blazing sunlight, and to render the vanishing of the planes in the infinite, is a thing that makes one dizzy to attempt." Another love affair is mentioned in his letters—this time with a girl who had been "originally a specimen of great value," but who now resembled, "a Cremona violin which had been spoilt by bungling repairers." The love affair, as usual, ended unhappily. The girl made an attempt on her life with poison. A scandal was averted by discreet family handling. Clearly Vincent in his thirties was still a problem child. He painted and starved and loved with an equal gusto. "I am prejudiced against women who wear dresses," he stated impatiently one day. He was at the time engaged in a study of the female nude. And because of lack of funds he found it difficult to obtain models. Meanwhile he was slowly maturing in his art. He had at last defined his goal. "Away with the old Renaissance masters! Away with the anatomy that is academically correct and artistically lifeless! We want anatomy that lives! Away with the insipid, cheerless studio colors! Most painters don't know a healthy color. They don't know life. If I paint peasant women, I want them to be peasant women." Harlots must be harlots. "My thoughts these days are full of Rembrandt and Hals"—and the lovely Dutch girls! "What an impression these girls make on me! I long to paint them even more than I long to possess them, though indeed I should like to do both." He painted and possessed them and neglected everything else. He neglected his stomach; he failed to have a hot meal for weeks at a time. He neglected his teeth. One by one they broke off, causing his mouth such intensity of pain that he swallowed his food quickly to keep from screaming aloud. Doctors warned him to ease up in his work or he would suffer a nervous breakdown. He urged his brother Theo to give up his job at Goupil's and to share with him a studio in Paris, believing that Theo had the makings of an artist in him. But Theo was far too practical a man to consent. Vincent went to Paris, studied the French impressionists and met the artist Gauguin. And then the warm winds of southern Arles lured his restless spirit. Arles was a land of riotous color. When the painter from the North, brought up in cold bleak landscapes among pinched peasant faces, opened his eyes on the profusion of flowers and the sparkling complexion of the Arlesiennes he would have been no more amazed if he had stepped into a magic city of the Arabian Nights. He had always been interested in Japanese landscape prints with their bright, assertive colors. Now it seemed to him that he had walked into the Japan of his dreams. Here was a country of pink blossoms and sparkling fountains and rose-colored peach trees. The women were beautiful, no humbug about that! They drank absinthe, those adorable little enchantresses of the South, and made love with a passion unexcelled in the North. Here was a wonderland under a hot, blazing sun. And Vincent was the man to paint it. He painted ten flower gardens in as many days. He painted a drawbridge crossed by a cart against a deep blue sky and orange-colored banks. His brush fairly burst into flame. He painted trees that "became possibilities which might give birth to a hundred other trees." He painted sunflowers that looked as if they would dissolve into light. To capture a few precious drops of the sun, that is what he must do! Brighter and brighter became the colors on his canvas, till they set his nerves atingle and the blood surging to his head. He drank alcohol incessantly, to keep himself in the state of excitement proper to paint the wild, exotic visions of his mind. He smoked continually, starved himself in his haste to keep on painting, painting, fourteen to seventeen hours a day. There was a demon inside him that drove him on. Always at this time he painted when the sun was at its greatest heat, for it was at this time that the colors of the landscape were most riotous and most fantastic to behold. The heat touched his brain, made him dizzy beyond belief. He went to bed every night with the hot rays of sunshine slowly etching their way into his reason. He plastered the walls of his studio with paintings of sunflowers and a series of pictures called *The Poet's Garden*. Gauguin arrived from Paris to share this studio with him. And Vincent was supremely happy. Occasionally a cloud passed over the horizon when he thought about the sacrifices Theo was undergoing to support him. What an angel of a brother! Sent him a hundred and fifty francs a month religiously, to keep his body and soul together. Once, in a fit of repentance, Vincent had written Theo: "Don't you realize that I should far rather give up painting than see you killing yourself to make money?" But enough of that! Give up painting! He was only joking, of course. He was only being heroic. And Theo was too kind to take him at his word.

Vincent continued to paint and to spend his evenings in the cafés. He bought himself a set of false teeth and he went to the brothels regularly. In his heart remained the painter's dream. Someday there would come upon the earth the "painter of the future," who would be such a colorist as had never yet been seen. And this dream repaid him for his hunger and his poverty and his rags. He asked his brother one day for a little extra money with which to buy a mattress "because," as he wrote naïvely, "I've been swindled by my landlord." Another time he wrote expressing Gauguin's great joy and gratitude to Theo for disposing of one of his pictures at fifty francs. On still another occasion he wrote that he was becoming hopelessly absent-minded. "If the storm within me gets too loud, I take an extra glass to distract me . . . My concentration becomes more intense, my hand more sure. That is why I dare almost swear to you that my painting will improve—*because I have nothing left but that.*"

Is this the end of the quest? A man of thirty-five, alone and dissipated beyond cure? Where is the beauty he has been seeking all these years? What has become of the evangelist who one day rebelled against a career in business and rushed to preach the gospel among the soul-hungry miners? "Often whole days pass without my speaking to anyone except to ask for dinner or coffee." Where is the faith that once moved him to take into his home a prostitute and to work for her regeneration? "I am dazed with the sun and the strain of managing large canvases." Where is the harvest long overdue? Where is the pure essence of his genius, after the patient years of strain and distillation through the alembic of his poverty and his suffering? "All I have to show is a carcass pretty well ruined and wits pretty well crazed for life . . . It has cost you, Theo, fifteen thousand francs which you have advanced me." Theo cautioned him against his excessive drinking. For, during these days, Vincent was hardly ever sober. And the World? Unfortunately it was only too sober. "Do you call this art?" gasped the young lady of fashion. And all the graybeard critics laughed in chorus.

VII

VINCENT became obsessed with the idea that he would not be alive come many more years. He felt he was going crazy. That hot sun of Arles! Those blood colors on canvas! The suffering, the starvation! Vincent speaks often of insanity and points out how many great men have fallen victim to it. These men sacrificed their wits to realize their ideal. "Our new painters are treated like madmen by society, and because of this treatment they actually become so." Or—"The more I am a crackpot, by so much more am I the artist." Still again—"The doctors will tell you that not only Moses, Mahomet, Christ, Luther, Bunyan and other religious leaders but also that artists like Franz Hals, Rembran and Delacroix were mad. Where, then, are the sane people?"

Indeed, the lodgings of Van Gogh and Gauguin were the lodgings of madmen. The two artists painted together, discussed art together, got drunk together and hurled wineglasses at each other. They would discuss the Impressionists, the Symbolists; they would fight over Delacroix, Daumier, Pissarro; and they would rush out of the studio without speaking to each other for days. Gauguin was a giant of a man. He had thrown over a tidy little fortune and had rushed to the South Sea Islands to paint and to live with the native women. Somewhere in Denmark he had left a wife. Now, on his return to France, he spent his time losing money at billiards, tramping through the museums and painting masterpieces. He was indifferent to money; he was indifferent to men. He was fascinated, however, by Vincent's sunflowers and brothel scenes. Vincent, in turn, admired Gauguin. The two artists applauded each other and cursed each other and were ready, for a time at least, to defend each other with their lives.

Vincent continued to mix his orange with his purple, his flaming yellows with his dazzling greens. He must steep the canvas with the burning sun, the wind-swept air, the pulsating shadows. He lived on ship's biscuit, milk and eggs and spent his brother's money on paints. He painted the night life in a café. "I have tried to express the terrible passions of humanity by means of red and green," he wrote Theo. "The room is blood red and dark yellow, with a green billiard table in the middle; there are four lemon-yellow lamps with a glow of orange and green." He painted fourteen sunflowers on a green-yellow ground. "My dear Theo, I am ravished, ravished with what I see. I went away to go on with a picture of a garden in sunshine. Then I brought it back and went out again with a black canvas, and that also was finished." Pale, sulphurous sunshine, pink houses with violet shutters! "I feel a relation between my colors and the music of Wagner. Sulphur and lilac! These colors give me extraordinary exaltation . . . I have no thought of fatigue."

He did the outside of a café, "with a terrace lit up by a big gas lamp in the blue night, and a corner of starry blue sky. I am not conscious of myself any more, and the pictures come to me in a dream . . . Just now I am not ill, but I should get ill without the slightest doubt if I did not take plenty of food and if I did not stop painting for days at a time . . . I have a fixed intention not to paint for at least three days . . . Perhaps I shall rest myself by writing . . . My last canvas is a row of green cypresses against a rose-colored sky, with a crescent moon in pale lemon . . . I am nearly dead with the work of the past week . . . I have just slept sixteen hours at a stretch, and it has restored me considerably . . . But I did a good week, truly, with five canvases." Thus he wrote on December 18 of the year 1889. And on December 21 a telegram was rushed to Theo summoning him in haste to Arles. Vincent, in a state of terrible nervous agitation and raging fever, had slashed off a piece of his own ear and had brought it as a present to a brothel girl. Theo took the first train and found Vincent lying unconscious in a hospital. He had gone mad in a tempest of waving oleanders and rose-colored skies.

VIII

HE RECOVERED from the attack and for a while seemed to be himself again. He went to the brothel girl and apologized for having sent her a piece of his ear in a fit of fever. She didn't mind; nobody minded. There had been similar cases. Everybody in Arles was a little bit mad. The south wind, the fantastically colored flowers. "I hope I have had simply an artist's freak," he wrote to Theo. He went back to work at his studio, this time without Gauguin. Gauguin had acted strangely about the whole thing. The day after the attack he had left Arles for Brittany and had washed his hands of the friendship. Vincent continued to paint. He was still weak and he suffered from insomnia. The only way he could sleep was by placing a dose of camphor under his pillow. The doctors assured him that he had merely cracked under the strain of hard work, that it was only a temporary ailment. They told him that such attacks often came to very impressionable people. To be sure, during the first days of his recuperation he had been haunted by continuous hallucinations. But these hallucinations had been reduced to a few nightmares a week by dint of his drugging himself with bromides. He begged the doctors to let him work full blast again. Why all this consultation and all this uncertainty? "Either shut me up right away in a madhouse—I shan't oppose it in case I'm deceiving myself—or else let me work with all my strength. . . ." That delirium of his, in which everything he dearly loved had been shaken, he refused to accept as a reality.

In February, a month after his discharge from the hospital, Vincent was taken to the hospital once more. He had imagined that people wished to poison him. As a matter of fact, ever since his first attack his neighbors had crowded around the windows of his studio and had pointed in whispers at the "madman." Whenever Vincent appeared at the window to get some air he was greeted with the shout, "Madman! Madman!" He was hounded by these outcries continually. "Look at the pictures he has painted—an insult to humanity! Look at his mutilated ear!"

He was released from the hospital once more. He wrote to Theo and urged him not to worry about his condition. "Again let us try to gulp it down, whatever it is. And I shall get along better if I know you have peace of mind."

Yet a couple of weeks later he returned to the hospital. Theo went wild with anguish, but he received no news. The doctors maintained a strict silence. Finally, in March, Theo received a letter from Vincent. "I seem to see so much brotherly anguish in your kind letters that I think it my duty to break my silence. I write you, in full possession of my faculties, not as a madman but as the brother you know. This is the truth." He then went on to explain that a number of his neighbors had delivered a petition to the mayor describing him as a man unfit to be at liberty. Whereupon the inspector of police had given the order to have him locked up in a cell. "You understand what a staggering blow between the eyes it was to find so many people here cowardly enough to join together against one man, and that man ill. Especially so, since I had done my best to be friendly with people and had no suspicion of their hatred." Well, was he not a madman who lived in a yellow house and plastered his walls with blinding pictures of sunflowers? "I told the mayor that I was quite prepared to throw myself into the water if that would please these good folk once for all; but that in any case, if I had inflicted a wound on myself, I had done nothing of the sort to them." He pleaded that if he went permanently insane people would not "meddle with me when I am busy painting, or eating, or sleeping, or taking a turn at the brothel since I haven't a wife. Now they are meddling with everything."

The doctors blamed it all on the coffee and the alcohol. But what else could he do? "To attain the high yellow note that I attained last summer, I really had to be pretty well strung up." The artist is a man with work to do, even if he loses his body and his mind in so doing. The true artist must sacrifice everything— health, happiness, personal respect, even life itself, on the altar of his art.

Vincent, however, was not by nature a martyr. "You must put aside any idea of sacrifice in this," he wrote Theo. "All through my life, or most of it anyhow, I have sought for something other than a martyr's career, for which I am not fitted. If I find trouble or cause it, I am honestly aghast at it."

When they were ready to dismiss him from the hospital again, he startled Theo by announcing that he desired to take up his residence at the St-Rémy institution for the insane, since he hated the idea of returning to his studio alone. He hoped the authorities of the institution would give him a room in which to paint to his heart's content. That was all he required. Meanwhile Theo must forgive him if his correspondence became slack. "I do not know whether I shall write very often henceforth, because not all my days are clear enough to enable me to write logically." Theo must not waste any pity on him. "In a way, it is only fair that having lived some years in comparatively good health, we should have our share of bad health sooner or later." Of course he would not have exactly chosen madness. But, after all, what was the ultimate difference between one sickness and another? "And as for my future, it is not as if I were twenty, Theo. I have turned thirty-six. And who knows? In spite of all, I may still have a number of almost normal years ahead of me . . . Oh, my dear Theo, if you could only see the olive groves just now!" At times, however, depression seized him. "If I were without your affection, Theo, my sufferings would drive me without remorse to suicide. . . . There is a point at which we have a right to protest against society and to defend ourselves." Theo was beside himself with grief. He was about to get married. He now needed for household expenses the allowance that he was accustomed to send Vincent every month. Vincent begged him to keep the money for himself and not to spend any more on his painting. For the chance of success, the chance of his ever gaining recognition as an artist, was now ridiculously slight. Indeed, he was convinced that an irresistible power had frustrated him at every step. There was but one thing left for him— to go to an insane asylum. And Theo had better not worry over him. "It is only too true that heaps of painters go mad. I shall always be cracked, but it's all the same to me. They have lots of room here in the hospital; there would be enough to make studios for a score or so of painters."

In the month of May he was admitted to the asylum of St-Rémy. He was given a room in which to paint. He covered his canvases with bright colors as a score of madmen looked on and helped him mix the paints. Vincent was very tender to his fellow inmates. "Though there are some who howl or rave continually, most of them get to know one another very well, and they help one another when their attacks come on." He described himself as a person who hardly had any hope or desire left in his heart. As for his painting, "it is only too doubtful whether painting has any beauty or use. But what is to be done? There are people who love nature even though they are cracked or ill; those are the painters." They must go on painting! A demon drives them on. "I have a cornfield very yellow and very light, perhaps the lightest canvas I have done. And the cypress is always occupying my thoughts."

Several days after this letter he suffered another attack. When he recovered he received good news. Theo's young wife had given birth to a baby boy. In addition Theo had sent him an article published in the *Mercure de France* by a young man of letters, Aurier, who went into a rhapsody on Vincent's pictures painted at Arles. He called Vincent the "torchbearer" of the new age and spoke of his colors in glowing metaphors. As Vincent read the article tears settled in his eyes. He wrote M. Aurier and told him that he was very grateful for the kind words but that they had been addressed to the wrong man. He explained that he owed everything to Monticello, who was the founder of the school of color at Arles. He urged Aurier to pay a visit to Goupil's and to look at some of Monticello's pictures of flowers. "And then, my dear sir, you will be able to give credit where credit is due."

Shortly after that Van Gogh went to Arles on a leave of absence from St-Rémy, and while painting there he was seized with another attack. They found him raving in the fields. His throat was so swollen he couldn't eat for four days. These attacks! "Abominable," he wrote to Theo in desperation. But he must continue his career as a painter. Painting, he felt, was an absolute essential for his recovery. And it was intolerable to remain idle for weeks, as the doctors ordered. They gave him very little hope for the future. They forbade him to do any work during his convalescence. They expected the attacks to return again and again. He read a good deal of Shakespeare and Voltaire to keep his mind in order. But he insisted on painting too. "I must paint were it only studies of cabbages and salads, for only through painting can I regain my sanity." During some of his attacks he lost consciousness for days, and in his periods of lucidity they forced him to sit behind barred windows for hours on end without moving a muscle. The doctors were interested only in stuffing him with food and getting him fat. He begged them to give him some manual work with which to engage himself. Perhaps he could learn the trade of blacksmith or carpenter. Finally, however, they allowed him once more to take up the brush. He made a study of the mad ward. What a perfect cycle he had completed! A study of the starving Belgian miners at twenty-five. A study of the suffering madmen of St-Rémy at thirty-seven.

He left the institution in March 1890. And for a time his life was happy. He became the godfather of Theo's little boy. Theo and his wife came often to see him. He took long walks with little Vincent, his nephew, and showed him the cows swishing their tails as they were milked and the roosters crying, "Cock-a-doodle-do."

And one fine day a great calm came over him. It was like nothing he had ever before experienced. Gone was the agitation of the spirit and the mad demon that had possessed him from his earliest childhood. He felt as if he were released from some great duty. He wrote Theo, "I am in a mood of nearly too great calmness to paint. . . ."

And then suddenly, on July 29, 1890, he put a bullet through his body. The end of the quest.

WHISTLER

Baltimore, Hatton Collection: *The Fish Wife*.

Boston, Museum of Fine Arts: *Little Rose of Lime Regis, Portrait of Rose Whistler*.

Chicago, Art Institute: *Battersea Bridge, The Silver Sea, Water at Southampton*.

Cincinnati, Art Museum: *Seascape*.

Cleveland, King Collection: *The London Fog*.

Detroit, Institute of Art: *Portrait of Himself*.

Glasgow, Corporation Art Gallery: *Portrait of Thomas Carlyle*.

Harvard University, Fogg Art Museum: *Sunday Morning, Domberg*.

London, National Gallery: *Cremorne Lights, The Little White Girl, Nocturne in Blue and Silver*.

London, Tate Gallery: *Nocturne in Blue and Gold—Old Battersea Bridge*.

New Orleans, Henderson Collection: *Chelsea Fruit Shop, Maud, The Red Note*.

New York, Frick Collection: *The Ocean, Portrait of Rosa Corder*.

New York, Metropolitan Museum of Art: *Cremorne Gardens, Connie Gilchrist*.

Paris, Luxembourg: *The Artist's Mother*.

Philadelphia, Pennsylvania Museum of Art: *Grand Canal in Venice—Moonlight*.

Pittsburgh, Carnegie Museum: *Portrait of Sarasate*.

Washington, Smithsonian Institution: *The Frozen Thames, Nocturne in Gray and Silver—Chelsea Embankment, Portrait of the Artist*.

Wellesley, Mass., Farnsworth Museum: *Study in Rose and Gold—The Neapolitan Girl*.

Worcester, Art Museum: *The Fur Jacket*.

James Abbott McNeill Whistler

1834–1903

WHEN James Abbott McNeill Whistler was a cadet at West Point he was very poor in chemistry. One day, at an oral examination, his professor asked him to discuss the properties of silicon.

"Silicon," began Whistler, "is a gas——"

"That will do, Mr Whistler," barked his examiner.

It was with no feeling of regret that Whistler was dismissed from the military academy for failure in chemistry. "Just think of it," he said many years later. "Had silicon been a gas, I would be a major general."

Imagine Whistler confined within the discipline of a military unit! Imagine the hurricane bottled up in a glass jar. The life of a soldier would have been the very last career in the world for this undisciplined, irrepressible, self-assertive and iconoclastic citizen of half a dozen countries. Born in America and educated in Russia, he lived at various periods in Italy and in the Netherlands and for the greater part of his life in France and in England.

His father, at the time of Whistler's birth (on July 10, 1834), was a civil engineer living in Lowell, Massachusetts. The nature of his work had turned his family into a tribe of gypsies. They were always on the go—from Lowell, Massachusetts, to Stonington, Connecticut; from Stonington, Connecticut, to Springfield, Massachusetts; and from Springfield, Massachusetts, to St Petersburg, Russia. James was eight years old when his family arrived in this imperial city of vanity, vodka and vice. Here he absorbed the elements of religion from his mother, who began the daily routine for her children with a recitation from the Psalms, and the rudiments of art from the teachers of the Imperial Academy. Throughout his life, religion and art remained his two absorbing passions. Though rarely a churchgoer, he was always a profound worshiper. His studio was his shrine, and his canvases were devout prayers of the brush—hymns of adoration to the glory and the beauty of the world.

His religion, however, unlike that of his mother, was pagan rather than Puritan. It was a religion of gaiety. In fair weather or foul, in the brief moments of his prosperity as well as in the long days of his hunger, he wore this gaiety of his like a boutonnière. His gaiety and his profundity. A symphony in white and black. Like so many of his paintings. Whistler was one of the supreme jesters and at the same time one of the most observant philosophers of the nineteenth century. Jesters, as Gilbert K. Chesterton reminds us, are the most serious people in the world.

The most serious and the most unpopular. Even as a child he shocked the Russian officials and caused his mother no end of anxiety with his double-edged tongue and his cynical laughter— a crackling *ha! ha!* that struck at the vanity of his listeners like the sudden explosion of two firecrackers. His mother warned him that he would lose his friends with this too effervescent cynicism of his. "Who cares for such friends?" he retorted, and his mother shook her head. There was no stopping her little Jamie' overbubbling spirit.

This overbubbling spirit was his most striking characteristic at the Pomphret School in Connecticut, whither his family had returned after the death of his father in 1849. It was his outstanding characteristic at West Point. "What!" cried his history professor. "Do you mean to tell me you don't know the date of the Battle of Buena Vista? Suppose you went out to dinner and the talk drifted to the Mexican War, and suppose someone asked you, a West Pointer, the date of the Battle of Buena Vista? What would you do?"

"Do?" replied Whistler. "Why, I'd have *nothing* to do with people who could talk of such things at the dinner table."

Good riddance, cried the authorities at West Point when Whistler was dismissed from the academy. No use trying to make a soldier out of a youngster with a sense of humor like that!

II

FOR A SHORT TIME he worked as an engraver of maps at the United States Geodetic Office. But he interspersed his geographical sketches with the caricatures of his superiors. He was told to go. The United States, he was advised, was no place for him. There was only one fitting spot for a queer fellow like him—the city of Paris.

And to Paris he went. He took his gaiety to the gayest of all places, the Latin Quarter, and soon became its guiding spirit— the unceremonious master of ceremonies to the bohemian vagabondia, the "no-shirt brigade." Taking a room up six flights of stairs, he "pawned his coat and ate his washstand and his wardrobe," as he explained to a solicitous friend, dressed like nobody else, flirted with the grisettes, led the dances at the students' balls and won the reputation of being the "Idle Apprentice of the Parisian Loafers." But this reputation was undeserved, for Whistler loved to paint as well as to play. Dressed in his loose black blouse, his broad-brimmed felt hat in his hand, he would sit for hours in the Louvre before a painting by Velasquez, studying, absorbing, measuring every line, analyzing every tint, memorizing beauty. It was during these years that Whistler acquired his prodigious visual memory. He knew a Velasquez painting by heart just as thoroughly as Toscanini knows a Beethoven symphony by heart. He learned to transcribe from memory every last technical nicety and tonal gradation of the pictures that he studied at the Louvre. And he made perfect copies of some of these pictures—copies that it was hard to distinguish from the original.

It was not, however, as a copyist that Whistler was eager to excel. For his genius was individual, unconventional, unique. Even in his earliest pictures, *At the Piano* and *The Little White Girl* for example, we find this individualistic note that makes a Whistler so unlike any other painting in the world. *At the Piano* is the picture of a woman in black, who plays at the piano, and of a little girl in white, who listens to the playing—a semiscientific, semimystical study in contrasts, a symphony of music in color. We find the same color symphony in *The Little White Girl.* This, too, is the half-realistic, half-poetic portrait of a woman, "Jo" Heffernan, the Irish girl who served him as a model and faithful companion for a number of years. In this picture the girl is seen in profile, with loosened hair, leaning languidly against a mantelpiece in front of a mirror, from which the reflection of her face looks back at the spectator. It is a study in white and red—the white muslin dress and the sad white face of the girl, the white mantel, the red hair, the red lacquer box on the mantelpiece and a spray of reddish pink azaleas that serve as a decorative arrangement on the canvas. There are bits of other colors, too, in the picture—a blue-and-white vase on the mantel and a Japanese fan of various tints that the girl holds at her side. But the white and the red predominate. When Swinburne saw *The Little White Girl* for the first time he was moved to translate into words the haunting effect of this picture:

WHISTLER

Come snow, come wind or thunder,
High up in the air
I watch my face and wonder
At my bright hair.
Naught else exalts or grieves
The rose at heart that heaves
With love of our own leaves, and lips that pair.

I cannot tell what pleasures
Or what pains were,
What pale new loves and treasures
New years will bear,
What beam will fall, what shower
With grief or joy for dower.
But one thing knows the flower, the flower is fair.

Whistler was deeply touched at this tribute, and he had the verses inscribed upon the frame of the picture. "I watch my face and wonder at my bright hair." This, in a sentence, is the keynote to the art of Whistler—Nature contemplating itself in the mirror and holding its breath at the reflection of its own beauty.

III

THE ACADEMIC WORLD was slow to recognize the genius of Whistler. Rejected by the Paris Salon, he was obliged at first to exhibit his pictures at the Salon des Refusées. Here he was in good company. For side by side with his own pictures hung the paintings of some of the greatest French artists whose work the academicians didn't possess the necessary stature to understand. The exhibition of the *Refused* was artistically if not financially successful. Napoleon III sponsored it, and the Empress Eugénie and the entire court came to see it.

Whistler was now becoming recognized in Paris as an unusual though incomprehensible painter. But, while his ears were filled with praises, his pockets still remained empty of money. He decided to seek his fortune in London.

His arrival in England was a bombshell. His gaiety scattered the fogs of London—and frightened the Londoners. They could understand neither his art nor his personality nor his clothes. They were scandalized one summer morning when he appeared on the streets with two umbrellas in his hands—a white and a black. When asked for an explanation he said that in the treacherous weather of London he wanted to be protected both against possible sunshine and probable rain. They called him a mountebank, a charlatan, a poseur. He was all of these things, but he was also a superb painter. And in his painting there was nothing of the charlatan. Indeed, those who knew him most intimately insisted that he assumed an insincerity in his behavior in order to startle an indifferent world into an appreciation for the sincerity of his art.

And after a time he succeeded. At first the people laughed at his eccentricities. They pointed him out as one of the "characters" of London—a character that seemed to have stepped out of the pages of a Dickens novel. They sniggered at his oversize topcoat, his long bamboo cane that looked like a fishing pole, his tieless but otherwise immaculate evening dress at the theater, the white lock of hair which he had combed and twisted into an exaggerated prominence. They came to his exhibitions, at which he strutted about with an impish pomposity, half king and half clown. And little by little they turned their gaze from the amazing artist to his amazing art. Amazing but sincere. *Amazingly* sincere. Genuine as a coin of the purest gold. Nothing of the poseur in that inspired priest who had sat worshiping upon the banks of the Thames, memorizing beauty, etching into his soul the very essence of the night, the starlight throwing a shimmer of blue and silver magic over the Battersea Bridge, the Wharf at Wapping or the Black Lion Wharf. Silent symphonies and sonatas, out of which the Earth speaks her secrets to the understanding heart. Not a single wasted line or false color or dishonest thought in these painted fragments of the Psalm of Life. If ever there was a serious and sincere painter, that painter was the Whistler of the Nocturnes. Or the Whistler of those other new glimpses into the human soul—the portraits which he called his Symphonies in White, in Gray and Green, in Rose and Purple, in Black and Gold, and those two supreme achievements in portraiture, the *Arrangements in Black and Gray*. These two *Arrangements* are the famous portraits of Carlyle and of Whistler's mother. Impatience and Serenity in old age. The man of the world, weary, disillusioned, cynical, disgusted with a life that promises so much and gives so little; and the woman in the home, tireless, hopeful, devout, contented with a life that brings the bitterness of mortality and the joys of motherhood. Philosophers, both of them. The one an apostle of mystical wisdom, the other a purveyor of homespun common sense. Carlyle, the worshiper of heroes; Matilda Whistler, the lover of children.

These two portraits, like most of the other paintings of Whistler, are so simple that they seem to have been dashed off with a few inspired strokes of the brush. But they are the result of long and painstaking labor. Tennyson, the master of the facile phrase, was once asked how he managed to round off such perfect expressions with such unpremeditated ease. "Unpremeditated?" said the poet of the Round Table as he puffed away at his pipe. "Why, man"—pointing to the first line in his *Crossing the Bar*, with its almost childlike simplicity—"it took me twenty pipefuls of tobacco to write this single phrase."

There is the simplicity of ignorance and the simplicity of genius. It took Whistler many anxious hours to acquire the "easy effortlessness" of his style. During the time that he was painting the portrait of Carlyle he was also engaged upon the portrait of a child, Miss Alexander. One day the old man and the little girl met at the door of the studio. Carlyle had just got through with a sitting, and Henrietta Alexander was coming in for one. The aged philosopher looked at the child, shook his head and murmured: "Puir lassie! Puir lassie!" And no wonder he sympathized with her. For the child was compelled to have seventy sittings before Whistler was completely satisfied with his job.

And yet there were times when, in spite of all his labor, he was unable to please his disgruntled sitters. He possessed too uncanny a faculty for bringing out their true character. To such people, whenever they presumed to criticize his work, his tongue was no more flattering than his brush. "Do you call this a good piece of art?" asked one of his sitters insolently. "Well," replied Whistler with a diabolical grin, "do you call yourself a good piece of nature?"

IV

WHISTLER FOUGHT HARD, just as he played hard and worked hard. He was merciless to his critics, especially to those whose criticism he considered either stupid or unfair. The dean of the British art critics, P. G. Hamerton, wrote a caustic review about one of his paintings, *Symphony in White No. III*. "A Symphony in White indeed! . . . Why, one of the girls has a yellowish dress and a bit of blue ribbon . . . She has reddish hair, and, of course, there is the flesh color of the complexion." This sort of unenlightened judgment was more than Whistler could bear. "Bon Dieu!" he wrote to the editor of the *Saturday Review*. "Did this wise person expect white hair and chalked faces? And does he then, in his astounding consequence, believe that a Symphony in F contains no other note, but shall be a continued repetition of F F F? . . . Fool!"

He never started a fight. But he never avoided one if somebody else started it. He hated salaciousness. But he also hated prudery. One of the Anthony Comstocks of the London Academy, a man by the name of Horsley, had attacked the practice of painting nude models from life. Whereupon Whistler painted a nude and sent it to the British Artists' Exhibition. Underneath the picture he wrote the words: "*Horsley soit qui mal y pense.*"

He ridiculed stupidity wherever he found it—among his students as well as among his critics. Some of his students came to him not because they had talent to paint but because they wanted their friends to admire their paintings. For these insincere worshipers in the temple of art he saved some of the keenest shafts of his wit. One of his students persisted in smoking a pipe while he painted. "Young man," said Whistler, "you had better stop painting. For you might get interested in your work and then your pipe would go out." Another student, a young lady, took exception to his criticism of her work. "Mr Whistler," she said, "I paint what I see." "Yes," he replied, "but wait till you see what you paint!"

Sometimes he turned the defense of his sarcasm into the weapons of a counterattack. This was especially true when his critics became abusive as well as destructive. When he exhibited his now famous *Nocturne in Black and Gold*—the picture of a skyrocket bursting through the night—he set upon it a price of two hundred guineas. Whereupon John Ruskin, usually so fair in his criticism, published the following injudicious attack upon this painting:

"For Mr Whistler's sake, no less than for the protection of the purchasers, Sir Coutts Lindsey ought not to have admitted works into the gallery in which the ill-educated conceit of the artist so nearly approached the aspect of the wilful imposture. I have seen, and heard, much of cockney impudence before now; but never expected to hear a coxcomb ask two hundred guineas for flinging a pot of paint into the public's face."

Enraged, and justly so, at this uncalled-for stab in the back, Whistler sued Ruskin for libel. During the cross-examination at the trial the attorney general, counsel for the defendant, tried to badger Whistler. It was a battle of wits.

Attorney General: Can you tell me how long it took you to knock off that *Nocturne?*

Whistler: I beg your pardon?

Attorney General: I am afraid that I am using a term that applies rather perhaps to my own work . . .

Whistler: As well as I remember, it took me about a day . . . I may have still put a few more touches to it the next day if the painting were not dry. I had better say, then, that I was two days at work on it.

Attorney General: The labor of two days, then, is that for which you ask two hundred guineas?

Whistler: No, I ask it for the knowledge of a lifetime.

Whistler won the case, but it was merely a moral victory. The judge ordered Ruskin to pay Whistler the compliment of an apology and nothing more.

V

WHISTLER made friends easily and easily lost them. "I'm always being asked out to dinner," he said, "but I'm never asked to the same house twice." One of the men with whom he dined frequently, however, was Oscar Wilde. Whenever they got together their associates knew that they were going to be treated to a duel of wits. For Jimmie Whistler and Oscar Wilde had the two sharpest tongues in the British Isles. A critic in the London *Times* wrote a striking if not altogether accurate summary of the difference between the two men: "With a mind not a jot less keen than Whistler's Oscar Wilde had none of the convictions, the high faith for which Whistler found it worth while to defy the crowd. Wilde had posed to attract the crowd. And the difference was this, that, while Whistler was a prophet who liked to play Pierrot, Wilde grew into Pierrot who liked to play the prophet."

Whistler was not quite so saintly nor Wilde quite so devilish as they are painted in this clever little study in contrasts. In reality they were both of them very human individuals who heartily enjoyed a laugh at each other's expense. And, more often than not, it was Whistler who got in the last laugh. His humor was more spontaneous, less polished, more explosive and more original than that of Oscar Wilde, who frequently borrowed his best bon mots from his friends. "Heavens," cried Oscar Wilde at one of Whistler's most effective epigrams, "I wish I had invented that!" "You will," replied Whistler dryly.

Once, in a heated argument, Oscar remarked, "As for me, I take my good where I find it." "Excellent," retorted Whistler. "This epigram needs but the change of a single word to make it perfect. What you ought to have said is this: 'I take *his* good where I find it.' "

A writer in *Punch* once referred to the wide range of the subjects discussed in the conversations of these two foremost London wits. Oscar, who was in Exeter at the time, sent the following wire to Whistler: "*Punch* too ridiculous—when you and I are together we never talk about anything except ourselves." Whereupon Whistler wired back: "No, no, Oscar, you forget— when you and I are together we never talk about anything except me."

Whistler's thrusts at Oscar, though sharp, were good-natured as a rule. They tickled rather than stabbed. But Oscar's sallies at Whistler were frequently ill-tempered as well as sharp. His arrows had poison at their tip. Whistler could never forgive that insulting epigram of Wilde's which all London was only too happy to adopt as its own: "With our James," said Wilde, "vulgarity begins at home; would that it might stop there."

Cut to the quick by this clumsy stab, Whistler parried the blow with another of his pungent thrusts: "A poor thing, Oscar, but for once, I suppose, your own."

The friendship between Whistler and Oscar Wilde, like most of the other friendships of Whistler, broke up in the end. To a lady who complained of the trouble that her friends gave her Whistler remarked: "Do as I do, madame, lose them."

No other man in England, indeed, had so perfect a talent for losing friends. He suffered from the consequences of an excessive honesty. "Suffered," however, is hardly the word. He actually *enjoyed* the consequences of his honest frankness. One of the gayest satires of the nineteenth century is his little pamphlet entitled *The Gentle Art of Making Enemies*.

VI

AND SO HE PAINTED, and exhibited, and entertained, and won friends and lost them, and defied the critics, and lived now in London and now in Paris, and attracted a small but enthusiastic school of artists who were blessed with "musical eyes," and began to make a comfortable though far from lavish livelihood, and at last, at the age of fifty-three, he took a wife. He married her on August 11, 1888.

The marriage was very happy but all too brief. His wife died of cancer just three months before their tenth wedding anniversary.

Whistler was never the same after the death of his wife. Gone was the old gaiety. Rarely now did he fling his head back in that cynical staccato laughter. It was a sadder and wiser man who gazed at the Thames out of the windows of his lodgings at the Savoy. He rarely sought the company of his fellows now but sat painting and etching the restless river as it drifted back and forth before his eyes. The Thames was a screen upon which the procession of life passed in constant review, and Whistler recorded the most arresting moments of that eternal procession. To the end he remained true to his calling—the calling of the painter prophet—to turn science into an art and art into a science. All art, he said, ought to be treated as a science, "the science of the beautiful." It was but another way of formulating the immortal idea of John Keats: "Beauty is truth, truth beauty." That is all, said Whistler, that any artist needs to know.

And now that he was drawing toward his own twilight Whistler became more than ever enamored of the night. He expressed this deep emotion that he felt for the night in words that are almost as supreme as his paintings:

"And when the evening mist clothes the riverside with poetry, as with a veil, and the poor buildings lose themselves in the dim sky, and the tall chimneys become campanili, and the warehouses are palaces in the night, and the whole city hangs in the heavens, and fairyland is before us—then the wayfarer hastens home; the workingman and the cultured one, the wise man and the one of pleasure, cease to understand, as they have ceased to see, and Nature, who, for once, has sung in tune, sings her exquisite song to the artist alone, her son and her master—her son in that he loves her, her master in that he knows her."

VII

HE SPENT the last few years of his life in a hopeless search for health. He went to Bath, to Corsica, to Holland; he took an occasional sea voyage; but his lost youth was nowhere to be found. Occasionally a flicker of the old fire would break through the ashes of his waning life. One day, at a lecture, he met a critic who in the past had done his best to keep him down. "Come now, Mr Whistler," said the critic, "be a gentleman and shake hands with me." Whistler drew himself up and with the old sarcastic ring in his voice replied: "It is because I am a gentleman that I refuse to shake hands with you."

But these outbursts became more and more sporadic. The fire was dying out. He who had never been afraid of life was now terribly afraid of death. He couldn't reconcile himself to the thought that so much of his remembered beauty must remain unrecorded. More and more his painting was now being interrupted by long sieges in bed. He was at work on a picture called the *Daughter of Eve*. He had felt ill for some time. For the spring of 1903 was cold, and the fogs of London had penetrated to his very marrow. But as the month of July brought summer days he rallied. On the seventeenth he ordered a cab for a drive. When he returned he sat down to work. A few minutes later the brush fell out of his hand.

He was refused the honor of a burial at Westminster Abbey. But he received a greater honor. For his body was laid to rest at the Old Chiswick Graveyard, the same burial ground which holds the remains of William Hogarth. And Hogarth was the man whom Whistler had always worshiped as the supreme painter of England.

RENOIR

Boston, Museum of Fine Arts: *The Grand Canal, The Seine*.

Chicago, Art Institute: *Chrysanthemums, Fruits of the Midi, Picking Flowers*.

Cleveland, Coe Collection: *Flowers in a Vase, Three Bathing Women, The Walk on the Seashore*.

Detroit, Institute of Arts: *Graziella*.

Harvard University, Fogg Art Museum: *At the Milliner's*.

London, Institute of Art: *La Loge*.

London, Tate Gallery: *The Umbrellas*.

Merion, Pennsylvania, Barnes Collection: *The Meadow on the Seine, The Spring*.

Minneapolis, Institute of Art: *Battledore and Shuttlecock*.

Moscow, Museum of Modern Art: *The Lady in Black, Reverie*.

Naugatuck, Connecticut, Whittemore Collection: *The Duck Pond, The Girl with the Cat*.

New York, Metropolitan Museum of Art: *Madame Charpentier and Her Children, On the Seashore*.

Northampton, Smith College Museum: *Madame Edouard Maître*.

Paris, Louvre: *The Bathers, Portrait of Madame Charpentier*.

Paris, Luxembourg: *Moulin de la Galette, The Reader, Two Girls at the Piano*.

Philadelphia, Pennsylvania Museum of Art: *Portrait of Mme Renoir*.

Philadelphia, Tyson Collection: *Bathers*.

St Louis, City Art Museum: *Portrait of the Artist's Father*.

San Francisco, Crocker Collection: *Prickly Pear and Flowers*.

Toronto, Art Gallery: *The Seine at Chatou*.

Washington, Duncan Phillips Gallery: *The Picnic Party at Lunch*.

Pierre Auguste Renoir

1841–1919

H̲E̲ W̲A̲S̲ A̲ S̲H̲Y̲ L̲I̲T̲T̲L̲E̲ M̲A̲N̲. His underlip thrust itself forward
and placed his entire mouth into a perpetual pout. His upper lip
and his chin were covered with a ragged tuft of hair. His cheeks
were sallow and wrinkled and gaunt. His entire face was what
you would expect of a tired old painter of seventy-eight—all but
his eyes. They were large and luminous. They shone far too
brightly for a man on the verge of eighty. They were more like
a child's. They burned with a fire that seemed to shrivel up the
yellow skin about them. They looked as if they would never be
stilled when the time came for death, as if they would return to
haunt the earth long after the rest of the body had been placed
away.

The old man sat in a wheel chair. He was all crumpled up like
a piece of ancient parchment. He was tortured with rheumatism.
Operation after operation had been performed on his feet, his
legs, his arms. His hands were twisted and thin, like the gnarled
roots of a dying oak tree. His fingers were deformed and useless.
Bands of linen were strapped over the palms to prevent the
fingernails from imbedding themselves in the flesh. A brush

rested between the thumb and the forefinger of the right hand. Painfully the old man moved his brush over a canvas on an easel before him. A few pecks with the brush, and then, to avoid reaching for a clean brush, a dip with the one he was using into a bottle of turpentine. The movement of the hand was perfunctory, mechanical, ghostlike. It moved through no strength of its own. It was the eye that lent its power to the hand. It was with the eye that Renoir painted, recording much of what he had seen and suffered. He had seen his sons, Jean and Pierre, go off to war against the Kaiser. Now they lay wounded in a hospital somewhere at the front. He had looked a short time ago on the sweetest and gentlest of wives for the last time. He had beheld the mystery of death and the misery of life. And now at last, after many years of searchings and sorrows, he had penetrated to the heart of nature. He had caught a glimmer of the truth—the unity of the human spectacle upon the stage and the directing of God behind the scenes. As the body of the painter grew weaker and more shapeless every day, the immortal part—the watchful, comprehending eye—had peered through the stained-glass window of its inspiration into the gigantic cathedral of immortality. And it had found there what it had always expected to find. For kneeling in prayer at the altar was a little child.

II

THROUGHOUT HIS LIFE Renoir had the spiritual temperament of a child. When he was asked how he managed to create his splendid colors he replied: "I don't know. I arrange my subject as I want it, and then I begin to paint—just like a child, if you please." Though there was a definite method to his artistic madness, there was no rigid formula, any more than there is a rigid formula for a child's expression of his happiness. He painted his canvases, as the child pours forth his laughter, out of the healthy superabundance of a joyous spirit. His art was as spontaneous as the formation of a snowflake, the growth of a flower, the song of a bird.

He was born (February 25, 1841) at Limoges. When he was four years old Renoir père, who was a tailor, moved with his family to Paris. At school one of his teachers was the composer Gounod, who recognized a musical talent in the child and advised him to become a musician. But Renoir had a greater talent for painting, and when he reached the age of thirteen certain magnetic forces had already set the compass of his genius. Owing to the poverty of his parents, he was obliged to become apprenticed to a manufacturer of glazed ware. He decorated porcelain and china cups—dainty little figures of grand dames and powdered fops for the parlors of the French bourgeoisie. Tinsel art for tinsel creatures! And yet his experience as a painter of porcelain enabled him to acquire two important qualities that were to characterize his later genius— a taste for transparent color and an ability to use canvas, like porcelain, as a decorative background for his pictures.

Renoir was abruptly dismissed from his job as a porcelain painter when the public suddenly developed a craze for machine-made rather than for handmade tableware. Renoir turned elsewhere for a living. He drew pretty designs for ladies' fans; he covered restaurant ceilings with frescoes; and he painted religious subjects on calico sheets for missionaries who set the canvas on four upright poles wherever they traveled and thus gave their heathen converts the illusion of praying in a Christian church. And then Renoir left all this and went to an artist's studio to learn how to paint real pictures.

III

ALONG WITH OTHER STUDENTS he spent many hours copying from the antique. One day his instructor bent over his shoulder to observe his progress. After he had watched him for a minute he tapped him impatiently on the arm. "Don't you realize," he said, "that the big toe of Germanicus ought to have more majesty than the big toe of the dealer around the corner? . . . Don't forget," he repeated as he walked away, "it's the big toe of Germanicus you are painting!"

This lack of regard for the pedal dignity of the honored dead did not prevent Renoir from placing a picture in the Salon at the age of twenty-two—something that Cézanne was unable to do throughout his life. Many of the painters of the new school had been refused admission to the Salon in that year—1863. They raised a great hue and cry. Some of them induced the adventurer emperor, Louis Napoleon, to open in their behalf a Salon des Refusées, where "the Rejected" were able to exhibit their works to the public. This secondhand gallery was crowded with the canvases of the mischief-making Impressionists. Some of the slighted artists, however, were dissatisfied with the exhibition at the Salon des Refusées. They wanted more individual attention for their work. And they took vigorous steps to secure this attention. Courbet, one of the forerunners of Impressionism, was typical of the energy of this school. He had made a mighty contribution to art by honestly labeling filth as *filthy*. Unsuccessful in his attempt to reach the public through the regular channels, he went in through the back door. He rented a vacant lot just outside the main exhibition gallery, erected a wooden hut with a huge sign reading *Courbet, Painter* and slept on the roof. Early in the morning on the first day of the exhibition a number of people were attracted out of curiosity to his hut. Courbet had just tumbled out of bed. Forgetting, in his excitement, that he was still in his flannel nightshirt, he rushed downstairs into the gallery and stood before his pictures, remarking as the visitors entered: "What beautiful painting! How magnificent! It's incredible! It's enough to take your breath away!"

Such were the frantic and often amusing attempts made by

the Impressionists and the other revolutionary artists of the day to attract the public to their wares. But the public, and especially the critics, remained for a time aloof if not downright hostile. They looked upon these experimenters in new aesthetic values, Courbet, Manet, Monet, as a dangerous rabble of radicals who were plotting to overthrow the established order in the kingdom of colors. Up to that period color had for the most part been impasted on canvas, creating a flat, opaque effect. But now these revolutionists proposed to paint color as three-dimensional and transparent as a crystal ball. Some of the more ardent of the Impressionists were said to have eliminated black as a color altogether and to have substituted the use of violets and deep blues. The term *Impressionist* was an epithet hurled by the scornful public at an early morning landscape of Claude Monet entitled *Impression*. Monet was the perfect target for popular abuse. He strove to record all his impressions on canvas, no matter how incoherent they might be. He was really a stream-of-consciousness artist, but more than that he called himself a man of science. He broke up all plastic form into little pin points of color, on the scientific principle of a prism intercepting the rays of the spectrum. He divided a beam of light into its prismatic components by placing tiny daubs of color in juxtaposition to one another, in such a manner that the spectator could get an atmospheric illusion only by stepping some distance away from the canvas.

Actually the great figures in the new school were not at all deserving of the public condemnation. Apart from the few sensation seekers they were solidly traditional at heart. They built their novelties on an orthodox foundation, as we shall see in the case of Renoir.

IV

RENOIR was labeled as one of the Impressionists because he had exhibited some canvases in their galleries. Furthermore, he was a gay young blade on the loose. What else could he be but an Impressionist? When the Franco-Prussian War broke out in 1870 he joined the French cavalry and spent the winter maneuvering in the snows around Bordeaux. Once peace was declared he left his carbine for the easel and moved to the left bank of the Seine, among the bohemian artists and the bankrupt idealists. He had not lost the burning desire to create something lovely out of the mess of paints on his palette. His soul was placid though the world was in upheaval. The Parisian workers had arisen in the Commune. They had barricaded the streets and drawn blood with their rifles. Renoir stayed at home. He suffered no personal danger, because he hadn't been particularly anxious to reform the world. As a matter of fact, he wasn't a reformer; he was a monk. He had taken the vows of the ancient order of Art. His altar was raised to Beauty. His senses were entranced in contemplation of her. He was more interested in drawing the female nude than in doing anything else in the world. The whole message of life for him lay in the lines of a woman's body. On one occasion a friend, looking at a recently painted nude study of Renoir's, suggested that the picture might be improved if the artist would give it a few extra finishing touches. "Nonsense," returned Renoir. "It's ready now. When I've painted a woman's back so that I want to touch it, then it's finished."

V

RENOIR was not an innovator. He was an orthodox painter of the beautiful moment in the eternal flux of things. He painted the study of a little French girl with a parasol. She was gloved in white. She wore a white muslin dress. A bonnet sat roguishly on her head. Her eyes were dark; they were two luminous pools in the white snow of her skin. She stood in a forest, refusing to budge, as if to defy the power of Destiny that was stretching out its hand to lead her away from this spot, from the certain serenity of the present into the restless uncertainty of the future.

This picture, entitled *Lisa*, was painted by Renoir at the age of twenty-eight. It was then that the public discovered him. He began to sell. People who had formerly bought his canvases merely out of friendship now took them out of the closet and hung them on the wall. Society opened its doors to him. Madame Charpentier, the wife of the opulent Paris book publisher, admitted him to her salon on an equal footing with such "greats" as the radical Émile Zola, the conservative Daudet, the voluble Gambetta, the eccentric Maupassant. Anybody who was accepted into the company of these successful intellectuals had definitely arrived. A friend visited his studio and discovered a sketch of the Moulin de la Galette, a beer garden of Paris. "You must do a picture of this from your sketch," the friend suggested to him. And Renoir set to work. He rented a house, surrounded by a large garden, in the neighborhood of the Moulin de la Galette, and he hired models to pose for him in the garden. The painting that resulted tingles with the joy of color. It is deluged with the wine of laughter. In the foreground a party of men drink and dine while two young women, one sitting on a bench next to the table, the other leaning with her hand on the shoulder of the first girl, smile happily. Behind them, on the right, stand two gentlemen in jaunty spring hats, chatting with friends. A few aristocrats in formal dress whirl around the floor with their demoiselles. One of the girls presses her escort with her cheek and sways to the music in a state of rhythmic intoxication. Renoir himself was intoxicated with the romance of life. He let others paint its sober realities. He was not interested in the drabness of the chimney sweeps and their drudging mates. He was interested only in the gaiety of the Prince Charmings and their Cinderellas, whether in homespun or in silk. There was to be no sadness to the songs he sang with his brush. For joyousness, he believed, lay at the core of life.

He painted a group of people picnicking in a pavilion under

the warm afternoon sun. One of them, in his trousers and his undershirt, his skin golden with the sun, sits astride on his tilted chair, facing its back. A young woman, wearing a hat trimmed with flowers, rests her elbows on the table. A thick-bearded fellow in his shirt sleeves, his muscles bulging prominently, a straw hat tipped at a rakish angle on his head, leans lazily against the railing. The other members of the group are represented in similar attitudes of carefree relaxation. "Life in those days was a perpetual holiday," wrote Renoir many years later, during the nightmare of the World War. "People knew how to laugh in those days!"

VI

HAVING EXPERIMENTED with various color effects, Renoir began to swing away from the so-called new school. He traveled through the leading art galleries. A visit to Italy, the home of the old Renaissance masters, convinced him that form was no less a property of painting than color. He feasted his eyes on the classical modeling of Raphael, Michelangelo, Donatello. He went to Spain and became so excited when he saw Velasquez' *Surrender of Breda* that he felt like "embracing the figures on the canvas." He learned from Velasquez the secret of the joy that radiates from the brush of the artist. To Renoir, as well as to Velasquez, a painting was as alive as a woman. "How I love to walk close to a painting and take it in my hands!" Renoir remarked on one occasion. "It is not enough for the artist to be a clever craftsman; he must love to caress his canvas too."

Renoir loved to caress his canvas. He has been abused for the "arrogant sensuality" of his work. To this charge he would plead guilty. He painted a series of women bathers in the nude—firm and fleshy, ample women with powerful joints. "Painting a woman," remarked a friend, "excited Renoir even more than embracing her." The public was astonished at his frank adoration of the human form. "These nude women of Renoir," wrote a critic, "are gardens—gardens of gluttony . . . inflated pneumatic figures, smeared with a sort of reddish oil, reclining in an orchard where they appear to be ripening . . ." "There are two forms of art, just as there are two kinds of love," wrote another critic. "And Renoir's particular form of loving— delicious though it may be—is not great art." Yet it is in the proper understanding of Renoir's sensuality that we may find the clue to his art. Renoir was not merely sensual in the ordinary sense of the word. He was more than that; he was a genius who sublimated sensuality into beauty. And thereby he is redeemed. The impulse to create art is in itself no more nor less dignified than the impulse to create children. But he loved to create art not for its utility to him nor for its transitory qualities but rather for its intrinsic worth. There was no lascivious leer in his eye as he took measure of his models. He esteemed them less for themselves than for their value as points of departure. "They are there only to set me going," he once remarked, "to permit me to dare things I should never have thought of inventing without them." Beauty in a woman was not sufficient. Renoir's sensuality was of a far more sensitive sort. "I can associate with the first dirty scamp who comes along—provided I find in him a skin which doesn't repel the light."

We are inclined to feel that sensual people are necessarily irreligious. But this is not true, especially in the case of great artists and great mystics. Renoir was an intensely devout soul. He once remarked that the strength of the ancient art rested upon the religious faith of the artists. "For them God was always present; man did not count. With the Greeks it was Apollo or Minerva; the painters of Giotto's time, too, had a heavenly protector. But man, in his modern pride, has chosen to reject this partnership, because it belittles him in his own eyes. He has driven out God; and in so doing, he has driven out happiness too."

The painter of the most exciting nudes in modern times was the most ascetic of spirits. To the very end his eyes went questing for beauty, even after his hands had been struck by paralysis and refused to work. In his last years he sat upright in his wheel chair, tortured with pain. But a mysterious, comforting smile stole across his face. "Really I am a lucky man, to be confined in one place," he told his friends. "Now I can do nothing but paint. And," he added with a gleam in his eye, "you don't need hands to paint."

He kept at his task of creating beauty through suffering until the last day of his life. On December 17, 1919, he rose from his sickbed after a fortnight's siege of bronchial pneumonia. He sat down at his easel and prepared to draw the picture of a vase.

"A pencil, please," he said to his attendant.

The attendant went into the next room to look for the pencil. When he returned the artist was dead.

CÉZANNE

Beverly Hills, California, Edward G. Robinson Collection: *Still Life with a Clock*.

Boston, Paine Collection: *Portrait of Himself, Portrait of His Wife*.

Chicago, Art Institute: *The Basket of Apples, The Pistachio Tree*.

Chicago, McCormick Collection: *The Bathers*.

London, Tate Gallery: *Landscape with Rocks*.

Merion, Pennsylvania, Barnes Collection: *The Drinker, Les Grandes Baigneuses, View of Gardanne*.

New York, Clark Collection: *Mme Cézanne*.

New York, Frick Collection: *Chestnut Trees*.

New York, Metropolitan Museum of Art: *L'Estaque* and many others.

New York, Museum of Modern Art: *Still Life with Apples* and a good many others.

Northampton, Smith College Museum: *The Road with the Bend*.

Paris, Louvre: *The Card Players, La Maison du Pendu*.

Philadelphia, Pennsylvania Museum of Art: *Mont Sainte-Victoire*.

St Louis, City Art Museum: *Mlle Marie Cézanne*.

Washington, Phillips Memorial Gallery: *Portrait of Himself*.

Paul Cézanne

1839–1906

A YOUNG COUPLE walked along Rue Lafitte in December 1895. They were in the midst of a heated argument. As they were passing the window of a shop where a group of Impressionist paintings were on exhibition the man caught the arm of the girl. The girl struggled for a moment and screamed. "How *could* you upset me like this?" The man forced her to look at the picture in the window for a few seconds and then released his hold.

"*That*," he replied, "will teach you to be respectful to me from now on." By way of punishment for the quarrel the husband had compelled his wife to look at a painting of Paul Cézanne, *The Nude Bathers*.

Cézanne was only one of a school of artists who had lately sprung up to plague the art lovers in France. This school of Impressionists made a very poor impression. "People don't buy the Impressionists yet," remarked an old collector in 1895. "For they find them ugly. But you'll see—they'll come around to buying them, no matter how ugly they are. Perhaps they'll even hunt them down just *because* they are ugly, on the theory that that very quality will guarantee big prices in the future."

It took a long time, however, for the public to "come around" to Cézanne's work. At the age of twenty-seven he had sent his first painting to the Salon at Paris. He didn't even receive a reply. He wrote the board a letter in haste and in anger. "I shall content myself with saying . . . that I cannot accept the ill-considered judgment of people whom I myself have not appointed to appraise me." He suggested that the board revive the former custom of exhibiting in the Salon des Refusées the paintings that had been rejected by the official Salon. In this way the public would become the judge. Cézanne got a reply to this suggestion. The board wrote him that it was beneath the dignity of art to re-establish such an institution.

Was it for such rebuffs that Paul Cézanne gave up his study of law and adopted the career of an artist, to his father's deep chagrin?

The Cézannes were solid countryfolk of Aix-en-Provence. The elder Cézanne, by dint of shrewd saving and hard work, had bought a small savings bank. When Paul was very young the father had given him a box of paints that he had purchased from a peddler. But he had no serious intention of making his boy an artist. It was all in fun. When Paul set about to paint in earnest and captured a second prize in school, Louis Auguste Cézanne was horrified. "Young man, young man, think of the future!" he cried. "With genius you die, with money you live!"

"But his name is Paul, isn't it?" persisted Mother Cézanne. She had dreams for her young son. Paul! Weren't Veronese and Rubens named Paul?

The father, however, was obdurate. His son must be a lawyer, or at least a businessman. He entered him in the law school—but to no avail. Paul spent his leisure time putting the French legal code into verse. He shared his poetic dreams with another young man at the gymnasium in Paris. "Poetry is a great thing; there is no salvation but in poetry," said that young man. His name was Émile Zola. The future great novelist and the future great painter were close friends. Together they discussed politics, literature and art—Socialism, De Musset, Hugo, Lamartine, Veronese, Rubens, Greuze. When, after a brief separation, the two met again Zola was beside himself with joy. "I've seen Paul!" he wrote to a mutual friend. "I've seen Paul! Do you realize all the melody that is contained in these three words?"

But Paul's father saw no melody in idle friendships and dreams. He called him to the bank at Aix-en-Provence. Paul stood at the counter and added figures. He passed money and stamped checks. A solid life! The father, however, was troubled with doubt.

> *The banker, Cézanne, with fear in his eyes,*
> *Sees a painter-to-be from his counter arise.*

The "painter-to-be" had too prodigal a temperament to be a lawyer or a banker. Hoarding money was not for him. At Paris he had scattered his coins to the winds. "Pardieu!" he had told the thrifty Zola, who had looked at him in amazement. "If I should die tonight, would you want my family to inherit the money?" Cézanne left the bank, threw away his lawbooks and rejoined Zola in Paris.

II

HE WAS PRODIGAL in his art. Dogmatically he divided all art into "husky" and "emasculated" painting. He was "husky." He was young, reckless, effervescent, unrestrained. He seized upon the husband of a woman who kept a soup kitchen. The husband was a night watchman who slept in the daytime. Cézanne induced him to pose in bed for him, painted him nude and sent the work to the Salon—with the ill success which we have already noted. Friends saw in his canvases nothing but a "dumping ground for paint." He was fond of spilling buckets of color upon canvas, they said. And Cézanne heartily agreed with them. What else could you expect from a fellow who was famous for wearing a red vest and for having enough money in his pocket to buy his friends a good dinner? He squandered cash and color. Confident? He had no use for the art critics, "the professors of daubery." A friend said, "Now that your painting has been refused at the Salon, what are you going to send them next?" "A pot of——" replied Cézanne. He had no use for the fashionable artists. When he was introduced to a group of them at the Café Guerbois he said to their leader: "You primp yourselves up like a pack of lawyers. You're not worth a cent!"

But he loved the masters. He visited the Louvre daily and copied their works. It was the Venetians he especially revered. The great Venetians, with their spendthrift colors. Unnatural? Of course! Better than Nature! He recalled a conversation he had had with his father. "My dear Paul," his father had said, "what good can painting do you? How can you hope to improve on what Nature has already done so divinely? You must be very, very stupid!" Very stupid indeed! "If I were you," Paul had replied, "I wouldn't worry about Nature, so long as Nature isn't worrying about your bank."

To paint Nature, to *improve* upon Nature, *that* was the business of Cézanne. His eyes were dazzled by the flesh colors of Rubens and the Baroque school. To him their world was the world of a giant dream. And—as he soon came to realize—a dream beyond his grasp. Great visions were for people who had eyes to see. But he hadn't those eyes. The truth, this fatal defect of his, struck him with a sudden force as he sat in the Louvre copying the epics of Tintoretto, the pastorals of Rubens. He had the feeling for color, but he lacked the instinct for form. His eyes were unable to recognize a three-dimensional space. It was as if he were invited to a banquet and all his hunger for the lavishly displayed dishes were nullified by his constitutional inability to sense their taste. At art school his teacher had said of him, "Cézanne has the proper temperament for a colorist;

unfortunately he has no ability for composition." He must set up a new style of his own; he must write a new language; he must turn all the old theories of aestheticism topsy-turvy and formulate an entirely new art on an entirely new basis to fit the idiosyncrasies of his genius. Or else he must go back to the bank and spend his life stamping checks.

III

THE WAR OF 1870 between France and Germany struck like a bolt out of the blue. France lost. The Socialists rose in rebellion, and Émile Zola wrote: "Cézanne, a new Paris is about to be born. It is our turn now!" Cézanne thought Zola was too sanguine. He joked about his friend's naïve optimism. Yet Émile Zola was right, at least so far as he himself was concerned. It *was* his turn now. He was to become a rich and famous writer, idolized by the smart set of his "new Paris." Cézanne, however, was destined to live a life of retirement and to endure many years of abuse from the critics of this selfsame Paris. For the one it was to be a new era of happiness and hope. For the other, the old era of despair. "When I behold that my house has not budged an inch, that my garden is just the same as it ever was," Zola wrote after the siege of Paris, "I am at last able to persuade myself that the two sieges are nothing but 'bogyman's stories.' " Not a chair in his house had been moved; not a plant in his garden had suffered! This was Zola's Paris, and he built cunningly upon its revolutionary tradition. But for Cézanne, postwar France was a nightmare. He had not gone back to his father's bank. Instead he had begun to develop a style of painting all his own, built around the strength and the weakness of his peculiar genius. He adopted a proud and independent credo: "Here is my work; I know you don't like it. If you come into my studio to buy it, so much the worse for you; no money refunded." He became interested in the work of those *enfants terribles*, Pissarro and Manet, and in Dr Gachet, an eccentric old art collector who had the audacity to mother them. And he became the most abused painter of the day.

Very few men in the history of art have attained the notoriety of disrepute that was Paul Cézanne's. His bad fame grew by leaps and bounds in the years that followed the Franco-Prussian War. Paris for him had developed into an unholy nightmare, though it sounded with a salvo of hosannahs for his old friend Zola. Cézanne sat at the café and talked shop with a few people who tolerated him. The "new Paris" found him a man in his early thirties, married, with a little son. Was it disconcerting to him that he had spent three decades of his life doing nothing that might bring him fame? A friend once entered his studio and was assailed "by huge canvases hung everywhere, so frightfully colored" that he stood "petrified." A parrot in the room screamed out, *"Cézanne is a great painter! Cézanne is a great painter!"* "My art critic," said Cézanne, pointing to the bird with a smile.

At last an acquaintance of Cézanne's, a man who professed to admire the badly drawn, brilliantly colored artistic curiosities of Cézanne's new art, bought one of his canvases—a study of nude bathers in which every rule and proportion of the female body had been violated. This purchaser, Choquet by name, didn't dare bring the painting home to his wife. Finally he suggested that a third person, a friend of the family, should pay a visit to him with the canvas, under the pretense of showing it to him, and that he should then, "absent-mindedly," leave it with him. The ruse worked, and the nudes entered Choquet's house for permanent residence.

As time went on Choquet became a genuine disciple of Cézanne's work and urged all his friends to buy his canvases. He never succeeded in making a single sale, however. One day, to be sure, he managed to force a small painting as a gift upon one of his acquaintances, but he prefaced his offer with the timid remark, "I am not asking you to bring it into your house, of course."

"I should hope not!" replied the recipient of the unwelcome gift.

Cézanne was a man with an imperfect vision. There was something always lurking behind the landscapes he tried to paint—something he never was able to grasp. The initiated whispered that he didn't have the simple powers of an ordinary draughtsman—and they whispered something like the truth. Yet he possessed the undying fire that made him carry on with his strange lack of gifts and his strange hidden powers. He worked obstinately. Once in a while he caught a glimpse of the Promised Land. Would he be like the great Leader of the Hebrews—forced by the Lord to retire from his pilgrimage just when he was about to arrive at the fulfillment of his dream?

IV

His FRIENDSHIP with Zola had progressed badly. Zola had become an artistic success; Cézanne was an artistic failure. Zola's books sold in the hundred thousands; Cézanne couldn't give away his pictures. Zola sat in his luxurious parlor and pondered occasionally, with an exaggerated theatrical sadness, upon the companionship of their younger days. Now they had drifted apart. It wasn't that any harsh words had ever passed between them. One fine day Cézanne stopped coming to see Zola, that was all. He was no longer at ease in Zola's house, with the fine servants, the splendid rugs and the self-satisfied complaisant Émile sitting at his luxurious desk. Émile had become a bourgeois. The maid had looked daggers every time Paul had failed to wipe his shoes on the mat before entering the drawing room. And then one day the great man of letters passed through Paul's native town of Aix on a lecture tour. When Cézanne heard of Zola's arrival he was painting in the fields. He threw down his palette and forgot about his painting, forgot about his troubles, his bitterness, his defeats. Zola was in Aix! His old friend! He hastened to Émile's hotel, overjoyed. The coolness he had felt for him was a thing of the past. But on the way he met a friend who told him, "No use—do not go to the hotel." On the previous day someone had asked Zola, now that he was in Aix, whether he wouldn't take a meal with Cézanne before he left. And Zola had answered that he had no desire to see that "dead one again."

Cézanne's eyes filled with tears. "The money-bloated idiot!" he raged, shaking his fist. He went back to his friendless paintings.

Then, suddenly, Cézanne's paintings began to sell. The younger set of artists in Paris, always on the lookout for something novel and something sensational, had acquired a new insight into Cézanne's master puzzles. They began to see "genius" where they had seen nothing before. A new religion was founded, and Cézanne was hailed as its prophet. Cézanne himself was slightly deaf, and he had to cup his hand behind his ear to catch the shouting of his newborn disciples. "Well, well," he remarked with a smile. "So they are putting my pictures into frames at last."

His neighbors in the province of Aix were amazed that his paintings were beginning to sell in Paris. Here in Aix Cézanne had for years offered his canvases to anybody who would come and get them. Unable to dispose of them in this way, he had abandoned a good many of them in the fields. Once Renoir had picked up a water-color sketch of *Bathers* that Cézanne had thrown away on the rocks. In the storeroom at Aix lay a rubbish heap of Cézanne's paintings, together with a broken bird cage, a cracked chamber pot, an old syringe. Friends, not wishing to insult the artist, had taken a few of the paintings for gifts and hidden them away in attics for the rats to eat. There now began an unholy scramble to recover these half-consumed "masterpieces." One old codger sold a small study which Cézanne had once given him as a token of friendship and retired from business on the price he got for it.

Cézanne was amused at the sudden stir he was making among the intelligentsia. A pack of idiots, he thought. Painting meant far more to him than fame. A pox upon those who praised him. A pox upon those who vituperated him. It was enough; he was Paul Cézanne, and he could tell this to any rude fellow he bumped on the street. What did the opinion of others matter to him?

As for his own estimate of his work, he was still painfully dissatisfied. Somehow he felt unable to express the intensity which beat upon his senses. Look at all the clouds, all the magnificent shapes and colors of Nature that he wanted to paint. Monet could; he had muscle. "Monet has not only muscle, but vision," he would murmur to himself. "And I?—I don't seem to possess the power to see."

V

CÉZANNE lived an almost celibate existence. Apart from his wife, women were to him "damn cats." Men he generally distrusted also. He suffered from a persecution mania. He felt that people were "trying to get their hooks into him." He hated the conventional professions. Teachers were stupid old women; scholars were asses. He even began to hate the old conventional painters—the men he had once so ardently admired. Rembrandt and Rubens, he said, should be "spat upon." When crowds stood before a masterpiece in the Louvre he felt like "blowing his nose and leaving the room." As the years wore on he became more and more of a misanthrope. The robust little peasant with the broad-brimmed hat, the heavy black beard, the solid step became, if you took his table talk seriously, the archhater of mankind and especially of the Salon that still refused to recognize his work. He was a curious mixture of self-depreciation and vulgar swagger. When Whistler, after looking at some of his landscapes, remarked, "If a six-year-old had drawn that on his slate his mother, if she were a good mother, would have given him a thorough spanking," Cézanne was enraged and hurt. His faith in himself was sadly shattered. And yet he blustered his way through the little streets of Aix, elbowing the sleepy villagers and shouting in proud defiance, "I am Cézanne!"

VI

ON OCTOBER 22, 1906, very few would have hazarded the statement that a great artist had just died. One painter, Henry Hamm, summed up the attitude of the majority when he wrote of Cézanne's work: "Its evident sincerity intrigues me; its clumsiness astonishes me." A decade before his death the *Revue d'Art* had published a searching though not altogether unfriendly analysis of Cézanne's work by George Leonte. "Because Cézanne has no other guide but his instincts," wrote Leonte, "he gropes, he hesitates . . . Can he really paint landscapes? He grasps their character, their color, their light . . . but he runs aground in the art of separating his planes and in giving the illusion of distance." Another contemporary critic spoke of the "awkwardness" of his design, the "heaviness" of his color. Still another critic summed up the general impression by calling Cézanne a workman of "remarkable gifts, but of troubled vision; not unskillful but made to appear unskillful by some manual infirmity." He had ideas, but he was incapable of expressing them, for "he seems not to know even the first principles of his craft." Two years before his death the air had not cleared. Some writers threw up their hands and confessed that Monsieur Cézanne was a painter whom the world would never be able to understand. Others, however, retorted: "Cézanne is not misunderstood; he is just incomplete." The man had a "fatal lack of facility." Most people criticized in whispers, for Cézanne had a "gang" of fanatical admirers, rough and ready to "beat up" anybody who was insolent enough to express his contempt for Cézanne's Chamber of Horrors. Cézanne, insisted these enthusiastic disciples, was a great, inspired, admirable painter. And the intimidated public agreed, but with the mental reservation —"The most admirable thing in his life was his perseverance in painting badly."

For a number of years a battle of bitter words has raged around the interpretation of Cézanne's art. His admirers have won out in the long run. Today Cézanne is an acknowledged master. The revolutionary qualities of his art, which repelled his contemporaries, are now generally regarded as the "auroral flushes" of a new era in painting.

What are these revolutionary qualities of Cézanne's art?

For one thing, there is an impersonal objectivity to his paintings—a complete detachment of the artist from his work, a characteristic which is at first sight disconcerting. All his landscapes seem to be represented in a strange absence of wind, of rustling foliage, of the play of light and shadow which make a scene alive, moving, real. The organic life is motionless. The atmosphere is rigid. It is as if the Creator had stopped breathing on the world He had made. Indeed, the "breath of life" is entirely absent from his scenes. Cézanne particularly shone in his painting of still life. The very characteristics which give the still-life objects of food and tableware firmness and grandeur appear, when applied to landscapes and people, rather confusing. Cézanne, when he painted a portrait, would tell the subject "to sit like an apple." "You wretch," he told Vollard one day, while he was doing his portrait, "you've spoiled the pose. Do I have to tell you again that you must sit like an apple? Does an apple move?"

Then, too, there is a neutral, timeless lighting, just as there is a neutral, motionless rigidity, to the paintings of Cézanne. The atmosphere that we see in a canvas by Corot, or by any of the other great interpreters of Nature, is surcharged with light and shadow; it glows with the green of foliage or with the blue of mountains in perspective. But a Cézanne landscape is completely devoid of atmospheric color in this sense. It is as if he did all his painting under a leaden gray sky.

But, most important of all, the illusion of space and perspective, which is the A B C of any elementary course in art, is completely disregarded in Cézanne. Small wonder that the critics grew red in the face when they first saw his pictures! There is no feeling of distance, no proper foreshortening of objects, no tension of planes, none of those conventional tricks which give an illustration its essential verisimilitude. In other words, there is no illusion of a three-dimensional reality in Cézanne's pictures. Cézanne revolutionized the entire intellectual conception of art, which had regarded distance and perspective as the primary values in the composition of painting. According to Cézanne, the primary quality in a painting is not perspective, but *structural form*. He does not see objects in relation to one another. "Everything in Nature," he said, "is an isolated cylinder or an isolated cube." The spectator finds it difficult to enter into Cézanne's dimension, for the simple reason that there is no such space dimension in his paintings. His "space" is completely independent of the body of his objects. All his objects, whether near or far, are massed together into an unrelated heap of sharply contrasted tints. The eye, according to Cézanne, cannot really see space. All it can see is structural form. And structural form, maintains Cézanne, depends not upon linear design but upon a solidity of color. The shapes of objects are obtained by a balancing of the adjacent areas of color. Cézanne created volumes of color with an authority that gives a monumental solidity to his work. He strips design to its primitive essentials. For him, design forms merely a line of demarcation between two patches of color. Cézanne aimed for an architectural logic beneath the ripple of atmospheric light.

He sought for essential structural ideas that had existed in eternity long before the artists had come to earth. All artists, he thought, made the mistake of painting what they saw and calling it reality. He wanted to catch the true reality beneath the appearance, the true order of form that only the intellect but not the eye can comprehend. His still-life subjects gave him an ideal opportunity for his experiments. The most famous of his still-life paintings is the *Compotier*. A group of apples, a knife, a napkin, a fruit bowl and a glass half filled with water are placed on a tablecloth. These objects are so solidly drawn that each seems to rest infallibly in its position, as if ordained to stay there by the Creator. The painted apples are much clumsier and denser than any real apples. The napkin and the knife are drawn in a rectangular sweep. The fruit bowl and the glass of water are heavy oblongs. If one does not appreciate the hand-writing of the artist, the picture seems awkward and ill drawn. Nevertheless there is a simple, logical relationship between the *colors* of the several objects. These colors are applied in a series of small, solid parallel strokes of the brush. They lie across the surface of the canvas without any regard for the contour of the forms. This painting, remarked one of Cézanne's admirers, may lack the illusion of life, but it contains the truth of eternity. To which a skeptic may reply, with Pontius Pilate, "But what is the truth?" Is the elemental solidity of Cézanne's studies in still life a glimpse of eternity or is it merely the result of a constitu-tional defect in Cézanne's vision? To answer this question categorically one must be more than an art critic; one must be a seer.

The same approach to the elemental, the same qualities of solidity that one finds in Cézanne's pictures of still life may be found also in his portraits. He approaches his subjects in a remarkably primitive manner. In his portrait of Madame Cézanne, for example, the model faces us squarely. She sits directly in the center of the canvas, rigidly upright. As if to set all the laws of composition at defiance, the chair she sits on is stiff and rectangular, giving a severe vertical sweep to the picture. The entire canvas possesses the symmetry of an Egyptian obelisk, a painted metaphor of monumental stability.

We find the same monumental stability—or, as his detractors would say, the same graceless incoherency—in his landscapes and his group paintings. His houses, his rivers, his mountains, his trees, his grass, his people—all his objects seem to defy not only the accepted physical but even the chemical and the mental and the moral laws of creation. But this, said Cézanne, is the sort of world we live in.

Whether Cézanne saw better than his fellow artists or was merely the victim of an eye disease that distorted the world in his sight will remain a moot question. But whatever the critics may say about the design of Cézanne's paintings, they are pretty unanimously agreed about his color effects. In the world of color Cézanne stands among the very great. As a young man he had set himself the task to excel Nature in the magic of her tints. In this task, most of his critics admit, he succeeded.

HOMER

Andover, Mass., Phillips Academy: *Eight Bells, On the Cliff, West Wind.*

Boston, Museum of Fine Arts: *Dory, The Fallen Deer, Fishing Boats, The Fog Warning, The Lookout—All's Well.*

Brooklyn, Museum: *Bear and Canoe, In the White Mountains, Shooting the Rapids.*

Chicago, Art Institute: *Adirondack Guide, Camp Fire, Coast of Maine, The Herring Net.*

Cincinnati, Art Museum: *Hauling in Anchor.*

Cleveland, Museum of Art: *Early Morning after Storm at Sea.*

Detroit, Institute of Arts: *Prout's Neck.*

New York, Metropolitan Museum of Art: *Bermuda, The Carnival, Gulf Stream, Harvest, Moonlight—Woods Island Light, Northeaster.*

Harvard University, Fogg Art Museum: *Fishing in the Adirondacks, Negro under Palm Tree.*

Northampton, Smith College Museum: *The Song of the Lark.*

Paris, Luxembourg: *A Summer Night.*

Philadelphia, Museum of Art: *The Life Line.*

Philadelphia, Pennsylvania Academy of Art: *The Fox Hunt.*

Pittsburgh, Carnegie Institute: *The Wreck.*

Toledo, Museum of Art: *Sunlight on the Coast.*

Washington, Corcoran Gallery: *A Light on the Sea.*

Washington, National Gallery: *High Cliff—Coast of Maine, A Visit from the Old Mistress.*

Washington, Phillips Gallery: *On the Cliffs, To the Rescue.*

Youngstown, Butler Art Institute: *Snap the Whip.*

Winslow Homer

1836–1910

How much more interesting Millet's paintings would have
been," observed an aristocratic old lady on Beacon Hill, "if
only he had painted a better class of people!" The same sort of
criticism has been directed against Winslow Homer. He has
been called crude, harsh, awkward, uncouth, a creator of the
commonplace and a vulgar interpreter of the distressed and the
dispossessed. Like Walt Whitman. His art deals with the obscure
lives of fishermen, soldiers, sailors, woodsmen, hunters, pioneers
—the toilers and the vagabonds and the sufferers of the human
race. The "barbaric yawp" of his brush possessed none of the
idiom of polite society, none of the daintiness of Copley, Black-
burn, Smibert, Sargent or any of the other popular drawing-
room painters of America. His was a new voice, racy with the
fresh raciness of a new world. Awkward? Unruly? Unkempt?
Yes, as awkward and as unruly and as unkempt as a northeaster
off the coast of Maine. And as majestic.

Like the good Lord, Winslow Homer created so many pictures
of common folk because he loved the common folk. And under-

stood them. No other artist in America had a better understanding of the human heart in homespun.

He knew the common people because he was one of them. He came of an old Massachusetts line of hard workers, devout worshipers and plain livers. His father, Charles Savage Homer, was a hardware dealer with a puritanical conscience and a thrifty soul. Winslow, the second of three sons, was born (on February 24, 1836) at 25 Friend Street, one of the oldest thoroughfares in the North End labyrinth of Boston.

When Winslow was a child of six his family moved to Cambridge. And it was here, in the shadow of Harvard College, that Homer received his first education.

There was nothing of the Harvard influence, however, in the training of Winslow's mind. His was a homespun character. He liked his games more than his books. Together with his two brothers, he spent many an hour fishing, swimming, boating and romping along the beaches of Cambridgeport. Here he developed an early taste for sketching. Wherever he went he drew pictures of his surroundings—simple little black-and-white representations of foot races and boat races, of the people at home, the pedestrians on the streets, the workers on the river front, the man with the wheelbarrow, boyhood sports of snap-the-whip and the-beetle-and-the-wedge. From that day until the end of his career Winslow Homer loved to create pictures that told a story. "Art for art's sake" was to him a meaningless phrase. A picture that didn't tell a story was as incongruous as a sentence that didn't contain a subject and a predicate.

His father was wise enough to recognize Winslow's story-telling ability through the medium of the drawing pencil. He took his boy out of school and apprenticed him to Mr Bufford, a Boston lithographer who had advertised for a boy "with a talent for drawing."

Homer's duties at Bufford's lithograph shop afforded him the spice of variety. He printed cards. He made pictorial decorations for book covers. He drew title pages for such popular songs as "Katy Darling" and "Oh, Whistle and I'll Come to You, My Lad." And finally he was entrusted with the important duty of designing on stone the portraits of the entire Senate of Massachusetts.

But this was not the sort of work he was interested in doing. One afternoon, when Homer was enjoying a half holiday, he went into Dobson's picture gallery. He stopped before a genre (storytelling) painting by Edouard Frère. An art connoisseur looked at him for a while and then walked up to him. "You like good paintings?" he asked.

"Yes sir . . . I intend to become a painter myself."

"Really? What particular line of work are you planning to take up?"

"Something like that, sir"—pointing to Frère's picture—"only a damned sight better."

II

ON HIS TWENTY-FIRST BIRTHDAY he left his apprenticeship and rented a Boston studio of his own. He was not a very prepossessing young man—rather short, slight, stolid; hazel eyes, a shock of thick brown hair, a bristling brown mustache and an incipient beard that grew on his chin in patches, like irregular tufts of grass on a rocky ledge. But he possessed a Yankee determination and a Yankee shrewdness. He knew how to work and how to sell his work. Anxious to make a more dignified appearance, as befitted a respectable young artist who was now in business for himself, he made a sketch of the most conceited dandy of the Boston boulevards, a Frenchman by the name of Paunceloup. He caught this man in his characteristic stride—head up, chest thrown out, coat perfectly tailored and perfectly pressed, a living model of the well-groomed young aristocrat. He took this sketch to his tailor and sold it immediately for a new suit of clothes.

His ability to catch the life of the city in its stride attracted the attention of the editors of *Harper's Weekly*. They began to buy his sketches of Boston—a street scene in April, a view of the Boston Common, a family reunion at Thanksgiving, a skating party on Frog Pond, a snowstorm on Tremont Street—sketches that were full of lifelike people and vigorous action, each of them a complete and interesting and dramatic story.

The editors of *Harper's* were eager to exploit his art, so distinctly superior to that of their other contributors. They suggested that he come to New York, so that they might be able to work more closely together. He acted upon their suggestion and, in the fall of 1859, set out for the newer and richer pastures of Manhattan.

He who travels away from home, observes the Latin poet Horace, changes his sky but not his mind. The mind and the genius of Homer, in spite of his removal to New York, continued to draw its sustenance from the New England soil.

III

THE EDITORS OF *Harper's* offered him a regular position on their staff. But he declined the offer because, as he said, he had already tasted freedom and he preferred it to slavery. "The slavery at Bufford's was too fresh in my recollection to let me care to bind myself again. From the time I took my nose off that lithographic stone, I have had no master, and never shall have any."

He remained a free lance. Like the true Yankee, he was self-taught, self-supporting. And he remembered the simple origins from which he came. He loved the underdog in the unequal struggle of life. Among the memorable drawings that he contributed to *Harper's* during his early years in New York were his studies of the *Two Great Classes of Society*—those who have more dinners than appetites and those who have more appetites than dinners.

His free-lance contributions to *Harper's* became more and more frequent and more and more remunerative. When the Civil War broke out he went to the front as the artist correspondent of that magazine. The pictures that he painted during this period were rarely pictures of battle scenes. His job was not to glorify war nor to condemn it, but merely to tell simple, realistic stories about the soldiers. And most of these pictures describe not the death but the life of the soldiers—in their tents, at their meals, around their bivouac fires, playing their games, singing their songs, telling their stories and reading the letters from their families at home. And, somehow, these pictures are more dramatic in their effect than many of the battle scenes of the conventional painters. There is genuine pathos in the efforts of the soldiers to pluck at the fleeting joys of life before they are called upon to face death. Homer produced almost all his effects indirectly. His war pictures are striking for what they leave out as well as for what they include. The sketch entitled *Wounded*, for example, depicts not the stricken soldier but his terrified wife as she reads the telegram. Homer was a master of the dramatic omission.

IV

By the time the war was over Homer had become not only an expert draughtsman but an honest critic of his own work. He was pitilessly candid in the appraisal of his shortcomings. Referring to one of his war sketches, the picture of a soldier being punished for intoxication, he said: "This thing is about as beautiful and interesting as a button on a barn door."

It was this candor, this readiness for self-criticism, that proved to be his best teacher. His purpose was to depict just exactly what he saw. If his hand failed to execute the promptings of his eye, he trained it, laboriously, faithfully, ruthlessly, until both hand and eye, working in perfect co-ordination, were able to produce a picture of which Homer the critic could say to Homer the artist, "Well done!"

And it was "well done" with the final pictures of the war. Completely satisfied with these specimens of his handiwork, he exhibited them and won the plaudits of an appreciative public. Here was an American artist who spoke in the American idiom. He had painted something vital, something new, something by which he would be remembered as one of the genuine painters of the world.

But it was not the war pictures that were to perpetuate the memory of Winslow Homer. These were merely a series of exercises in drawing and painting. They were to prepare him for his real work which was to come later on.

And what was his real work? To this question not even Homer himself as yet knew the answer. When the right moment came he would know. For the present, however, he must keep on practicing, painting, criticizing his work, preparing himself for that solemn moment when he would hear the call. He took a trip to Europe. He studied the old masters, but he did not copy them. They were skillful, beautiful, at times sublime, but they did not speak his language. He was a Yankee, a free citizen of a free world, a world that had broken away from the traditions of the past. It had a new story to tell. It was building a new tradition. It was singing a new song. The song of Walt Whitman. Of the Divine Average. Of the heroism that dwelt in the simple soul. Of the sacrifices that men made for their fellow men. Of the beauty that was America.

He returned to New York and tried to depict this beauty in a series of American historical pictures. And when he finished these he said once more, "Well done, but it is not quite the thing that I want to do." He then turned, for his inspiration, to the toilers and the farmers of America, white and black. He painted them in their homes, in their schools, at their seasonal occupations—*A Winter Morning, Shoveling Out; Gathering Berries;*

Market Scene, White Mountain Wagon; The Country Store; New England Factory Life, Crossing the Pasture; The Noon Recess; The Visit (to the emancipated slaves) *from the Old Mistress; A Happy Negro Family in Virginia.* "These pictures," wrote the editor of *Harper's Weekly,* "are beautiful poems." But Homer was not yet completely satisfied. He was still looking for that supreme inspiration.

And then one day he painted a picture of a different sort—*Winter at Sea.* He looked at it when he finished it. *This* was the theme for which he had been searching. This, from now on, was to be his inspiration. Winslow Homer had become the Poet Laureate of the Storm. His job henceforth was to paint the Saga of the Sea.

V

WINSLOW HOMER had never felt at ease in the city. And now that he had discovered his affinity with the ocean he left New York and built himself a cottage on the rocky seacoast of Maine. Here, in the little fishermen's village of Prout's Neck, he remained for twenty-six years, from 1884 until his death in 1910.

Prout's Neck is a rugged promontory that juts steeply into the northern Atlantic. The air is a blended fragrance compounded by those two supreme alchemists, the pungent pine grove and the salty sea. And the solitary wildness of the scene appealed mightily to the solitary genius of Homer. His house was set back, at a safe distance from the ocean. But he built himself another little place, a portable, boxlike shelter, with a window facing the sea. Here, in easterly weather, he would shut himself in like a diver, way down among the cliffs, and paint the fury of the ocean as it broke into mountains of spray over his head.

But it was not always stormy at Prout's Neck. There were days, especially in the summer months, when the sunlight moved like a caress over the water and the Atlantic stretched itself like some lazy animal and purred its delight in a million ripples of laughter. And Homer transferred to his canvases this innumerable laughter of the sea, just as he had transferred its tumultuous rage.

He loved the sea, in its fury as well as in its calm. For months at a stretch he lived alone, with the sea as his only companion. With this comrade to talk to, to study, to paint, Winslow Homer had become all sufficient to himself. In a little garden which he had laid out behind his cottage he planted all the vegetables that he needed. One summer he even raised a crop of tobacco. He learned how to sweat and dry the leaves, and he went to a factory in Portland where he took lessons in making his own cigars.

For recreation he devoted a section of his garden to the raising of old-fashioned flowers—primroses, marigolds, cinnamon pinks, heliotropes, pansies, nasturtiums, petunias—simple, democratic citizens in the flower republic of New England. Unpretentious Yankee growths like himself.

He loved his work in his garden. And his more strenuous work too. For, physically as well as mentally, he was a man of the toughest fiber. No soft-muscled aesthete he. Stick to your artistic faith, stand alone and endure—that was the sum and substance of his character. Cooking his own food, washing his clothes, repairing his house, building a stone fence around his garden, hauling his provisions from the grocer—these were but a few of the hobbies of his spare hours. He had guts, this Homer of the New World Odyssey, the poet who painted the ocean epic of America.

VI

HE PAINTED the first great picture in his long series of sea pieces in 1884. He called it *The Life Line*. It is the story of a shipwreck, but there is no ship on the canvas. Homer, the master of the dramatic omission, represented the tragedy of the sinking ship in a much more effective manner. He painted the rescue of one of the passengers who had been taken off the ship. This rescue brings home to the mind of the spectator not only the terrors of the sea but the ingenuity and the courage of man. Across the upper part of the picture, in the hollow between two mountains of water, a life line stretches from ship to shore. Suspended from the line by means of ropes and pulleys, a life chair is seen swinging toward the land. In the chair sits a sailor, bearing in his stalwart arms the unconscious figure of a girl. Her face is white. Her dress, saturated with salt water and torn by the violence of the sea, clings about her limp form. Her right arm hangs limply toward the waves. The sailor's features—and here we have another of the painter's dramatic touches—is hidden by a scarf which the tempest has whipped around his face. Had Homer painted the sailor's face, he would have created two centers of equal interest. He would have destroyed the unity of the picture. But he knew better. He wanted the spectator to concentrate not so much upon the courage of the rescuer as upon the helplessness of the rescued. Ingenuity? Bravery? Yes. But, over and above it all, the tragic littleness of humanity in the midst of the raging sea.

This tragic littleness of man appears to an even more poignant degree in Homer's *Gulf Stream*, a picture which he painted while on a visit to the South. A shipwrecked Negro lies stretched out in a sailless and oarless lifeboat, drifting aimlessly over the blue Caribbean waters. The craft is surrounded by a number of sharks who wait, with hungry mouths wide open. In the far distance a merchant ship passes along the horizon. Nobody on board has observed the exhausted sailor, who is too weak even to be aware of this last disappearing hope of rescue. There is but one end to this grim and ghastly story—the sharks.

Homer is not often, however, the painter of pessimism. The Poet Laureate of the Ocean, he presents it in all its moods. And he presents his seamen, "the peasants who plow the waves for their sustenance," in all *their* moods. He shows them hauling their nets, returning with their day's catch, dancing with their girls on the beach, pulling at the anchor chain with their hearty *heave-ho*, rowing to their ship at night, while the waves are "kissing the moon," watching the incoming boats with their spyglass from the shore or attending to the everyday heroisms of the sailor in their simple, unheroic way.

Out of these everyday duties of the sailor, unglamorous bits of shipboard routine, Winslow Homer drew his inspiration for two of the most glamorous deep-sea classics of America—*The Lookout* and *Eight Bells*.

The Lookout, a night scene on shipboard, was painted in the moonlight and was never retouched by daylight—a feat which not even Whistler had ever dared to attempt. In this picture Homer has captured, as perhaps no other painter has ever succeeded in capturing, the quintessence of the poetry of a night at sea. A starry sky overhead, a furrow of white foam underneath; and in between, the ornamental bell of a ship, a corner of the deck, a couple of ropes and the bearded face and the uplifted hand of a sailor. These are about the only details in the picture. And yet the effect is one of vast spaces, lonely hours, fearless toil. The sailor, who is on the lookout, has just shouted, "All's well!" His mouth is still open, and his hand is just completing the gesture that has accompanied his call. The head of the sailor, with its oilskin hat, its sharp features and its grizzled hair, looks as if it had been modeled out of bronze. The eternal watchman of the sea. "Sleep, my mates! The stars are out, the sea is smooth, the ship is safe. All's well!"

Equally impressive in its poetic simplicity is *Eight Bells*. Two bearded sailors, painted at two-thirds length, are standing on the deck of a ship. Both of them wear oilskin hats and heavy reefing jackets. The chief figure, who occupies the center of the picture, stands facing the sea, with his back to the spectator. He holds a telescope in his two hands and he is busy "shooting the sun"—that is, taking the latitude of the ship. His assistant, at the right, is seen in profile. He bends over a chronometer, intent upon taking the ship's longitude. The only part of the vessel that the spectator can see is the upper part of the bulwarks rising from the deck, just behind the assistant's back. The sea is churning with foam. The ship has just outridden a heavy storm. The clouds are still swirling in tattered masses of grim gray vapor, but here and there the sky is trying to break through in little patches of blue. To the sailors, a prosaic detail of every-day routine—the taking of the ship's position at noon. But to the spectator, a thing of magic and awe—the reading of the daily signposts on the unmarked highways of the sea. The unconquerable ocean conquered by the ingenuity and the perseverance of man. This is the secret of the spell cast upon the spectator by *Eight Bells*—by all the other sea epics of Winslow Homer.

Winslow Homer was not exactly a hermit. He loved the company of his intimate friends, and for them his table was always laden with dainty tidbits of his own preparation. But he tried to avoid strangers, especially those who belonged to the obnoxious tribe of celebrity hunters. Whenever he painted outdoors in the summertime a swarm of buzzing boarders from the near-by hotels would cluster around him and disturb him. Finally he hit upon the expedient of shooing them away with his gun—unloaded, of course. His Yankee sense of humor never failed him. One day a man came all the way from New York City to Prout's Neck to make his acquaintance. When he arrived at Homer's cottage there was no answer to his knock. He went off in search of the artist among the cliffs. Presently he met a man in a ragged suit of clothes, rubber boots and a derelict felt hat. The old fellow was carrying a fish pole in his hand.

"I say, my man," said the New Yorker. "Can you help me find Winslow Homer?"

"And what if I can?"

[*311*]

"I'll give you a quarter."

"Where's your quarter?" asked the fisherman.

The New Yorker handed it over. The fisherman pocketed the money and turned to the inquisitive stranger. "I am Winslow Homer."

He avoided society not because he despised people but because he wanted to be undisturbed in his work. His genius, like a huge and sturdy oak tree, needed plenty of earth and air for expansion. It was Goethe, we believe, who said: "Talent is nurtured in a crowd; genius, in solitude."

VII

"Silence, and evening star, and one clear call for me." The call came on September 29, 1910.

Winslow Homer was a young man when he died—only seventy-four. He had hoped to live to a far more advanced age. And he had good reason for his hope. He came of a stock that refused to die. Both of his grandfathers had lived to be over eighty-five, and his father had died at the age of eighty-nine. His two brothers survived him.

Success had come to him early in life. He had earned much and spent little. Yet he left only forty thousand dollars when he died. What had become of all his money? Let the postmaster of Prout's Neck give the answer to this question:

"If any man ever had a setback, Mr Homer was the first to help him. He was good to the poor. We shall miss him for a long time . . ."

"Blest is the work of genius," once observed an Eastern sage, "but twice blest is the memory of the Just."